First World War
and Army of Occupation
War Diary
France, Belgium and Germany

17 DIVISION
50 Infantry Brigade,
Brigade Machine Gun Company
(9 February 1916 - 23 February 1918)
and Brigade Trench Mortar Battery
(2 December 1915 - 25 March 1916)

WO95/2004/3-4

The Naval & Military Press Ltd
www.nmarchive.com
Published in association with The National Archives

Published by

The Naval & Military Press Ltd

Unit 10 Ridgewood Industrial Park,
Uckfield, East Sussex,
TN22 5QE England
Tel: +44 (0) 1825 749494

www.naval-military-press.com

www.nmarchive.com

This diary has been reprinted in facsimile from the original. Any imperfections are inevitably reproduced and the quality may fall short of modern type and cartographic standards.

© Crown Copyright
Images reproduced by permission of The National Archives, London, England, 2015.

Contents

Document type	Place/Title	Date From	Date To
Heading	WO95/2004 50 MG Coy Feb 1916-Feb 1918 17 Div-50 Inf Bde		
Heading	17th Division 50th Infy Bde 50th Machine Gun Coy Feb 1916-Feb 1918		
Miscellaneous	17 50 M G Coy Vol 1		
Miscellaneous	XVII 50 M.G. Coy App To Vol 1		
War Diary	Havre	09/02/1916	11/02/1916
War Diary	Godewaersvelde	12/02/1916	12/02/1916
War Diary	Reninghelst	12/02/1916	14/02/1916
War Diary	Trenches	14/02/1916	18/02/1916
War Diary	Reninghelst	19/02/1916	20/02/1916
War Diary	Trenches	21/02/1916	08/03/1916
War Diary	Reninghelst	09/03/1916	11/03/1916
War Diary	Steam Mill	12/03/1916	15/03/1916
War Diary	Merris	16/03/1916	21/03/1916
War Diary	La Creche	22/03/1916	22/03/1916
War Diary	Armentieres	23/03/1916	31/03/1916
War Diary	Houplines	01/04/1916	01/04/1916
War Diary	Trenches	02/04/1916	06/04/1916
War Diary	Armentieres	07/04/1916	13/04/1916
War Diary	Trenches	14/04/1916	22/04/1916
War Diary	Armentieres	23/04/1916	30/04/1916
War Diary	Armentieres Frenches	01/05/1916	09/05/1916
War Diary	Armentieres	10/05/1916	12/05/1916
War Diary	Estaires	13/05/1916	13/05/1916
War Diary	Morbecques	13/05/1916	14/05/1916
War Diary	Wardrecques	14/05/1916	15/05/1916
War Diary	Muncq Neurlet	16/05/1916	12/06/1916
War Diary	Morlancourt	13/06/1916	23/06/1916
War Diary	Heilly	24/06/1916	27/06/1916
War Diary	Ville	28/06/1916	28/06/1916
War Diary	Ribemont	29/06/1916	30/06/1916
Heading	50th Inf. Bde. 17th Div. War Diary 50th Machine Gun Company. July 1916		
Heading	War Diary 50th Machine Gun Company July 1st 31st 1916 Vol 5.		
War Diary	Ville To Meaulte	01/07/1916	06/07/1916
War Diary	Fricourt	06/07/1916	11/07/1916
War Diary	Moliens Vidame	12/07/1916	15/07/1916
War Diary	Mon Fliers	15/07/1916	22/07/1916
War Diary	Conde Hanguest	23/07/1916	24/07/1916
War Diary	Dernancourt	25/07/1916	31/07/1916
Heading	50th Brigade. 17th Division. 50th Brigade Machine Gun Company August 1916		
Heading	50th M.G. Coy. Agst 1916 Vol 6		
War Diary	Dernancourt	01/08/1916	03/08/1916
War Diary	Bellevue Farm	04/08/1916	04/08/1916
War Diary	Pomiers Redoubt	05/08/1916	13/08/1916
War Diary	Dernancourt	13/08/1916	15/08/1916
War Diary	Le Meillard	15/08/1916	16/08/1916

War Diary	Villiers L'Hopital	16/08/1916	17/08/1916
War Diary	Halloy	17/08/1916	18/08/1916
War Diary	Bayencourt	19/08/1916	19/08/1916
War Diary	Hebuterne	20/08/1916	31/08/1916
Miscellaneous	Messages And Signals.		
Miscellaneous	Note		
Miscellaneous	Messages And Signals		
Miscellaneous	A Form Messages And Signals		
Heading	50th M.G. Coy. Sept 1916 Vol 7		
War Diary	Hebuterne	01/09/1916	16/09/1916
War Diary	Caumesil	17/09/1916	19/09/1916
War Diary	Mezerolles Bernatre	20/09/1916	21/09/1916
War Diary	Neuilly L'Hopital	22/09/1916	30/09/1916
Heading	War Diary of 50th Machine Gun Company Machine Gun Corps October 1916 Vol 8		
War Diary	Neuilly L'Hopital	01/10/1916	06/10/1916
War Diary	Maison Ponthieu	07/10/1916	07/10/1916
War Diary	Remasnil	08/10/1916	10/10/1916
War Diary	Grenas	11/10/1916	11/10/1916
War Diary	Souastre	12/10/1916	13/10/1916
War Diary	Hebuterne	14/10/1916	18/10/1916
War Diary	Bayencourt	19/10/1916	19/10/1916
War Diary	Halloy	20/10/1916	20/10/1916
War Diary	Talmas	21/10/1916	21/10/1916
War Diary	Franvillers	22/10/1916	22/10/1916
War Diary	Meaulte	23/10/1916	27/10/1916
War Diary	Mansel Camp	28/10/1916	31/10/1916
Heading	50th Machine Gun Company Vol 9		
War Diary	Les Boeufs and Vianity	01/11/1916	13/11/1916
War Diary	Edgehill	14/11/1916	14/11/1916
War Diary	Moliens Vidame	15/11/1916	16/11/1916
War Diary	Camps En Amienois	17/11/1916	30/11/1916
Heading	War Diary For The Month of December 1916 For 50th Machine Gun Coy. Vol 10		
War Diary	Camps En Amienois	01/12/1916	13/12/1916
War Diary	Longpre	14/12/1916	14/12/1916
War Diary	Treux	15/12/1916	24/12/1916
War Diary	Les Boeufs & Vicinity	25/12/1916	31/12/1916
Heading	War Diary For January of 50th Machine Gun Company Vol XI		
War Diary	Mansel Camp	01/01/1917	08/01/1917
War Diary	Morval Sector	08/01/1917	15/01/1917
War Diary	Guillemont	16/01/1917	17/01/1917
War Diary	Corbie	18/01/1917	24/01/1917
War Diary	Sallisel Sector	25/01/1917	31/01/1917
Heading	War Diary For February 1917 50th Machine Gun Company Vol 12		
War Diary	Sallisel Sector	01/02/1917	04/02/1917
War Diary	Bronfay Camp	05/02/1917	06/02/1917
War Diary	Sallisel Sector	07/02/1917	10/02/1917
War Diary	Bronfay Camp	11/02/1917	14/02/1917
War Diary	North Copse Sector	15/02/1917	20/02/1917
War Diary	Montauban	21/02/1917	21/02/1917
War Diary	Meaulte	22/02/1917	28/02/1917
Heading	War Diary 58th Machine Gun Coy. March-1917		
War Diary	Meaulte Warloy	01/03/1917	14/03/1917

War Diary	Beauval	14/03/1917	14/03/1917
War Diary	Bouquemaison	15/03/1917	15/03/1917
War Diary	Oeuf	16/03/1917	23/03/1917
War Diary	Rebreuvette	24/03/1917	31/03/1917
Heading	War Diary For April 50th Machine Gun Coy Vol 14		
War Diary	Rebreuvette	01/04/1917	05/04/1917
War Diary	Ambrines	06/04/1917	07/04/1917
War Diary	Le Hameau	08/04/1917	08/04/1917
War Diary	Agnez	09/04/1917	09/04/1917
War Diary	Vicinity of Arras	10/04/1917	10/04/1917
War Diary	Arras	11/04/1917	11/04/1917
War Diary	Feuchy	12/04/1917	16/04/1917
War Diary	Arras	17/04/1917	18/04/1917
War Diary	Feuchy	19/04/1917	25/04/1917
War Diary	Arras	26/04/1917	26/04/1917
War Diary	Sombrin	27/04/1917	30/04/1917
Heading	War Diary May-1917 50th Machine Gun Company M.G.Corps. Vol 15		
War Diary	Sombrin	01/05/1917	02/05/1917
War Diary	Arras	03/05/1917	04/05/1917
War Diary	Yhuts L.1.B.	05/05/1917	09/05/1917
War Diary	XVII Corps Left Div Sector	09/05/1917	16/05/1917
War Diary	St Nicholas	17/05/1917	20/05/1917
War Diary	XVII Corps Left Div Sector	21/05/1917	26/05/1917
War Diary	St Nicholas	27/05/1917	31/05/1917
Map	Plouvain		
Miscellaneous	Miscellaneous Orders		
Miscellaneous	A Form. Messages And Signals		
Heading	War Diary June 50th Machine Gun Coy. Vol 16		
War Diary	Grenas	01/06/1917	19/06/1917
War Diary	St Nicholas	20/06/1917	20/06/1917
War Diary	In The Line	20/06/1917	22/06/1917
War Diary	In The Trenches	23/06/1917	29/06/1917
War Diary	St Nicholas	30/06/1917	30/06/1917
Heading	War Diary July 1917 50th M.G.Coy		
War Diary	St Nicholas	01/07/1917	08/07/1917
War Diary	In The Trenches	09/07/1917	12/07/1917
War Diary	In The Line	12/07/1917	17/07/1917
War Diary	Line	17/07/1917	19/07/1917
War Diary	In The Line	20/07/1917	21/07/1917
War Diary	Line	21/07/1917	22/07/1917
War Diary	In The Line	23/07/1917	23/07/1917
War Diary	St Nicholas Camp	24/07/1917	26/07/1917
War Diary	St Nicholas	27/07/1917	31/07/1917
War Diary	XVII Corps Left Div Sector	01/08/1917	16/08/1917
War Diary	St. Nicholas	17/08/1917	24/08/1917
War Diary	Fampoux	25/08/1917	31/08/1917
Miscellaneous	50th M.S Coy		
Map	Maps		
War Diary	Fampoux	01/09/1917	09/09/1917
War Diary	St Nicholas Camp	10/09/1917	16/09/1917
War Diary	Greenland Hill Sub Sector	17/09/1917	23/09/1917
War Diary	Arras	23/09/1917	23/09/1917
War Diary	Manin	24/09/1917	25/09/1917
War Diary	Berlencourt	26/09/1917	04/10/1917
War Diary	Proven Area	05/10/1917	09/10/1917

War Diary	Coppernole Camp	09/10/1917	12/10/1917
War Diary	Martins Mill	13/10/1917	16/10/1917
War Diary	Boesinghe Proven	17/10/1917	17/10/1917
War Diary	Parana Camp Proven (e 17 d 12)	18/10/1917	20/10/1917
War Diary	Le Riecle	21/10/1917	21/10/1917
War Diary	Bertehem	22/10/1917	07/11/1917
War Diary	Solfernio Camp	08/11/1917	13/11/1917
War Diary	Drop Houses	14/11/1917	20/11/1917
War Diary	Cardoen Camp	20/11/1917	20/11/1917
War Diary	Drop Houses	20/11/1917	20/11/1917
War Diary	Cardoen Camp	21/11/1917	25/11/1917
War Diary	Mortar Camp	25/11/1917	30/11/1917
War Diary	Langemarck Sector Drop Houses	01/12/1917	04/12/1917
War Diary	Langemarck Sector	05/12/1917	05/12/1917
War Diary	Mortar Camp	06/12/1917	07/12/1917
War Diary	Bertehem	08/12/1917	10/12/1917
War Diary	Ouest Mont	11/12/1917	13/12/1917
War Diary	Bertehem	14/12/1917	14/12/1917
War Diary	Le Transloy	15/12/1917	22/12/1917
War Diary	Bertencourt	23/12/1917	23/12/1917
War Diary	Old British Front Line Havrincourt	24/12/1917	26/12/1917
War Diary	Trescault	27/12/1917	28/12/1917
War Diary	Fresquieres	28/12/1917	30/12/1917
War Diary	Fresquieres Sector	30/12/1917	31/12/1917
War Diary	Graincourt Sector	01/01/1918	06/01/1918
War Diary	Sanders Camp	07/01/1918	13/01/1918
War Diary	Coy In Line Graincourt Sector	13/01/1918	13/01/1918
War Diary	Graincourt Sector	14/01/1918	26/01/1918
War Diary	Sanders Camp	27/01/1918	31/01/1918
Miscellaneous	Headquarters 12th Division		
Miscellaneous	HQ 17th Division	01/03/1918	01/03/1918
War Diary	Sanders Camp	01/02/1918	01/02/1918
War Diary	Left Brigade Sector	02/02/1918	13/02/1918
War Diary	Sanders Camp	14/02/1918	19/02/1918
War Diary	Graincourt Sector	20/02/1918	23/02/1918
Heading	WO95/2004 50 T M Batty Dec 1915-Mar 1916 17 Div-50 Inf Bde.		
Heading	17 Div. 50 Bde 50 Trench Mortar Bty 1915 Dec To 1916 Mar		
Heading	50th Trench Motar Batty Dec Vol I		
War Diary	Map 28 Square G 18a SE of Poperinghe	02/12/1915	07/12/1915
War Diary	Railway Wood	12/12/1915	02/01/1916
War Diary	Hooge	27/01/1916	30/01/1916
War Diary	Right Sector Armentiegres	19/03/1916	25/03/1916

WO95/2004

SD MG Coy

Feb 1916 - Feb 1918

17 Div - SD Inf Bde

17TH DIVISION
50TH INFY BDE

50TH MACHINE GUN COY

FEB 1916 - FEB 1918

17

50 M G coy

Vol 1

XVII

50 M G Coy
app to Vol 1

Army Form C. 2118

WAR DIARY
or
INTELLIGENCE SUMMARY
(Erase heading not required.)

No 50 Coy. Machine Gun Corps

Feb. '16 to Feb. '18

Place	Date 1916	Hour	Summary of Events and Information	Remarks and references to Appendices
Havre	Feb 9.	3 P.M.	Arrived.	
"	" 11	8.15 P.M.	Left.	
Godewaer-velde	" 12	3 P.M.	Detrained.	
Renninghelst	" 12	11 P.M.	Arrived after five hours march	
"	" 13	11 A.M.	Officers toured trenches to be taken over	
"	" 14	10 A.M.	Company inspected by General Pilcher G.O.C. 17th Division.	
"	" 14	4 P.M.	Company left for the trenches. via Dickebush. Shrapnel Corner. H.Q. installed at Voormezeele.	
Trenches.			Positions occupied by guns were as follows. Dickebush, Voormezeele, P2A. 23.13.5.8. New Trench, Sardine Box, La Poste, Spoil Bank. One section ordered to go to the following Posts. M 24. M 26. Canal Post. Hill Top. But received contrary orders to last two positions from O.C. Infantry, who ordered them to go across YPRES Cousines Canal & help in the Counter Attack against the Germans who had captured the BLUFF that night. Counter Attack was not successful. During evening two guns from Dickebush

WAR DIARY or INTELLIGENCE SUMMARY

Army Form C. 2118

(Erase heading not required.)

Place	Date	Hour	Summary of Events and Information	Remarks and references to Appendices
Trenches	Feb 15	10 P.M.	brought up to Voormezeele and two guns at Voormezeele sent to V.H. and September Post. All sections reported that night except the section sent on to the BLUFF. No 52 M.G. Coy. relieved gun in September Post & this gun brought back to Voormezeele. Received reports of casualties.	
	16		1 Officer missing. 1 man missing. 8 wounded. 4 guns were reported missing - two brought in later by section sergeants.	
	17		Two guns recovered. Kept in reserve at Spoil Bank. Gun from Sardine Box moved to French trench.	
	18		Company less one section relieved by No 52 M.G. Co. and marched back to Reninghelst.	
	19		Remaining section relieved.	
Reninghelst	20	4:30 P.M.	Rested. Guns tested etc.	
			Half the Company left Reninghelst and relieved half No 52 M.G. Co in the following posts. Canal Post. Hill Top. Voormezeele. M 23 B. M 26.	

1875 Wt. W593/826 1,000,000 4/15 J.B.C. & A. A.D.S.S./Forms/C. 2118.

WAR DIARY
or
INTELLIGENCE SUMMARY
(Erase heading not required.)

Army Form C. 2118

Place	Date	Hour	Summary of Events and Information	Remarks and references to Appendices
Trenches	Feb 21	4.30 P.M.	Remainder of Coy left Reninghelst and relieved remainder of No 52 M.G. Coy in the following posts:- U 27, U 24, U 28 La Poste, Spoil Bank, Eclme No 7, Arundel Farm, French Trench, September Post.	
	22.	4-6 P.M.	Heavy bombardment. Gun in U 28 fired on BLUFF during night.	
	23.		Artillery Duel during day. — ditto —	
	24.	7-9 P.M.	Work done on Emplacements. Indirect fire carried out from [Voormezeele]	
	25.		— ditto — Situation quiet	
	26.		Gun in U 24 moved to R 5. Enemy bombarded about 4 P.M. one officer wounded.	
	27.		Quiet all along the line	
	28.		Slight Bombardment. Work on Emplacements done Canal Post Emplacement fell in. No Casualties.	
	29.		Heavy bombardment. Canal Post emplacement built up with assistance of R.E.s Gun in U 26 changed to U 25.	

WAR DIARY or **INTELLIGENCE SUMMARY**

Army Form C. 2118

No 50 Coy Machine Gun Corps

Place	Date 1916	Hour	Summary of Events and Information	Remarks and references to Appendices
Trenches	Mar 1		Action on the BLUFF. Fierce artillery bombardment by British 4:30 to 6.30 P.M. Indirect fire from gun at Middle Farm from 6 P.M. and all through the night. Pte Wilkinson won the D.C.M. for carrying messages through heavy shell fire. Lyns in M 28 fired all night till 4 A.M. 2/3/16 on to New Years Trench and other parts of the BLUFF.	
	2		Our artillery opened up a heavy bombardment from 4:10 A.M. Our infantry took the BLUFF. Indirect fire used from our guns from Middle Farm, La Poste, Spoil Bank. Celere No 1. Trench. Lyns in M 28 & M 27 also fired. Indirect from 4.30 A.M. to 6.30 A.M. 2/Lt H R Halden & L/Corp Sturgeon in M 28 recommended for honours. German bombarded heavily all day. Several emplacements and dug-outs were knocked down. Casualties 4 killed 2 wounded. 1 attd man killed. Spoil Bank in particular was heavily bombarded.	
	3		O.C. Coy, & a party of the Dorsets dug out some bodies buried. Coy which took place.	

O.C. [signature] J.B.C./& A. A.D.S.S./Forms/C. 2118.

Army Form C. 2118

WAR DIARY
or
INTELLIGENCE SUMMARY
(Erase heading not required.)

Instructions regarding War Diaries and Intelligence Summaries are contained in F.S. Regs., Part II. and the Staff Manual respectively. Title Pages will be prepared in manuscript.

Place	Date	Hour	Summary of Events and Information	Remarks and references to Appendices
Trenches	Mar 4		Very quiet. Stores salvaged from dug-outs & emplacements recovered from Canal Post - kept in reserve at Spoil Bank. Guns in M26, M27, M28, La Poste, Hill Top, Canal Post. Relieved by No 52 M.G. Co.	
"	5	6:35 P.M.	Voormezeele shelled heavily.	
"	7		Coy H.Q. Guns in Voormezeele Trench, September Post. R5 M23 relieved by No 52 M.G. Co.	
"	8		Guns in Spoil Bank, Celwe No.7, Arundel Farm relieved by No 52 M.G. Co.	
Reninghelst	9		Coy rested.	
"	10		Billeting officer sent ahead to Strazeele for billeting purposes. Coy rested. Baths. Lewis gear checked etc.	
"	11		Coy paraded at 10 a.m. and marched via Locre & Bailleul to Steam Mill near Outersteene where Coy was billeted.	
Steam Mill	12-14		Coy rested. Parades as ordered by O.C.	
"	15		Coy paraded at 10 A.M. inspected by G.O.C. 17th Division and marched to Merris where Coy was billeted	
Merris	16-17		Programme of work arranged by G.O.C. V Corps.	
"	18		Coy inspected by G.O.C. V Corps. carried out.	

Army Form C. 2118

WAR DIARY
or
INTELLIGENCE SUMMARY
(Erase heading not required.)

Instructions regarding War Diaries and Intelligence Summaries are contained in F. S. Regs., Part II. and the Staff Manual respectively. Title Pages will be prepared in manuscript.

Place	Date	Hour	Summary of Events and Information	Remarks and references to Appendices
Merris	Mar 19		Coy Baths & Church Parade	
"	20		Programme of work carried out.	
"	21	10 AM	Coy paraded and marched to LA CRECHE. No 6 M.G. Coy on the way, arrived at La Creche area, passed & shared billets with No 61 M.G. Coy for the night	
La Creche	22	6.30 P.M.	Coy paraded and marched to Armentieres via Steenwerck & Nieppe	
Armentieres	23		Coy billeted here. 17th Division in the line. 50 & 13 Div in reserve	
"	24		Coy paraded for various inspections, kit, etc.	
"	25		T.G.M. on dgt Craft. He was reduced to rank of corporal. Officers toured trenches east of Armentieres. Coy, carried out programme of work	
"	26		Church Parade. Officers toured Left & centre of Divisional line. Draft of 14 men arrived from Grantham.	
"	27		Guns tested. Coy baths.	
"	28		Coy officers & sergeants toured the trenches to be taken over by them.	

Army Form C. 2118

WAR DIARY
or
INTELLIGENCE SUMMARY
(Erase heading not required.)

Place	Date	Hour	Summary of Events and Information	Remarks and references to Appendices
Armentières	March 29		Company relieved No 52 M.G. Co. in the trenches as follows. Coy. H.Q. at Tissage. Guns in Cambridge House. SS& North SS& South. Irish Ave. The But. Panama. Fry Panama. Frying Pan. Trench 83. Campbell Cop. Sentry Loft. Monument. Distillery. SPX. SPY. SPZ. Plank Ave. Relief completed at 4.15 P.M.	
"	30		Hostile aircraft very active. Germans shelled slightly. Emplacements & dug-outs being built & improved by our Teams. O.C. visited all gun positions during the day.	
"	31		No guns in action. Work on emplacements & dug-outs carried on. German machine guns very active.	

SOMME Coy
XVth Bde M.G. Coy
50th Bde M.G. Coy
Vol 2
Army Form C. 2118

WAR DIARY or INTELLIGENCE SUMMARY
(Erase heading not required.)

April 1916

Place	Date	Hour	Summary of Events and Information	Remarks and references to Appendices
Houplines	Apr. 1		Coy H.Q. and vicinity heavily bombarded. One direct hit. Work done on Emplacements and dug-outs. German machine guns very active.	
Trenches	" 2		Two guns moved from Fy Panama to Trenches 75 and 77. Reinforcement officer arrived. Machine guns & aircraft on both sides very active. Gun in Trench 75 in action during the night. Work done on Emplacements & dug-outs	
	" 3		Guns in Trenches 75 and 77 in action during the night, firing mainly at working parties. Indirect fire carried out from Point C 28 c 63½. sheet 36 on to C 30 central & vicinity. 2000 rounds fired.	
	" 4		Gun in Trench 77 in action. Indirect fire work done on emplacements and dug-outs. Emplacement hit. Gun from Camp hill dop moved to Trench 81. Gun from Distillery moved to Trench 79.	

Army Form C. 2118

WAR DIARY
or
INTELLIGENCE SUMMARY
(Erase heading not required.)

April 1916.

Place	Date	Hour	Summary of Events and Information	Remarks and references to Appendices
Trenches	April 5		Guns moved from Cambridge House to Trench 82 from Irish Ave. to Trench 64. Gun moved from Plank Ave. to Trench 88. Gun in Trench 81 fired at working parties. Gun in Trench 75 fired at enemy Tramway. Work done on Parapets. Indirect Fire Emplacements. Gun in Trench 77 swept enemy parapet & fired at working parties. Guns in Trenches 75 & 82 also fired at working parties. Work continued on dug-outs and emplacements.	
"	6.		Relieved by No 52 M.G. Coy. Reliefs completed at 4.30 p.m.	
Aventines	7		Company carried out programme of work. L'cpl Sturgeon presented with a "card" for gallantry on March 2.	
"	8.		O.C. Coy toured trenches with O.C. 52 Coy. Company carried out programme of work & paraded for Baths. Zeppelins reported.	
"	9		Church Parade.	

Army Form C. 2118

WAR DIARY
or
INTELLIGENCE SUMMARY
(Erase heading not required.)

April 1916

Place	Date	Hour	Summary of Events and Information	Remarks and references to Appendices
Armentières	April 10		Company went on a Route march. Full marching order. Route Nieppe. Steenwerck. Erquinghem.	
"	11		Company carried out programme of work. 2 officers reconnoitred Defences of Armentières. Company held a concert.	
"	12		Company carried out programme of work. Vicinity of Ry. Station shelled by the Huns. Received order "All leave suspended after the 18th of this month."	
"	13		Company carried out programme of work. Transport inspected by G.O.C. Officers went to the French warfare school to inspect Jut emplacements.	
Trenches	14		Company relieved 52 Coy in the trenches. Relief completed 6.30 P.M.	
	15		Gun in trench 77. fired at enemy Machine Gun & silenced it. Strong lines estry ranged. Zeppelin reported. Plane for indirect fire worked out	

Army Form C. 2118

WAR DIARY
or
INTELLIGENCE SUMMARY
(Erase heading not required.)

April 1916

Place	Date	Hour	Summary of Events and Information	Remarks and references to Appendices
Trenches	April 16.		Guns in Trenches 77, 79, 81 fired at enemy wire during the night. Guns in Trench 79 fires on by two enemy machine guns. Work on dug outs & emplacements done. Pte J Lewis killed by sting bomb near SP2. Guns in Trenches 83 & 78 fired at enemy front line. Gun from the Monument fired indirect from position from de la Buterre at enemy's front line & supports from sheet 36 C 23 b.1.0. to C 19 d 5.5. 3500 rounds were fired. Gun from Cemetry Right fired Indirect from Position C 22 o 9.2. at enemy's front line & supports from C 29 d 1.2. to Brune Rue and along road to I 6 central. 3500 rounds were fired. Guns in Trenches 75, 77, 79, 81 fired at enemy's snipers & Machine guns.	
"	17		8 C. toured trenches with R.E. officers to select emplacements & work done on emplacements & dug outs. May 36 pivot mountings suggested as permanent fixture in front line	

WAR DIARY
or
INTELLIGENCE SUMMARY

(Erase heading not required.)

Army Form C. 2118

April 1916.

Place	Date	Hour	Summary of Events and Information	Remarks and references to Appendices
Trenches	April 18		German machine guns very active. Guns in Trenches 77, 79 fired at enemy machine guns. Gun in Trench 81 fired at working parties. Gun in Trench 84 did damage to working parties. Gun in Trench 84 silenced an enemy machine gun. Work done on Dugouts & emplacements. Indirect fire emplacement fired up in a house at Houplines. Indirect Fire carried out from Farm de la Buterne on to L'epinette Avt Road. 2750 rounds fired. Indirect fire carried out from C.16 & 11. on to Frelinghein and along road to La Houlette. 600 rounds fired. Indirect fire carried out from a house at C.27 to 9.8. on to L'aventure at C.30 central. 1500 rounds fired. Gun in Trench 81 fired at enemy machine gun. Work done on dug-outs & Emplacements	

Army Form C. 2118

WAR DIARY
or
INTELLIGENCE SUMMARY
(Erase heading not required.)

April 1916

Place	Date	Hour	Summary of Events and Information	Remarks and references to Appendices
Trenches	April 19.		O.C. and Divisional M.G. Officer visited Indirect Fire emplacements. 2/Lt E.W. Davis arrived from England to join this Coy. Gun in Trench 88 fired at enemy Machine Gun in a house at Les 4 Hallots enemy Machine Gun in Trenches 75, 77, 79, 81 fired over Japan. Guns in Trenches 75, 77, 79, 81 fired over parapet towards the enemy wire. Germans retaliated with whiz-bangs, H.E. Rifle Grenades etc. Work done on dug-outs & emplacements.	
"	20.		Our artillery active H.E. & whiz bangs around H.Q. & vicinity. O.C. visited trenches 75 & 77. Took working party up to help repair damage. Zeppelins reported. Gun in S.S. 88 North fired Indirect from position C.1.6.d.1.1. at Trolley Road from Telinghem to La Houlette. 2250 rds were fired Indirect fired Indirect from Ferm de la Butene	

Army Form C. 2118

WAR DIARY
or
INTELLIGENCE SUMMARY
(Erase heading not required.)

April 1916.

Place	Date	Hour	Summary of Events and Information	Remarks and references to Appendices
Trenches	April		on to enemy front line between C 23 central and I 17d 5.5. Les 4 Hallots Farm was also fired at. 2500 rounds were fired. Guns in Trenches 75, 77, 79, 81, fired over the parapet towards the enemy. Work done on emplacements, dugouts, carrying parties supplied for taking up material to Trench by 5 for front parapet being built.	
	21.	11:30 AM	H.E. & shrapnel dropped around Tissage.	
		4 P.M.	Our Artillery bombarded the German front line. Machine guns joined in as follows between the hours of 4 & 5 P.M. Gun in C.16.d.1.1. fired Indirect at Enemy front line at Rue Rue & vicinity. 2000 rounds fired. Gun in House at C 27 L.7.8. fired Indirect at Enemy front line at Rue Rue & vicinity. 1250 rounds fired. Gun in Farm de la Butene fired Indirect at Y'epinette Britt Rd. 1250 rounds fired. Gun in white I 4 b 2 5 fired Indirect at C.30 Central to C 30 d 3.6. 1500 rounds were fired. Gun from behind barricade on Australia	

1875 Wt. W593/826 1,000,000 4/15 J.B.C. & A. A.D.S.S./Forms/C. 2118.

WAR DIARY or INTELLIGENCE SUMMARY

Army Form C. 2118

April 1916.

Place	Date April	Hour	Summary of Events and Information	Remarks and references to Appendices
Trenches	22.		Road at C.28 d 8.1. at enemy subsidiary line. 500 rounds fired. Lynn in Trench 7 fired 700 rounds at enemy Front line. Lynn in Trench 77 fired 750 rounds at Enemy Front Line. During the night Lynns in Trench 81 had a duel with an enemy Machine Gun & also fired at working party. Work done on dugouts & emplacements.	
	23.		H.E. & whizz bangs dropped around the trenches. 5.2 H.L.I. Coy. relieved us in the trenches. Reliefs completed at 7 pm.	
Armentiers	24 & 25		Church Parade. O.C. ordered by the Brigade to inspect loophole in the front line. Working party sent up to work on dug outs in the trenches. 2 O/R. inoculated. Remainder of Coy. carried out programme of work.	
"	26		Working Party. Inoculation party. Working party had to return at 3 p.m. owing to our artillery bombardment of the German front line.	

WAR DIARY
or
INTELLIGENCE SUMMARY

Army Form C. 2118

April 1916.

Place	Date	Hour	Summary of Events and Information	Remarks and references to Appendices
Arrentières	April 27, 28			
"	29		Germans retaliated at 6.30 P.M. Our artillery opened a short while after. Company ordered to stand to. Weeping gas shells sent over by Germans. Working party for the trenches. More men inoculated.	
"	30		Company Relieved No 52 M.G. Coy in the trenches.	

50th Bde M.G. Coy

WAR DIARY or INTELLIGENCE SUMMARY
Army Form C. 2118
XVIISO M.G Coy Vol 3
May 1916

Place	Date	Hour	Summary of Events and Information	Remarks and references to Appendices
Armentières Trenches	May 1		Gun in T.88 fired at enemy new trench after each artillery salvo as did guns in T.83 & 84. Work done on emplacements and dug-outs. "Tub" position shown in front of T.78 & 79 by O.C.	
	2		Guns in T.75, 77, 79, 81 fired at working parties. Guns in T.84, 83, 88. fired at enemy new trench at intervals during the night. Work done on emplacements & Dug-outs. Indirect fire emplacement commenced. Tub put into position. Heavy Bombardment on both sides. German machine guns very active.	
	3		B.Q. and vicinity shelled. Guns in T.75 & 81 fired at working parties. Work done on dug-outs & emplacements. Tub put in position in front of T.77.	
	4		Hostile aeroplanes busy. Strong lines shelled. Gun	

T 82 fired at enemy carrying party. Gun from
Cemetery Right fired Indirect from near Cabaret
Ave. at L. Aventine Gun in T 75, J 9, fired
at working parties. Gun in T 79 fired Indirect
at German trenches opposite T 82. Gun from
Monument fired Indirect from C 28 0 63 at
C 30 central and vicinity. B 00 mounting
Gun in position in front line. Work also
on Dug-outs and emplacements. "Tub" position
improved.
H.Q. & vicinity shelled also front line in
direction of T 6. Gun in T 82, 83 &, 9 6, 7 9, 8 1.
fired at working parties. Dap dug to Tub.
Work done on emplacements & dug-outs. Heavy
bombardment on both sides between 7.30 P.M. & 9.15 A.M.
Gas alarm sounded. Pte Davis D. wounded

WAR DIARY
or
INTELLIGENCE SUMMARY
(Erase heading not required.)

Army Form C. 2118

Place	Date	Hour	Summary of Events and Information	Remarks and references to Appendices
	6.		T.77 heavily shelled. Trench Mortars sent into T.92. Work done on emplacements, dug outs etc. M.G. Gun in T.79 put out of action by stray M.G. bullet.	
	7.		Guns in T.75, 87, 88 fired at working parties. Gun from monument fired indirect from fine Gun from Butte on to enemy new trench suspect de la B. attone established with Trench Mortars. "Tut" Enemy emplacements & dug outs "Line Position" damage. Work done on emplacements & dug outs "Line Position" disguised at T.77. New Indirect Line Position completed at T.79. New relieved by 52 M.G. Coy Relief completed at 7. P.M.	
	8.		Coy rested and cleaned guns etc.	
	9.		Nine inefficient men sent to Étaples. Coy carried out programme of work. Supplied working party for the trenches	

Army Form C. 2118

WAR DIARY
or
INTELLIGENCE SUMMARY
(Erase heading not required.)

Place	Date	Hour	Summary of Events and Information	Remarks and references to Appendices
Paradis	10		O.C. went on leave. Coy cleaned Guns. Baths Parade. Working Party for Trenches supplied.	
	11		Musts to Parade. Inspections etc. Orders for move received.	
	12		Billeting Party sent on ahead. Coy left at 11.40 P.M. and landed over to new Billets.	
Estaires	13	2 PM	Arrived. Coy rested till 10 PM. Paraded at 12.30 noon. Passed thro Berguin & La Motte.	
Morbecque		6 PM	Arrived & rested.	
	14	9 PM	Coy paraded and moved off at 9.15 AM. Passed Blaringhem. One man fell out on the march.	
Wardrecques		1.45 PM	Arrived & rested.	
	15	9 PM	Coy paraded and moved off at 10 PM. Passed thro. St Martin, Tilques, Molle, and eventually arrived at destination.	
Muncq Nieurlet		6 PM	Arrived & rested.	

WAR DIARY
or
INTELLIGENCE SUMMARY

(Erase heading not required.)

Army Form C. 2118

Place	Date	Hour	Summary of Events and Information	Remarks and references to Appendices
Munkq Neuville	16.		Muster Parade. Repacked limbers ready to move at 2 hours notice. German aeroplane over.	
	17.		Conference of C.O.'s at Bde. H.Q. early. Coy. carried out Field Training, including galloping limbers over rough country. Officers reconnoitred road to Aubigny.	
	18.		Coy. paraded for purposes of an attack. Firing on the Range carried out. Field Training, an attack on Aubigny. Reinforcement officer & 21 Other Ranks arrived.	
	19.		O.C. returned from leave. Coy carried out Field Training, Mechanism etc. Night scheme carried out.	
	20.		Coy carried out programme of work. Firing on the range.	

Army Form C. 2118

WAR DIARY
or
INTELLIGENCE SUMMARY
(Erase heading not required.)

Instructions regarding War Diaries and Intelligence Summaries are contained in F. S. Regs., Part II. and the Staff Manual respectively. Title Pages will be prepared in manuscript.

Place	Date	Hour	Summary of Events and Information	Remarks and references to Appendices
Hinges hamlet	21		Coy carried out programme of work. Reconnoitred ground for Bttle of the Day.	
	22		Bathing Parade. Coy carried out Tactical Scheme. Coy. paid in the evening.	
	23		Coy. carried out programme of work. Supply of Ammunition demonstrated by one section of Brigade Field Day. Coy out from 4 a.m. to 8 p.m.	
	24		Coy had inspection etc. Bombardment heard in distance.	
	25			
	26		2nd in command went on leave. O.C. inspected sections. Coy carried out programme of work.	
	27		Remainder of Coy inoculated. Lt. Costellogue	
	28		Church Parade	
	29		Officers witnessed 51 & 52 R.G. Coys in Field tactics set them by Div. Commander	

Place	Date	Hour	Summary of Events and Information	Remarks and references to Appendices
Hunstanton	30.		Conference of C.O.'s & adjts at B. de D. Q. Instructions for Div: scheme received. Divisional Field Day. Coy out from 12.30 noon to 1.30 p.m.	
	31.		Coy. cleaned guns etc. Lecture on Gas at Policeoir. Received orders for Divisional Route March.	

WAR DIARY or INTELLIGENCE SUMMARY

Army Form C. 2118

50 Bde M.G. Coy:
June 1916

Place	Date	Hour	Summary of Events and Information	Remarks and references to Appendices
Muncq Nieulet	1		Company paraded for Divisional Route March inspected by GOC 17th Division one officer attended Gas lecture at Moule	
	2		Company carried out programme of work	
	3		Company took part in a Divisional Field day	
	4		Company had Church Parade	
	5		Company took part in a Brigade Field Day	
	6		Company carried out programme of work special attention being paid to Indirect Fire	
	7		An Kit Inspection. Reinforcement Officer 2/Lt E.W. Davis arrived	
	8		Company went on a route march and carried out scheme ordered by Brigade	
	9		Company carried out tactical scheme – orders to move received	
	10		OC went on advance with OC's & other units in Brigade	
	11		Company entrained at Audruicques, detrained at Longeau and then marched 5½ miles to Buire, and stayed the night.	
	12		Orders to move to Molancourt received. Company started at 10 AM and arrived at Molancourt at 2.30 PM. Coy met by OC orders received that "A" & "B" sections had to go up to the trenches at night. OC accompanied sections to the trenches.	
Molancourt	13		OC & 2nd in command went up to the trenches at 4 AM. The two sections relieved two sections of the 11th M.G Coy and took over emplacements at Kingston Rd, 85 Street, Support Clapham Cut, adult Rd 74th. We noticed our artillery strafing in this part of the line. advanced AR situated 71 N q. H 2. H.Q and 2 sections at Morlancourt	

WAR DIARY
or
INTELLIGENCE SUMMARY

Army Form C. 2118

50th Bde M.G. Coy
June 1916.

Place	Date	Hour	Summary of Events and Information	Remarks and references to Appendices
Mohammed 1/4	15		Half Coy in rest paraded for Inspection etc. Half Coy in line worked out alternative emplacement in S.H. Floor for dug out, put in in th Noticable Hot the Genuine one Rifle Grenade Harrassen fires Officers + Sgts in rest toured trenches, rest from OC 52 M.G. Coy. Rumours received of coming attack.	
	16		Half Coy in rest paraded for Battle at Bruen rear foremen arrived. Dug out in S.S strengthened.	
	17		OC and two officers toured trenches in 63 Bde area. Half Coy in rest paraded Eroplane + Gas Helmet drill and fatigues. We notice our 8" guns here on and suddenly noticed in this part of the line: Heavy bombardment on the part of the Fd at night.	
	18		Half Coy in rest paraded for church Parade OC OC52 M6 Coy toured trenches. "B" and "C" section relieved "A" and "D" sections. Relief complete 7.30 PM More bombardment heard at night.	
	19		OC and 2 officers went to Pont Rideon to take ranges and also went to 63rd Bde area	
	20		OC and 2 officers toured trenches in 63 Bde area Half Coy in rest paraded for fatigues. Returns made T/Mort officer safely taken it at night the rest	
	21		officers of 54 M.G. Coy Half Coy in rest paraded for alarm and Gas Helmet drill etc OC and one officer visited sections in the line at night. Issue of clothing Funky at our station from railway. No result noticed Germans busy	
	22		2 officers and 4 Sgts went to Pont Rideon t Rouele ave Survey St Heoif Coy in rest paraded for Pay. Relief orders received we meet officer of 91 M.G. Coy	

WAR DIARY
or
INTELLIGENCE SUMMARY

(Erase heading not required.)

Army Form C. 2118

50 Bde MG Coy
June 1916

Place	Date	Hour	Summary of Events and Information	Remarks and references to Appendices
Montauban	23		Coy relieved by 22nd M.G. Coy. Company marched by sections to Heilly, arriving later at night and quartered in tents	
Heilly	24		Muster Parade. Gun cleaning etc. OC attended a conference of OC of Bde and received orders for the attack. Coy paraded for Bath.	
	25		Steady Bombardment prior to the attack. Coy paraded for Church Parade and for work. OC lectured officers NCOs on the coming attack.	
	26		Company with 6 MGs with the Bde in support by GOC 17 Div. Sections returned into Brigade. One gun being let into the light Coy order issued for "B" section to move to Ville by night & officers reconnoitred to Ville. Remainder pencil arrangements	
	27		received for 3 remaining sections to move to Ville to conform Coy left Heilly at 2 PM and marched to Ribemont where we billeted and marched off by 9 PM on to Ville	
Ribemont to Ville	28		Coy left Ribemont 6.12 PM and marched in a Bivie to Ville arriving there we attack had been postponed 48 hours. Returned to Ribemont, which we did. Report received from OC "B" section as follows. 2 Guns OK Guns in position at tunnels, n plan uts, Knyton Rd, Guinea St. 2 Guns able to fire at Fricourt. Gun fired on enemy for 1 hour during the night	
Ribemont	29 30		Company carried out programme work Company marched to Ville	

50th Inf.Bde.
17th Div.

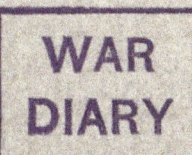

50th MACHINE GUN COMPANY.

J U L Y

1 9 1 6

17/ July
50 M.G. Coy
Vol 5

Confidential

WAR DIARY
50th Machine Gun Company
July 1st to 31st 1916

WAR DIARY or INTELLIGENCE SUMMARY

Army Form C. 2118

50th Bde. M.G. Coy.

Month: JULY

Place	Date	Hour	Summary of Events and Information	Remarks and references to Appendices
VILLE to MEAULTE	1	6.0am	Company left VILLE and marched to MEAULTE. The big offensive started by the BRITISH at 7.30am. Position of Company B section in reserve at MEAULTE, one section in KINGSTON RD. Section in KINGSTON RD via "D" Section fired on FRICOURT VILLAGE at 3am "A" Section ordered up to Bde HQ and sent to KINGSTON AVENUE. Attack on FRICOURT WOOD not successful. German machine guns did excellent work. 8pm remainder of Coy moved up to Bde HQ. and the guns placed in position to his indirect on FRICOURT WOOD should they be needed. G.O.C. 17th Division held a conference of C.O's at HQ at 12mn.	
	2	1.0am	Guns of "A" section in ENGLISH TAMBOUR at 1.0am fired down German communication trench and front line and several Germans were seen to be hit by our fire. We received orders that the 51st Bde relieved our Bde. Relief complete about noon and orders received back to MEAULTE independently, and than on to VILLE and rest. Before being relieved Guns of "A" Section in RONDAKA AVENUE fired on FRICOURT from WING CORNER to WICKED CORNER with good effect. Company cleared Guns a/c. Deficiencies on Kits inclined for. We learn that the BRITISH FORCES have taken MAMETZ, MONTAUBAN, FRICOURT, CRUCIFIX TRENCH. Company fired by all day.	
	3		Company paraded for Baths. O.C. and second in command ordered by Bde to reconnoitre to FRICOURT. One another slid my tray.	
	4		Company went on short route march. O.C. and two officers reconnoitre ground around FRICOURT.	
	5		Company paraded for Physical Exercises and gun cleaning etc. O.C. and two officers reconnoitre ground around FRICOURT. Company left VILLE at 8pm, arrived at MEAULTE at 9pm, neither operation entrained there on to FRICOURT about 11.30pm owing to congestion of traffic. "B" and "C" section took up positions RAILWAY ALLEY for indirect fire anywhere. "A" Section was ordered to report to O.C. KING FUSILIERS QUADRANGLE TRENCH. "D" Section HQ remained in reserve at WICKED CORNER. O.C. made his HQ with Bde HQ at FRICOURT station.	
FRICOURT	7		Artillery bombardment commenced at 1.25am. 50th Bde attacked QUADRANGLE SUPPORT and ACID DROP COPSE at 2am. attack not successful. at 8am 52nd Bde again attacked objectives. Yet 4 YORKS attacked MAMETZ WOOD in conjunction with 38th Div on right attack not successful. Artillery bombarded at 4.30pm. E.YORKS and DORSETS attacked MAMETZ WOOD again at 8pm not successful. Reports received from section officers as follows:— "B" Section. Took up position 1am in RY ALLEY sunk H Guns from 1.55am to 2.25am 3 guns fired on the CUTTING from X17a 05 to X17b. 4500 rounds expended. from 7.30am to 8.20am 3 guns fired on the CUTTING as above and one gun fired on PEARL WOOD from 8.40am to 9.15am 3 guns fired on North edge of MAMETZ WOOD on line from X18 55 to 513 & 69. 3000 rounds expended. 4.30pm - 5.30pm 3 guns fired on North edge of MAMETZ WOOD as above. 4000 rounds expended. One gun fired on PEARL WOOD 1250 rounds expended. 4.40am to 6.20am 3 guns fired 600 rounds each as of MAMETZ WOOD as about 5000 rounds expended. 1/R moved to X28 a 67½. "C" Section took up position Ry. ALLEY about 1am took up to guns and laid on a.m of (A) Martindeque lunch at point X28a 67½. Firing being about 15°apart. These Rounds X18a 23 & 4 features Northedge of MAMETZ WOOD between points X17b 64 and X18 2 3. (B) ENEMY WOOD X18 a 53 (C) Entire Rondo X18 a 23 & 4 features Northedge of MAMETZ WOOD. During one commenced at 7am and gun fired. 1875 Wt. W593/886 1,000,000 4/15 J.B.C. & A. A.D.S.S./Forms/C. 2118. erased for 1½ hours. 2000 rounds per gun fired.	

Instructions regarding War Diaries and Intelligence Summaries are contained in F.S. Regs., Part II. and the Staff Manual respectively. Title Pages will be prepared in manuscript.

(Erase heading not required.)

WAR DIARY or INTELLIGENCE SUMMARY

Army Form C. 2118

Unit: 50th Bde. M.G. Corps

Place	Date	Hour	Summary of Events and Information	Remarks and references to Appendices
FRICOURT	7		Rapid firing 7 1/2 m/m team were wounded by shrapnel. Section Sergeant kept the gun going. Shortly killed all dawn. At 3am 4.5.30am all guns fired on western edge of MAMETZ WOOD and at ground between MAMETZ WOOD and German second line. Afterwards firing station unknown. Similarly to FRICOURT WOOD at X26d 50 at 5pm on ground of action by an H.E. Shell. From 7.30pm all guns concentrated on western edge of MAMETZ WOOD and the gun firing and up from section in reserve. Section returned to FRICOURT WOOD during the night. "A" Section:- Section went up to FRICOURT VILLAGE & LOZENGE WOOD reporting to O.C. Manx Fusiliers. Relaying officers and supported to advance H.Q.–N.F. in CRUCIFIX TRENCH motivated to remain where we were and attack by on and DROP COPSE was occupied & go on and take up positions. Then attack failed to material to stand in LOZENGE WOOD in the afternoon. 2 H.E. shells dropped in middle of gun team destroying 1 gun. 1 injured all gun plan. In the evening ordered to report receive action at WICKED CORNER. "B" Section:- remained in reserve ordered to go forward and consolidate should attack succeed.	
	8		O.C. and second in command visited "C" Section in R.Y. TRENCH at 9 a.m. Immediate attacks delivered between 5pm and 2 a.m. 9/7/16. Dorsets took WOOD TRENCH. "B" Section ordered "B" Section by night. Reports received from action officers as follows:- "B" Section received orders to move at 4 pm and moves to B.C. Y1h. Yortea. In BOTTOM WOOD arrived there 4.15 a.m. 2 guns placed in position at X29 a 5y & 5/R were wounded during this period. One gun placed in position at X29 a 25 about 5 a.m. and one gun at X29 c 39 (in old German trailing position) and all guns under orders of O.C. Yrk York KR.– "C" Section:- About 8 a.m. enemy registered and an H.E. on the corner of FRICOURT WOOD N.R.R.R. and on R.F. ALLEY SECTION withdrawn to million TRENCH. Section Sgt. and two No. 1s receiving great unstinting recovery in this attack under shell fire. At 12 noon and at regular intervals till 6 p.m. the section indirect and MAMETZ WOOD at ranges X23 b 48 & X24 a 25 and X24 a 25. From 5.30 p.m. to 6.30 p.m. guns employed support of WOOD TRENCH & STRIP TRENCH (3 rounds) Dorsets in attack up QUADRANGLE ALLEY & QUADRANGLE. Indirect Battalion 2/R. wounded. Rhodes to Dorsets officer in front that one gun was last fired and good effect. "A" Section. 10pm section went up to relieve "B" Section in BOTTOM WOOD. Relay carried by dawn. "B" Section start in reserve to help & carry out assistance to the sections, communications are kept up by orderly and no gun was sent into action.	
	9		C.O. visited reserve Section at 10 am. "B" Section attained "C" Section at 3pm. O.C. visited "B" Sec by night also visited "A" Section. Reserve received from Section as follows: "B" Section reserve relieve "A" Section at 2 am. Section remained in reserve corner & waited. "C" Section. Bivouac 12.30pm and 3 pm guns fired indirect STRIP TRENCH from units X24 c.03 northwards to corner of WOOD & STRIP TRENCH and along edge of wood to point X24 a 35. Also fired then help in the attack on STRIP TRENCH 3. Relieved to "B" Section and retired to WICKED CORNER & to in reserve.	

WAR DIARY
or
INTELLIGENCE SUMMARY

Army Form C. 2118

50th Bde M.G. Coy.

July.

(Erase heading not required.)

Place	Date	Hour	Summary of Events and Information	Remarks and references to Appendices
FRICOURT	9		"B" Section relieved "C" Section in WILLOW TRENCH at 3.30am. Rifle indirect on STRIP TRENCH until 4.15am at 11.25pm. 2 guns fired indirect along a line about 100x N of QUADRANGLE SUPPORT until 12.20mn. 2 guns ready to support if BOTTOM WOOD is relieved. Rem of "A" Below guns, Slow range fire at 1am 10/7/16. "A" Section. About 10am we fired on enemy making attack in STRIP TRENCH when we observed a gap of QUADRANGLE SUPPORT TRENCH where it joined the WOOD. Fire was successfully directed on these at 11mn 1 gun moved into QUADRANGLE TRENCH.	
	10		Attack on MAMETZ WOOD commenced at 6.15am and eventually taken CONTALMAISON also attacked + taken. Many fighting took place all day + night. Division relieved by night. Reports received from Section as follows:- "B" Section. 12.30am left WICKED CORNER with 2 guns and arrived at WILLOW TRENCH at 7am. At dawn turn J indirect fire went laid on block in MAMETZ WOOD and on fire from XY2QY to MSLH. Between 4.55am and 5.15am each gun fired about 500 rounds. Gun fired first with two guns on N side of MAMETZ WOOD firing at irregular intervals till 3.30pm. At 4.20pm received orders to move to RY ALLEY and at 5.10pm opened fire which was going on the outskirts and finished at 5.55pm at 7.30pm had orders to move back to WICKED CORNER arrived here about 9pm. "C" Section remained in reserve at WICKED CORNER and ready to carry out gun-gun. 7a+13 cutting wire. "D" Section. At 1am 2 guns moved up to BOTTOM WOOD and were subject to severe + shelling. 10/7 having remained fire partly exposed, carried messages from them gun on "D" Section at HIMAM TRENCH 5am. 2 guns in WILLOW TRENCH fired at N.W portion of MAMETZ WOOD. At noon gun moved as RY ALLEY the N.side of MAMETZ WOOD until we retired on the enemy's second line at 4.4pm when they retired to prs N.side around MINE from CONTALMAISON. Ate fired from 5pm to 8pm about 8mm fire 600 gun were ordered to WICKED CORNER and ink 2 guns from BOTTOM WOOD were also withdrawn to WICKED CORNER. "A" Section. After attack on STRIP TRENCH gun in QUADRANGLE SUPPORT filed subsequently at enemy who were retiring their trenches 2 guns moved about QUADRANGLE in WOOD Divison as target about retiring accounted for several of the enemy. At 5pm the guns were captured. 2nd Lieut J.CHAN, Sgt CLEWS + LCpl J.plumer were responsible for the defence of the guns in the front line at 2am 11/9/16 relieved by a section of 110 M.G. Coy. GEORGETOWN which we secured till 12 noon. We left DRANOUTRE to follow to road to our entire division company entrained at 12 noon and arrived at ESPAEU at 8pm then marching to MOLLIENS VIDAME + company acted in billets.	
MOLLIENS VIDAME	12		Company rested and general clear up O.C. addressed Coy at 5pm. Transport arrived about 8am.	
	13		H.O.T.R. reinforcements reported. Coy paraded for inspection 2.O. Run gun ever equipment officer here attached from the Overseas.	

1875 W: W593/826 1,000,000 4/15 J.B.C. & A. A.D.S.S./Forms/C. 2118.

WAR DIARY or INTELLIGENCE SUMMARY

Army Form C. 2118

50th Bn. M.G. Coy

July

Place	Date	Hour	Summary of Events and Information	Remarks and references to Appendices
MOISLAINS VERMAND	14		Company cleaned guns etc. and received new clothing etc. Company hand cart at 12:30 pm was received officially in return.	
	15		Company moved off at 6 am and marched through MONTAGNE, FAYET, LABREA MOUCHES, ARRAINES, SOREL LIERCOURT, PONT REMY, BÉNARNICOURT and arrived at MONFRIERS at 2:30 pm and were temporarily settled in billets.	
MONFRIERS	16		Company paraded for Rifle inspection etc. 207th reinforcements were on hand 16 in number 6 O.R. and 52 M.G. Coy. Company paraded for Church Parade at 5 PM.	
	17		Company paraded for fatigues and inspection. Visited by G.O.C. 50th Bde. who informed us that we were the first Canadian unit on the site of property. Arrangements for school on the	
	18		Company carried out programme of work.	
	19		do — do — do	
	20		do — do — do (Bodiream - BRUCHA(?)P)	
	21		do — do — do	
	22		A Bomps entered a match to No. 2 M.G. Coy. Company carried out programme of work. Transport moved off on retreat. Preparation made for move. Company moved off at 5 pm via ARRY-AIMAGET ETAPE and arrived in CONDÉ about 9:30 pm when men were issued hot tea. All day spent at 10:45 pm and marched to HANGUEST where we slept in the attic all night.	
CONDÉ HANGUEST	23		Company entrained at 5 am arrived RIBEMOUNT when we detrained at 11 am. Marched to billets in town new	
	24		Company temporary billeted	
DERNANCOURT	25		Company cleaned guns etc. and prepared for inspection	
	26		Company carried out programme of work. Officers attended a demonstration of STOKES GUNS.	
	27		— do — do — Lectures took part in on Divisional Ground to Brady received	
	28		no military subject.	
	29		Company carried out programme of work. Bathing Parade. Company rest time.	
	30		— do — do — do at MÉRICOURT.	
	31		Church Parade. Clo attended companies of E/O's at MÉRICOURT. Company carried out programme of work. Bathing Parade. Orders for further relief for overseas received.	

50th Brigade.
17th Division.

50th BRIGADE MACHINE GUN COMPANY

AUGUST 1 9 1 6 ::::::::

Vol 6

50/17

50th M.G. Coy.

Agst 1916

WAR DIARY or INTELLIGENCE SUMMARY

Army Form C. 2118

50 M G Coy. — August 1916 —

Place	Date	Hour	Summary of Events and Information	Remarks and references to Appendices
BERNAY COURT	1		Company carried out programme of work and deficiencies etc. made up. Operation Orders received.	C/w
	2		Company moved off at 7A.M. and marched to BELLE VUE FARM camp near ALBERT. Schemes during Combined Sights. C.O. lectured Sergeants on ALBERT	C/w
	3		Company carried out drill after tea. Ran at Rugby. very active at night.	C/w
BELLE VUE FARM	4		Company carried out advanced stage work in M.G. tactics. 2 officers rode to POMIERS REDOUBT. Reconnoitre positions occupied by 51 M.G. Coy. Operation Orders received. Company moved off at 6.40 P.M. via trench passing by FRICOURT and MAMETZ and arrived at POMIERS REDOUBT about 8.30 P.M. Company sub div. in shell holes and trenches. Second in command with left behind at Bde Report. BELLE VUE FARM. Transport lines at WING CORNER. Artillery on both sides very active all day.	C/w
POMIERS REDOUBT	5		Company stood by. C.O. and 4 officers toured line occupied by 52 M.G. Coy. Operation Order received in the afternoon to relieve this Coy. First Section started out at 3 P.M. H.Q. installed in MONTAUBAN ALLEY. Portion of Sections as follows:— "A" and "½ B" Sections in reserve at MONTAUBAN ALLEY S26d. "B" Section went into Support line at GEORGE STREET. S16a 9.6, S16 b 5.½, S16 b 3.5/2 . S16 c 5.5. These guns being able to cover ground between GEORGE St. and HIGH WOOD and can be usefully employed for indirect fire on SWITCH TRENCH and HIGH WOOD. 2 guns of "B" Section went up to LONGUEVAL and went into PICCADILLY position, one at Corner of DUKE ST. and NORTH ST. Second gun at S17 d. 9/2 sweeping ground between PICCADILLY and NORTH ST. Second gun at S17.8.18 and covers PICCADILLY. "C" Section went up to PEARS ST. Guns went to positions as follows. No 1 gun at S11c 0.8. Being able to enfilade ORCHARD STREET. No 2 Gun at S11c 3.6. enfilading ORCHARD LANE. No 3 Gun at S11c 4.5. sweeping ORCHARD ST. and TEA LANE. No 4 gun at S11c 10.5. sweeping ORCHARD ST. and NORTH St. Sergt Major in Charge in Relief completed 8.30 P.M. Sugt MAJOR in Charge in advanced dump near the GREEN DUMP where Section sent down for Rations and work, and bright down managed from the guns. From there first observation brought their Linings to H.Q. Communication also kept up by orderly with the Transport. Sigl. Station installed at the Dump for connection with Brigade Signals. one O/R was wounded during the relief. B.O. watched GEORGE ST guns during the evening. Enemy artillery fired great attention to CATERPILLAR VALLEY. Reports received from sections as follows. B. Section. about 11.30 P.M. Heavy shrapnel and H E in region of front line in HIGH WOOD and west of it. Fire red rocks shewn sent up and Indirect fire with two guns and continued until 12 M.N. 2000 rounds expended. Target SWITCH TRENCH and its immediate rear from S.5 6.30 to S.4 a 5.5. Traversing fire used. W.O. Dawe Tarvin worked on aeroplane exciting employer to S. Catherine Machine position commanded on right of front gun. Casualties NIL "C" Section Guns in Harness from front line during our forward went. Everything clear except — Casualties. Killed 1 O/R. wounded 1 O/R. wounded 1 O/R. CPL Strungen. Displayed great coolness. when the shell which caused these casualties fell, and set overlaid example to his men. Recommended for D.C.M. Heaps. B. Section. Nothing to report. Shelled all day but not	C/w

1875 Wt. W593/826 1,000,000 4/15 J.B.C. & A. A.D.S.S./Forms/C. 2118.

WAR DIARY or INTELLIGENCE SUMMARY

Army Form C. 2118

50 M.G. Coy.

August 1916.

Place	Date	Hour	Summary of Events and Information	Remarks and references to Appendices
POZIERS REDOUBT	6		Reports received from Sections as follows:- "D" Section all correct. Casualties Nil. "C" Section all correct. Casualties Nil. We observed indirect fire from "B" section in support going into the German front line. "B" Section Gun in action. 2. Between 9.20 P.M. and 10.40 P.M. - 11.15 P.M. and 12 M.N. Each gun fired 3500 rounds. Target, TEA LANE, S.12.a.9 to S.6.c.65, SWITCH TRENCH from S.6.c.65 to S.6.d.46 (critical search from S.11.c.74 thro' Tea Sup.wt. to S.6.d.77. FLERS ROAD from S.12.a.22 to S.12.b.79 and all TEA SUPPORT. S.12.a.25 to S.12.b.9. all emplacement to have been strong'd thus, by resetting with sandbags, and an extensive emplacement made for tail gun. Casualties wounded a-dury O/R. 1. - Ends. Germans shelled CATEPILLAR VALLEY and MONTAUBAN ALLEY heavily at night.	Chui.
	7		In 1 Section Relief carried out. Half "D" Section in reserve relieved 1/2 "D" Section in the line at LONGUEVAL. "A" Section relieved "B" Section in SUFFOLK - GEORGE ST. "B" Section relieved "C" Section in PEAKE ST. "C" Section and 1/2 "D" Section returned to reserve at POZIERES REDOUBT. either Bde and Coy HQ had been withdrawn to. We still kept an advanced Coy HQ at MONTAUBAN ALLEY. Relief completed by 8.30 P.M. Guns in Support co-operated with artillery during bombardment between 5.30 P.M. and 6.30 P.M. "C" Section reported. Wounded. O/R.1. and wounded a-duty O/R. 2. Casualties POZIERES REDOUBT and MONTAUBAN ALLEY at night. Reports received from Sections as follows:- "A" Section Casualties Nil. "B" Section, at 6.25 P.M. in order to cover the 6th Dorsets, Jack-O on consol of WOOD LANE and ORCHARD TRENCH at S.11.c.4.8. we put up a barrage of fire. Shots Round that point and cont.d firing until 6.45 P.M. "D" Section Casualties Nil.	Chui.
	8		During our artillery bombardment between HAM and 6 A.M. 1 gun of "A" Section fired indirect as follows. (A) Shelling FLERS ROAD from end of Tea TRENCH (b) along TEA LANE. (c) Sending rounds onto from HIGH WOOD (d) on SWITCH TRENCH Hill behind SWITCH TRENCH. 8000 rounds expended. 2/Lt. H.R. MALDEN admitted to hospital sick. an efficient eye and evacuated. Reports received from section as follows:- "D" Section all correct. Casualties Nil. "A" Section. Everything quiet. Unable to fire on West Jetta we are digging a new trench. Casualties Nil. "B" Section all correct. Quiet night. Casualties Nil. DELVILLE WOOD shelled heavily by the enemy. Guns in return. One gun fired from a position about S.11.c.2.5 between 7.40 P.M. and 8.30 P.M. 1000 rounds. Employed, and searched S.12.a.10 and region. FLERS ROAD, Tea LANE area and behind SWITCH TRENCH. We were laid on a spot where we could see no bolts bursting. We fired in hopes of catching a sup.Post moving relief. During the night an emplacement was needed with sandbags enlarged and strengthened, and on obtaining his emplacement about. Bomb the advance dump and gun a-longueval. C.R. was ordered to embury fire. previously in the day he had moved thro' fires of ground fire. Recommended for Military Medal. Guns not touching. Stoney escape.	Chui.

WAR DIARY or INTELLIGENCE SUMMARY

Army Form C. 2118

50 M.G. Coy.

August 1916

Place	Date	Hour	Summary of Events and Information	Remarks and references to Appendices
POZIERES REDOUBT	9		Intention relief carried on. "C" Section relieved "B" Section in front line. "B" Section returned to reserve. Relief complete by 9.30 P.M. O.C. 41 M.G. Coy paid us and sections as follows:- "A" Section was shelled but quiet. Condition Nil. Biggest difficulty was getting rations and water. Casualties comet. O/R. 1. "B" Section all correct. Condition Nil. "C" Section all correct. Bombarded afresh water during the night. Casualties.	Chui.
	10		C.O. Lt. Col. Bell round front line guns in the early morning. 2.0 P.M. "A" M.G. Coy. Storm round C.O. rest. the O.C. Bde round front line guns in the afternoon. 2/Lt. W.R. Transom wounded in the eye at 3 P.M. Had difficulty in reserve relief the line. Relief complete 10.30 P.M. Reports received from the Huns as follows:- "A" Section in the line. Relief complete. Fired 500 rounds at HIGHWOOD and SWITCH TRENCH. Each gun made a covering attack and put 1 gun on front line. "B" Section. Situation unchanged and quiet. Heavy bombarded along up a barrage on the right. Several shells falling near the tramway of the dugout. Piccadilly & barely during the night. Casualties Nil. "A" Section all correct. Casualties Nil.	Chui.
	11		The following order was issued by O.C. Section. "Wherever artillery bombards front line co-operate by firing indirect will two of our guns. Targets as follows:- No.5 and 6 guns situated TEA LANE ground between SWITCH TRENCH and Tea Support. No.7 gun ROTT ST. to FLERS ROAD. No.8 gun lines to retaining from S.12.a.6. to S.6.C.6.6. No.8 gun to traverse Ten Support. Hand over Sections Reports received from Sections as follows:- "A" Section. Enemy fairly tranquil/quiet during the night, front line shelled for several hours. Enemy put up a barrage just behind front line. Trench in front of PEARSST. Communication trench is now bursted. Relief was carried out by day. Trench is taken up the position on the unfinished - and is called DORSET TRENCH, on extreme left gun lone in the sufficient. Casualties Nil. "A" Section Gunner killed O/R one. During the night we completed the artillery bombardment. Casualties Nil. "B" Section quiet at present. Casualties Nil.	Chui.
	12		Situation quiet. Relieved by 41 M.G. Coy during the night and early hours of the morning.	Chui.
	13		Relief complete. 8.30 A.M. Company marched back, by Sections, to an old camp near DERNANCOURT. Hot meal handed by our cooks and company paraded for baths in the evening.	Chui.
DERNAN COURT	14		Transport moved off at 6.30 A.M. under orders of the Brigade T/pt. officer. Company paraded for inspection etc. operation orders received.	Chui.

1875. Wt. W593/826. 1,000,000. 4/15. J.B.C. & A. A.D.S.S./Forms/C. 2118.

WAR DIARY or INTELLIGENCE SUMMARY

Army Form C. 2118

50 M.G. Coy. — August 1916 —

Place	Date	Hour	Summary of Events and Information	Remarks and references to Appendices
DERNANCOURT	15		Company paraded at 1.30AM and marched via TREUX and BUIRE to MERICOURT where we entrained and went to FIENVILLIERS CANDAS, where we detrained about 12 noon. Company then marched via AUTHEUX and BOISBERGUES to LE MEILLARD where accommodation had been arranged for us. Company rested the remainder of the day. Operation orders received.	CLIII
LE MEILLARD	16	10.00AM	Company paraded at 10.00AM for inspection. C.O. addressing the Company. Company paraded at 2.40PM and marched via FROHEN & PETIT and FROHEN & GRAND to VILLIERS L'HOPITAL. Accommodation arranged for men but not for officers. Operation orders received.	CLIII
VILLIERS L'HOPITAL · HALLOY	17	9.30AM	Company paraded at 9.30AM and marched via FROHEN & GRAND, MAZEROLLES, DOULLENS to HALLOY arriving about 4PM. No transport was on the march. Accommodation arranged for the Company during the day. Company cleaned guns during the day.	CLIII
	18	4PM	G.O.C. Brigade & O formed trenches around HEBUTERNE during the evening. Paid out in the evening.	
	19		Four officers went ahead to HEBUTERNE to reconnoitre positions. Company received orders to move to BAYENCOURT via PAS and SOUASTRE arriving about 4.30PM and waited for transport of ammunition etc to where 1st of M.G. Coy received.	CLIII
BAYENCOURT	20	8.30AM	Company loaded by Sections. First Section starting out at 8.30AM. Relief completed by 12 noon. Excellent help. Positions of Company as follows: Transport and A Section at COYNEUX. H.Q.at HEBUTERNE. "B" Section at SONIS [2 guns] WARWICK and CROSS ST [Yankee & YIDDISH No.2], "D" Section at WOMAN [2 guns each of them at AEROPLANE TRENCH by day] YANKEE & YIDDISH No.2. "C" Section Bell Position in HEBUTERNE for anti-aircraft and aircraft. One of these guns in need of repair. YIDDISH No.2 by night. Actuated at WELCOME ST under an officer are 3 signallers. HEBUTERNE was shelled slightly during the night. Reports received from Sections as follows: A Section Gun machine N.C. Casualties N.E. wood done. Indirect fire day out reinforced and shots fire Sentry put at @ Section. Very quiet during the night threat of YANKEE engaged by M.G. fire. Casualties N.I. @ Section. Everything quiet and correct. Gun in action N.E. Casualties N.I. CO visited B Section gun by night.	CLIII
	21		CO visited D Section gun by day. First cart out at Dump. Buyers. Casualties accidentally wounded O/R 1. Indirect fire shoots perform for proposed Gen Lot of F which was even hastily cancelled Reports received from Sections as follows "B" Section at 10.5 PM lost night 2 guns on WOMAN, was called out for emergency concentration torsion E1.BE + F.B.E. H50 minutes enfilade gun ceased fire on second at 10.20 PM Guns at YANKE and YIDDISH located Casualties NIL "C" Section and found during being operated on the following targets EX.E. FM5 EM2 EN Hostile	CLIII

Wt. W593/826 1,000,000 4/15 J.B.C. & A. A.D.S.S./Forms/C. 2118.

WAR DIARY or INTELLIGENCE SUMMARY

Army Form C. 2118

50 M.G. Coy.

August 1916.

Place	Date	Hour	Summary of Events and Information	Remarks and references to Appendices
HEBUTERNE	21		ETCH, EPTE Trenches, CEMETRY, K4d.4½.7½, K11.B.½.6, K5.c.6.11. Time of firing 10PM-11PM. Casualties Nil. B Section Everything quiet and correct. Own in action 2. Son.s. ¾ Left Gun at 10.5 PM Commenced firing on trench at entrance to ELBE Communication trench and carried on until about 11 until 10.15PM. Right Gun fired on ROSSIGNOL WOOD. at the same time. 250 rounds fired at each target ceased fire when ordered. Casualties Nil. Gun ST Gun were taken in positions and remained there on stand down to stand to. German MG's very active around HEBUTERNE at night. Co mounted C Section guns by day in company with D. Warnock M.G officer. Report is received from Sections as follows: B Section all correct can watches Nil. C Section all correct Casualties Nil.	Chu.
	22		Casualties Nil. 1/F emplacement improved.	Chu
	23		Gas alert given at 3AM. all Sections stood to. no gas discharged. The 60 toot G.O.C. Both around our front line gun positions. artillery on both sides rather more active than usual. Reports received from Sections as follows: "C" Section all guns and correct gun tested Casualties Nil. B Section Very quiet Casualties Nil. B Section all correct casualties Nil.	Chu
	24		1st Section relief carried out. "C" Section relieved "D" Section "D" Section went back to reserve. Report from Sections as follows: "C" Section Nothing to report Casualties Nil. "A" Section Two guns fired at the hursts of ranging on the following points. K4d.44, K5c19, K11.B.16. Results unfortunately unobtainable. The following how is introded, fired at intervals during the night. K11.B.16 and K5.c.19. Total expenditure of ammunition 2500 rounds. B Section all quiet except 1st Gun fire four shells around WARWICK. Casualties Nil. Own in CROSS ST fired 250 rounds in conjunction with anti-aircraft gun at an hostile aeroplane. It retired. Emplacement H and Sons have been improved, lines of fire corrected and laid. Reports received from Sections.	Chu
	25		Reports from Section as follows: all quiet casualties Nil. 1st improved trench in emplacement at SONS. CROSS St gun fired at enemy aero plane. German MG's active at night.	Chu
	26		at 3.00 AM enemy sent over several shells, trench mortar, machine guns also played on our trenches, this lasted for quarter of an hour. Two new fragment officer can report. 2/Lt. S.N. Rowbotham and 2/Lt. W. Bowerbank. Reports from Sections as follows:- "C" Section Nothing to report Casualties Nil and fired B Section. Everything Quiet and correct one of our patrols was observed at 11PM by enemy and fired on MG's and bombs used. Casualties wounded O/R 1. Own in action. CROSS ST gun fired 250 rounds at hostile aeroplane. Work done. SONS a new open emplacement on right WARWICK operations emplacement commenced close to gun house position on right. CROSS ST firing gun Maxim being improved Guns on tested A Section 2 guns fired indirect from K4d.97 to K11.a.9.7. left gun commencing at 10.45 PM to 12 MN. and along the line from K4d.97 to K11.a.9.7. left gun commencing	

WAR DIARY or INTELLIGENCE SUMMARY

Army Form C. 2118

50 M.G. Coy. — August 1916.

Place	Date	Hour	Summary of Events and Information	Remarks and references to Appendices
HEBUTERNE	26		on the former point and the night gun on the latter. Safety measures were adopted. Rounds expended work done return of emplacement. Casualties nil.	Cu
	27	2100.	work. off as turned the line and was fired at portions and crossed objects. Several shells of different calibre dropped into HEBUTERNE during the day. C.O. visited in L.G. reference to co-operation between french guns. C.O. of Hungry visited 51 M.G. By to ascertain capability of his guns and arrange co-operation. Between flank corps to ascertain from sections. A Section one gun in action against hostile aeroplane. conjunction with anti- aircraft gun. aeroplane retired. Work done. Fire Emplacement. Casualties nil B Section Guns in action. Nil Casualties Nil work done CROSS ST trench made similar and red emplacement repaired. alternative emplacement carried on work at WARWICK alternative emplacement at SONIS completed. C Section Gun in action Nil Casualties Nil work done open emplacement started at WOMAN YANKEE YIDDISH.	Cu
	28		C.O. lectured at BAYENCOURT on the tactical handling of Machine Guns. D Section guns used to stores on skates. In preservation relief carried out "A" Section relieved B Section. A Section B Section returned to reserve. Baths arranged for the Company. Reports received from Sections as follows: A Section Guns in action Nil Casualties Nil. Work done. Emplacement at SONIS slightly built up in form of L.G. gun by two layers of sandbags, and in front of left. By new layer front and head cover completed. Platform of emplacement of WARWICK Sep. R.H. relieved by one layer of new alternative emplacement nearly completed, only two layers of sandbags. Traverse & Platform. C Section Guns in action Nil gun in CROSS ST increased by making small clearing in front. YANKEE / outpost emplacement 13 our Casualties Nil work done YIDDISH emplacement erected. It back at also saved 1 ft. alternative emplacement of night gun emplacement at NO MAN's land. Nil Casualties Nil all covert at relay activity in front D Section Guns in action. Guns all tested outside during the day.	Cu
	29		Reports from Sections as follows. C Section Guns in action Nil Casualties Nil work done. Improvements of M.G. Gun position carried out. Steps two red in H Platoon. skid material Gun from Y. did also moved to YVONNE in reserve. A Section Gun in action Nil Casualties Nil work done SONIS night post & emplacement finished and left both emplacement repaired. WARWICK. Both emplacements repaired. CROSS ST. Boards for both sections given. Heavy bombardment on night tops line S Section work to report. Very quiet during night. Casualties Nil. C.O. lectured Seigon 4 on trench duties as not for the Burrow M.G. officer wet ran the shell ground. Report received from Section as follows: - A Section Guns in action 2, at SONIS firing between 10-3 PM and 10.50 PM at the following target. K1c95 – K11d12, K12A 1/2, 2 1/2 – K12d9.9, K12B19 – K12 & 62 are kill at 2 – K11d 2.6. Ammo expended: work done. Bombs on bassinet founded at SONIS. Revolving armour C emplacement founded from WARWICK finished. Casualties Nil.	Cu
	30			

WAR DIARY or INTELLIGENCE SUMMARY

Army Form C. 2118

50 M.G. Coy.
August 1916.

(Erase heading not required.)

Place	Date	Hour	Summary of Events and Information	Remarks and references to Appendices
HEBUTERNE	30		B Section Walderne on Intermit Fire on Pheasant but quietly during rest of day weather. Cavalleri N.E. D Section Gun in action 3. A t WOMAN. 2 guns fired 1500 rounds at YANKEE 1 gun fired 300 rounds. Target. Enemy Communication Trenches. ELBE, EPTE, ETCH and CEMETRY. No dam Wd. Branch put into dugout at WOMAN and YVONNE. Proposed gun at BIVOUAC but might did not externalize our gun. Could not be warned because firing at the right time from the Enemy.	Clear
	31		Several Shrapnel fell into HEBUTERNE during the morning. New M.G. Shoots Tested. Gas at 10 Off. Arranged but did not externally. Report from C Section Gun in action W.O.M.A.N fired 200 rounds at EPTE and ETCH communication trenches from 11.15 p.m – 11.30 p.m. Gun walker N.E. Wald on Stores of YVONNE. Enemy placement wood sent up shell flare. Left emplacement at WOMAN improved Bulk Branch put down. Another gun in action N.E. refused men at corner and disused Repaired track backup to emplacement at both ends. D Section watching enemy of sent cart on N.T. Ready in starting on right portion. Cavalleri N.E.	Clear

MESSAGES AND SIGNALS.

Army Form C. 2121.
(In pads of 100.)

SECRET

TO { 10 4/7 Yorkshire Rgt
7 E/ Yorkshires Regt

Sender's Number: V 58

Warning	orders	not	10 4/YORK
Rgt	and	7 E/YORK	Regt
will	be	prepared	to
move	into	the	GREEN
LINE	tonight		Relief
over	his		issued
later			

From: SD Bde
Time: 9.30 am

P Barker Capt.

Note.

In the War Diary of 31st July 1917. the 4th Divn was said to be on the left of the Battn this should read "Royal Naval Division.

REC

Attached to War Diary Aug/17

MESSAGES AND SIGNALS. Army Form C. 2121.

TO: 50 M.G. Coy

Sender's Number: SV 61
Day of Month: 20

Warning Order.
50 M.G. Coy will relieve
the 52nd M.G. Coy tonight.
Relief orders follow.
Acknowledge.

From: 50 Bde
Time: 12 10 pm

"A" Form.
MESSAGES AND SIGNALS.

Army Form C. 2121.
(In pads of 100.)

TO { 7 Yorks
     6 Dorset

Sender's Number.	Day of Month.	In reply to Number.	AAA
SV75	21		

Noon aaa
The 7th Yorkshire Rgt and 6 Dorset
Rgt will be prepared
to move into the line
tonight
orders follow.

From 50 Bde
Place
Time 12 45 pm

Bucks Capt

"A" Form.
MESSAGES AND SIGNALS.

Army Form C.2121 (in pads of 100).

TO: Savage

Sender's Number: G946
Day of Month: 14

WARNING order aaa School will relieve SAVAGE tonight on right bde front aaa. Necessary reconnaissances to be carried out forthwith aaa Relief of M.G. bays will take place 24 hours later aaa On completion of relief advanced SCHOOL will withdraw to CUTTING aaa SAVAGE on relief will move to St. NICHOLAS area originally occupied by SCHOOL aaa Advd dhq will close at CUTTING 3 pm opening same hour at present rear hq aaa SENIOR M.O. will move from present position to advanced dhq after 3 pm aaa ACKNOWLEDGE aaa Addd Savage School Senior reptd all concerned

From: STRONG Adv
Time: 4/30 am

"A" Form.
MESSAGES AND SIGNALS.

Army Form C.2121
(in pads of 100).
No. of Message _____

Prefix _____ Code _____ m.
Office of Origin and Service Instructions.

Fullerphone

| Words | Charge |

Sent
At _____ m.
To _____
By _____

This message is on a/c of:
_____ Service.
(Signature of "Franking Officer.")

Recd. at _____ m.
Date _____
From _____
By _____

TO { SASH
     SWAP

| Sender's Number. | Day of Month. | In reply to Number. | AAA |
| SV 949 | 13 | | |

To assist you tonight 18 Pdrs. will open at 10/30 pm burst of fire continuing for 10 minutes on CHARLIE as far South as safety limit CUTHBERT and COD aaa Rate of fire 4 rounds per 100 yards of trench per minute aaa During burst slopes of GREENLAND HILL in I.8.a. and c will be searched with shrapnel aaa similar burst at same rate for same time will be fired as follows aaa 7/15 pm on Northern half CHARLIE 8/25 pm as for burst at 10/30 pm 9/35 pm Southern end WIT and WEART aaa Attacking infantry should check watches at each burst aaa 18 Pdrs will maintain intermittent fire on CHARLIE from safety limit on South to sunken road throughout day aaa acknowledge addressed SWAP and SASH

From SAVAGE
Place
Time 5/55 pm

The above may be forwarded as now corrected. (Z) Sd) P.S. Barber Capt

Censor. Signature of Addressor or person authorised to telegraph in his name.

* This line should be erased if not required.
750,000. W 2186—M509. H. W. & V., Ld. 6/16.

"A" Form.
MESSAGES AND SIGNALS.

Army Form C.2121 (in pads of 100).

TO: Savage

Sender's Number: G.927
Day of Month: 13

AAA

SAVAGE will capture CURLY trench tonight 10pm aaa To assist inf. attack 18 pdrs. will open at 10.3pm burst of fire continuing for 10 minutes on CHARLIE as far south as safety limit CUTHBERT & COD aaa Rate of fire 4 rounds per 100 yds. of trench per minute aaa During burst slopes of GREENLAND HILL in I8A and c a b searched with SHRAPNEL aaa Similar bursts at same rate for same time will be fired as follows aaa 7/15pm on Northern half CHARLIE 8/25pm as for burst at 10.3pm 9/35pm southern end WIT & WEARY aaa Attacking inf should check watches at each burst aaa 18 pdrs will maintain intermittent H.E. fire on CHARLIE from safety limit on south to Sunken Road throughout day aaa ACKNOWLEDGE aaa addd Savage reptd School. Senior. Secure. Roe. Ship. Cardinal. Rosangus

From: Strong
Place:
Time: 6.55pm

"A" Form.
MESSAGES AND SIGNALS.

Army Form C.2121 (in pads of 100).

Prefix	Code	m.	Words	Charge	This message is on a/c of:	Recd. at	m.
Office of Origin and Service Instructions.			Sent			Date	
			At m.		Service.	From	
			To			By	
			By		(Signature of "Franking Officer.")		

TO { SANE. SASH. SWAP. SATIN. SATISFY. SANDAL. STRONG

Sender's Number.	Day of Month.	In reply to Number.	AAA
SV.934	13		

Moves and reliefs tonight as follows SATIN relieves SASH details to be arranged between COs aaa on relief SASH will move to CLOVER. CUSHION. CLARK. CADIZ aaa one company and Hqrs will move to GREEN line now occupied by SATIN aaa SANE will move two companies from GREEN line to CHILI where they will come under orders of SWAP aaa These Coys to arrive in CHILI by 9pm aaa SWAP will move two coys back to GREEN line aaa Relief of SWAP by SANE will be carried out tonight as soon after 11pm as situation allows aaa Inter battalion boundary if CURLY is taken will be 150 yds S of CURLY and * CHAPLAIN South of junction with CASH to left battalion thence westward present battalion boundary

* Two coys SWAP moving to CHILI and CLASP

From: SAVAGE
Place:
Time: 2/35 am

(Z) H. Simson Capt.

"A" Form.
MESSAGES AND SIGNALS.

Army Form C.2121 (in pads of 100).

TO: SWAP. SASH. SATISFY. SENIOR. SANE. SATIN. STRONG   by Fullerphone

Sender's Number: S.V.936   Day of Month: 13   AAA

SWAP will rush CURLY trench tonight at 10pm aaa SASH will co-operate by working North in CURLY and behind and just east of it aaa Artillery will fire bursts of 10 minutes from about 11pm on CHARLIE and on COD and CUTHBERT and neighbouring targets so as not to attract attention to any one point aaa One of these bursts will begin on CHARLIE COD and CUTHBERT at zero plus three minutes aaa SWAP will establish a flag as far NORTH in CHARLIE as possible aaa The front line is to be held at all costs aaa Active patrolling will be carried out aaa Acknowledge

From: SAVAGE
Place:
Time: 2pm

"A" Form.
MESSAGES AND SIGNALS.

Army Form C.2121 (in pads of 100).

TO: SWAP. SASH

Sender's Number.	Day of Month.	In reply to Number.	
SV.936	13		AAA

From other intelligence received Corps believe enemy may have withdrawn to line CANDY. COST. WHIP. aaa SASH is pushing down CURLY as far as possible this morning aaa. If possible SWAP to send patrol into North end of CURLY aaa low flying aeroplane was not fired on at 7am from CHARLIE or CURLY this morning aaa SWAP to report early definitely whether enemy holds S end of CHARLIE and CURLY aaa Troops on right occupied half ROEUX and took 50 prisoners.

From Place: SAVAGE
Time: 11am

"A" Form.
MESSAGES AND SIGNALS.

Army Form C.2121 (in pads of 100).

TO SWAP

Sender's Number.	Day of Month.	In reply to Number.	A A A
SV.984	13.		

SASH has rushed post at junction CURLY and CUPID stop established 40 yards up CURLY aaa opposition slight five prisoners aaa SWAP to make preparations for capture of remainder of CURLY and submit proposals

From SAVAGE
Place
Time 8/15 am

"A" Form.
MESSAGES AND SIGNALS.

Army Form C.2121 (in pads of 100).

TO: Savage

Sender's Number: G.898
Day of Month: 12
AAA

Continuation G.888 and G.891 aaa Operation will now be limited to capture of junction of CUPID and CROOK and establishment of advd. post as far up CURLY as possible aaa line CUPID-CROOK-CHAPLIN-CASH to be made good and connected up aaa Operation will be carried out not later than 10/30 pm without arty. preparation aaa ACKNOWLEDGE aaa Added RECIPIENTS G.888

From: STRONG
Place: Advn
Time: 9/5 p

"A" Form.
MESSAGES AND SIGNALS.
Army Form C.2121 (in pads of 100).

TO: SATIN

Sender's Number: S.V.906 Day of Month: 12

No relief tonight aaa SATIN will send two companies up to CUSHION trench at 9.30pm where they will come under orders of OC SASH

From: SAVAGE
Time: 8.12pm

"A" Form.
MESSAGES AND SIGNALS.

Army Form C.2121 (in pads of 100).
No. of Message _____

Prefix .... Code .... m.	Words	Charge	This message is on a/c of:	Recd. at .... m.
Office of Origin and Service Instructions.				Date ....
	Sent		.... Service.	
....	At .... m.			From ....
....	To			
....	By		(Signature of "Franking Officer.")	By ....

TO { **SASH SWAP STRONG.**

Sender's Number.	Day of Month.	In reply to Number.	
* S.V.904	12		AAA

Tonight SASH will rush the german stop at junction of CUPID and CURLY and will establish strong posts at junction of CUPID and CROOK with advanced post and stop as far north up CURLY as possible aaa OC SASH will make all arrangements and notify Zero hour aaa There will be no artillery preparation aaa Two companies SATIN will move up to CUSHION trench and come under orders of OC SASH aaa line to be held is CUPID - CROOK - CHAPLIN - CASH - CUBA aaa SASH will hold CUPID and CROOK disposing of SATIN as required aaa SWAP will hold CHAPLAIN - CASH and CUBA aaa Operation must be started so as to be finished before 10/30pm tonight aaa Addd SASH repeated SWAP STRONG

From **SAVAGE**
Place
Time 8/40pm

The above may be forwarded as now corrected.   (Z) W. Johnson Capt.
Censor.   Signature of Addressor or person authorised to telegraph in his name.

* This line should be erased if not required.

"A" Form.
MESSAGES AND SIGNALS.

Army Form C.2121
(in pads of 100).
No. of Message _____

Prefix ..... Code ..... m.	Words	Charge	This message is on a/c of:	Recd. at .... m.
Office of Origin and Service Instructions.				
....	Sent		.... Service.	Date ....
Place	At .... m.			From ....
....	To			
....	By		(Signature of "Franking Officer.")	By ....

TO { Savage

Sender's Number.	Day of Month.	In reply to Number.	
G 891	12		A A A

Continuation G. 888 aaa attack deferred aaa Zero will be notified later aaa Acknowledge aaa Warn all recipients G 888

From Strong Adv
Place
Time 6/50 am

The above may be forwarded as now corrected. (Z)

Censor. Signature of Addressor or person authorised to telegraph in his name.

* This line should be erased if not required.

"A" Form.
MESSAGES AND SIGNALS.

Army Form C.2121 (in pads of 100).

PRIORITY

TO SASH

Sender's Number: SV 903
Day of Month: 12

SV 694 is cancelled aaa detailed instructions follow for rushing stop at junction of CUPID & CURLY

From: SAVAGE
Time: 4/50 pm

(Sd) B Rowley

"A" Form.
MESSAGES AND SIGNALS.
Army Form C.2121
(in pads of 100).
No. of Message

Prefix .... Code .... m.
Office of Origin and Service Instructions.

Priority

Words | Charge
Sent
At.................m.
To
By

This message is on a/c of:
..................Service.
(Signature of "Franking Officer.")

Recd. at.................m.
Date..................
From..................
By..................

TO — Savage

Sender's Number: Y889 | Day of Month: 12th | In reply to Number: | AAA

One Bn. SCHOOL will move to Green line N of LEMON TRENCH H.10.D head to arrive 9.30pm aaa Bn. will come under orders of SAVAGE on crossing brown line aaa Bn. Comdr to report in advance to Adv SAVAGE H.Q. H16.B.6.5. aaa Acknowledge aaa. Addsd SCHOOL reptd SAVAGE

From STRONG
Place
Time 6.25pm

"A" Form.
MESSAGES AND SIGNALS.

Army Form C.2121 (in pads of 100).

Prefix .... **Code** .... m.
Office of Origin and Service Instructions.

Urgent Priority

Words | **Charge**

Sent At .... m.
To ....
By ....

This message is on a/c of:
.... Service.
(Signature of "Franking Officer.")

Recd. at .... m.
Date ....
From ....
By ....

TO { Savage

Sender's Number.	Day of Month.	In reply to Number.	AAA
G.888	12		

SAVAGE will attack CURLY TONIGHT at 9pm from direction CUPID and CASH aaa A local barrage will be put down on CHARLIE to within 150 Yds. of Junction with CASH - CUTHBERT - COD to RAILWAY line about J.14.a Central aaa Crest of GREENLAND HILL North of rly. will be swept by 60 pdrs. aaa WHIP crossroads and North Eastern portion of CHARLIE will be also be kept under fire aaa Barrage will be maintained intense for ten minutes and then slow for twenty minutes aaa Putting down of barrage will be signal for attack aaa ACKNOWLEDGE aaa Addsd SAVAGE. SENIOR. SODE. SAR. SECURE. repeated Corps. HA

From STRONG
Place
Time 6/10pm

"A" Form.
MESSAGES AND SIGNALS.

Army Form C.2121 (in pads of 100).

TO	SANE SATIN		

Sender's Number.	Day of Month.	In reply to Number.	AAA
S.V.695	12		

Warning order aaa SATIN relieves SASH and SANE relieves SWAP late tonight aaa CURLY will be rushed at 9pm by SWAP and SASH

From SAVAGE

"A" Form.
MESSAGES AND SIGNALS.

Army Form C.2121 (in pads of 100).

TO: SWAP   SASH

Sender's Number: SV694
Day of Month: 12
AAA

Continuation SV688 aaa Time 9pm instead of 8.30pm aaa Signal for rushing CURLY will be fall of barrage to isolate it at 9pm aaa Acknowledge aaa Stokes ordered to cooperate aaa Rifle Grenades will be of great use aaa Barrage will not come down on CURLY but is arranged to isolate it aaa SASH will rush from CUPID and SWAP from CASH aaa SATIN relieves SASH and SANE relieves SWAP tonight orders follow.

From: SAVAGE
Place:
Time: 5.50pm

(Sd) H.J. Simson Capt.

"A" Form.
MESSAGES AND SIGNALS.

Army Form C.2121 (in pads of 100).

TO: SWAP SASH

Sender's Number: S.V.688
Day of Month: 12

From O.P. can see much movement of our men in CUPID and CROOK and in CASH aaa It looks as if we held junction of CUPID and CROOK and also some of CURLY aaa SWAP and SASH will send Officers patrols to clear up situation and report by 8pm definitely aaa SASH will make all preparations to capture junction of CUPID and CURLY tonight and SWAP will prepare to take junction of CASH and CURLY and CURLY up to junction CURLY·CUPID·CROOK exclusive aaa Prepare to rush objectives without Artillery preparation at 8/30pm aaa C.O's to arrange details together aaa Aeroplane will probably call for flares about 6/30 pm this evening aaa Acknowledge

From: SAVAGE
Place:
Time: 4/30pm

"A" Form.
MESSAGES AND SIGNALS.

Army Form C.2121
(in pads of 100).
No. of Message ____

Prefix ____ Code ____ m.	Words	Charge	This message is on a/c of:	Recd. at ____ m.
Office of Origin and Service Instructions.				Date ____
____	Sent		____ Service.	From ____
____	At ____ m. To ____ By ____		(Signature of "Franking Officer.")	By ____

TO { Savage

Sender's Number.	Day of Month.	In reply to Number.	AAA
* G 883	12		

Continuation G.848 aaa In order to ensure safety flank and of railway GOC considers that in addition CURLY must be made good and joined to CASH tonight aaa One Bn. SCHOOL will be placed at your disposal, in Bde reserve if you require it aaa Report what Arty support you require aaa Re your SV.682 G.O.C. considers you should send Staff Officer up to ascertain definite situation about CROOK if you have not already done so aaa Acknowledge addso Savage rept SOME SCHOOL SENIOR.

From STRONG
Place
Time 3/5 pm

The above may be forwarded as now corrected.   (Z)
Censor.   Signature of Addressor or person authorised to telegraph in his name.
* This line should be erased if not required.

"A" Form.
MESSAGES AND SIGNALS.

Army Form C.2121
(in pads of 100).
No. of Message _____

Prefix .... Code .... m.	Words	Charge	This message is on a/c of:	Recd. at .... m.
Office of Origin and Service Instructions.				Date ....
....	Sent		.... Service.	From ....
....	At .... m.			
....	To			By ....
....	By		(Signature of "Franking Officer.")	

TO { Savage

| Sender's Number. | Day of Month. | In reply to Number. | A A A |
| * G.404 | 12th | | |

Refe your G.883 aaa SCHEME have been put at the disposal of G.O.C. SAVAGE as for 6pm tonight at half an hours notice to move aaa resent position of SCHEME railway cutting H7D95.40 aaa O.C. SCHEME has been ordered to get in touch with G.O.C. SAVAGE aaa Addd Strong advd G. reptd SAVAGE

From SCHOOL
Place
Time 5/25pm

The above may be forwarded as now corrected. (Z)

Censor. Signature of Addresser or person authorised to telegraph his name.
* This line should be erased if not required.
750,000. W 2186—M509. H. W. & V., Ld. 6/16.

"A" Form.
MESSAGES AND SIGNALS.

Army Form C.2121 (in pads of 100).

Prefix .... Code .... m.	Words	Charge	This message is on a/c of:	Recd. at .... m.
Office of Origin and Service Instructions.				Date ....
	Sent		.... Service.	From ....
	At .... m.			
	To		(Signature of "Franking Officer.")	By ....
	By			

TO { Savage

| Sender's Number. | Day of Month. | In reply to Number. | A A A |
| G.378 | 12th. | | |

Absolutely essential that junction of CUPID and CROOK be made good aaa This will be done after if not possible by day aaa Addressed SAVAGE repeated Senior Some aaa acknowledge

From STRONG
Place
Time 1/20 pm

"A" Form.
MESSAGES AND SIGNALS.

Army Form C.2121 (in pads of 100).

TO	SWAP SANE

Sender's Number: SV 66
Day of Month: 12

2 Coys SANE now moving to COPPER placed at disposal of SWAP and come under orders of OC. SWAP

From: SAVAGE
Time: 10/10 am

"A" Form.
MESSAGES AND SIGNALS.
Army Form C.2121 (in pads of 100).

TO: SANE

Sender's Number: S.V.663

AAA

Move two companies to COPPER and endeavour to get touch with SWAP reporting if they require support

From: SAVAGE
Place:
Time: 9am

Sd B Barber Capt

"A" Form.
MESSAGES AND SIGNALS.

Army Form C.2121
(in pads of 100).
No. of Message ....

Prefix .... Code .... m.	Words	Charge	This message is on a/c of:	Recd. at .... m.
Office of Origin and Service Instructions.				Date ....
....	Sent		.... Service.	From ....
....	At .... m. To By		(Signature of "Franking Officer.")	By ....

TO { SANE SATISFY SANDAL
SATIN SAMPLE by Fullerphone

| Sender's Number. | Day of Month. | In reply to Number. | A A A |
| * S.V.647 | 11 | | |

Objectives taken aaa O.O.143 comes into force

From SAVAGE
Place
Time 11.45 am

(Z) (Sd) H.J. Simson Capt.

Censor. Signature of Addressor or person authorised to telegraph in his name.
* This line should be erased if not required.

"A" Form.
MESSAGES AND SIGNALS.

Army Form C.2121
(in pads of 100)
No. of Message _____

Prefix ___ Code ___ m.	Words	Charge	This message is on a/c of:	Recd. at ___ m.
Office of Origin and Service Instructions.	Sent			Date ___
	At ___ m.		___ Service.	From ___
	To ___			By ___
	By ___		(Signature of "Franking Officer.")	

TO { **SWAP**

Sender's Number.	Day of Month.	In reply to Number.	
S.V.64a	11		AAA

Objectives taken aaa OO.143 now comes into force aaa Acknowledge

From **SAVAGE**
Place
Time 11 am

The above may be forwarded as now corrected. (Z) Lt. H. Simson Capt
Censor. Signature of Addressee or person authorised to telegraph in his name.

* This line should be erased if not required.

"A" Form.
MESSAGES AND SIGNALS.

Army Form C.2121 (in pads of 100).

TO: SASH

Sender's Number: S.V.638
Day of Month: 11

AAA

Operations take place tomorrow as in OO.143 aaa Report by 4 am where you have assembled

From: SAVAGE
Time: 10.45 am

Bd/ H.J. Simson Capt

"A" Form.
MESSAGES AND SIGNALS.

Army Form C.2121
(in pads of 100).
No. of Message ....

Prefix .... Code .... m.	Words	Charge	This message is on a/c of:	Recd. at .... m.
Office of Origin and Service Instructions.				Date ....
....	Sent		.... Service.	From ....
....	At .... m.			
....	To		(Signature of "Franking Officer.")	By ....
	By			

TO: SANE · SCHEME · SWAP · SATIN · SASH · SATISFY · SANDAL · STRONG · SCHOOL · SENIOR · SNAKE

Sender's Number.	Day of Month.	In reply to Number.	AAA
* S.V.6	14		

Tonight the brigade front will be reorganised on a three battalion front instead of two. aaa SCHEME will move two coys to CUBA from present left boundary to CUT inclusive with one company in CHILI one company in GREEN line Hqrs relieves SANE Hqrs in CUBA aaa on relief by SCHEME SANE will move South and take over front from CUT inclusive to present right boundary relieving SWAP aaa on relief SWAP moves back to St. NICHOLAS aaa SANE Hqrs moves into CLARKE Trench aaa SATIN stands fast but 2 coys SCARF come into support relieving 3 coys SASH now attached SATIN aaa SWAP will supply 8 guides to SCHEME to report to Bde. Hqrs 6pm aaa SANDAL and SATISFY stand fast aaa on completion reliefs tonight G.O.C. SCHOOL takes over command from SAVAGE aaa tomorrow night ROE will relieve SANE. SATIN

From
Place
Time

The above may be forwarded as now corrected. (Z)

.... Censor. Signature of Addressor or person authorised to telegraph in his name.

* This line should be erased if not required.

750,000. W 2186—M509. H. W. & V., Ld. 6/16.

"A" Form.
MESSAGES AND SIGNALS.

Army Form C.2121

TO	10th W York	7th York	53rd Field Amb
	7th E York	50th M.G Coy	78th Field Coy RE
	6th Dorset	50th T.M. Battery	

| Sender's Number. | Day of Month. | In reply to Number. | AAA |
| Sr 550 | 4. | | |

All units to be prepared to move to Y huts in L1B about 6 AM tomorrow morning

From
Place: 50th B.de
Time: 8.10 AM.

"A" Form.
MESSAGES AND SIGNALS.

Army Form C.2121 (in pads of 100).

TO: SASH SATIN SCHOOL

Sender's Number: SV4
Day of Month: 10
AAA

Tonight two coys SCARF will relieve 3 coys of SASH now attached to SATIN aaa SATIN will find guides from SATIN Hqrs forward aaa SASH will provide guides up to SATIN Hqrs from Bde Hqrs reporting there 8pm aaa On relief SASH moves back to ST. NICHOLAS guides will meet at cutting H 8 a 00 aaa addd SASH SATIN repeated SCHOOL

From: SAVAGE
Place: 4.25am
Time:

"A" Form.
MESSAGES AND SIGNALS.

Army Form C.2121 (in pads of 100).
No. of Message ....

Prefix .... Code .... m.	Words	Charge	This message is on a/c of:	Recd. at .... m.
Office of Origin and Service Instructions.	Sent		.... Service.	Date ....
....	At .... m.			From ....
....	To			
....	By		(Signature of " Franking Officer.")	By ....

TO { SAVAGE

| Sender's Number. | Day of Month. | In reply to Number. | A A A |
| G 953 | 14 | | |

ROE will take over STRONG line up to CUT inclusive I.y.1.15 night 15/16 aaa Accordingly Bttn SAVAGE holding this portion of line will remain until relieved by troops ROE aaa SCHOOL will tonight relieve remainder SAVAGE and will take over SENIOR line night 15/16 up to CURSE inclusive aaa GOC SCHOOL will assume command SAVAGE front on completion relieve left Bttn SAVAGE tonight aaa Bde H.Q. will remain as at present SCHOOL maintaining ato hq in PUDDING aha Rear

From
Place
Time

"A" Form.
MESSAGES AND SIGNALS.

Army Form C.2121
(in pads of 100).

boundaries will be notified later aaa Relief of SATISFY will take place night 15th/16th. aaa Acknowledge aaa Adds SAVAGE. SCHOOL. SENIOR. ROE. SHARE reptd SAND Salvar

From Strong Adv 1.25 pm

"A" Form.
MESSAGES AND SIGNALS.

Army Form C.2121 (in pads of 100).
No. of Message

Prefix .... Code .... m	Words	Charge	This message is on a/c of:	Recd. at .... m
Office of Origin and Service Instructions.				Date ....
....	Sent		.... Service.	From ....
....	At .... m			By ....
....	To		(Signature of "Franking Officer.")	
....	By			

| TO | SAVAGE | | | |

| Sender's Number. | Day of Month. | In reply to Number. | AAA |
| * G 485 | 14 | | |

ROE will take over STRONG line up to CVT exclusive IYD.13 night 15/16 aaa Accordingly Battalions SAVAGE holding this portion of the line will remain until relieved by troops of ROE aaa SCHOOL will tonight relieve Remained SAVAGE aaa Your Battalion will take over this part of the line tonight from SANE in CUBA and SWAP in CASH and CHAPLIN aaa Send representatives to reconnoitre aaa Relief not to start before 8pm aaa Relief to be arranged between OC Battalions aaa Bruton SCHOOL hq. adv. in PUDDING reference H16B86. acknowledge aaa Addd SCHEM repl. SAVAGE. SCARF

From: School
Place:
Time: 2/30pm

"A" Form.
MESSAGES AND SIGNALS.

Army Form C.2121 (in pads of 100).

TO: SAVAGE . SCHEME

Sender's Number: G 436
Day of Month: 14

ROE will take over STRONG line up to CUT exclusive S 4 D.1.3 night 15th/16th aaa Accordingly battns SAVAGE holding this portion of the line will remain until relieved by troops of ROE aaa SCHOOL will tonight relieve remaining SAVAGE aaa Two companies of your battn. will relieve headquarters and 3 companies of SASH about CADIZ aaa Send representatives to reconnoitre aaa Relief not to start before 8pm aaa Relief to be arranged between OC Battns. aaa Position SCHEME hq. advanced is in pudding reference H 16 B.8.6. acknowledge aaa Addsd SCARF repld Savage Scheme

From: SCHOOL
Place:
Time: 2/30pm

"A" Form.
MESSAGES AND SIGNALS.

Army Form C.2121
(in pads of 100).
No. of Message ....

Prefix .... Code .... m.
Office of Origin and Service Instructions.

Words | Charge
Sent
At .... m.
To ....
By ....

This message is on a/c of:
.... Service.
(Signature of "Franking Officer.")

Recd. at .... m.
Date ....
From ....
By ....

TO { Savage

Sender's Number. | Day of Month. | In reply to Number. | A A A
* G.961 | 14 | |

Additional to G.958 aaa SCHOOL will relieve supporting troops to right Bn SAVAGE tonight aaa Ack aaa Adds Savage School Res

From: Strong 2/16 pm
Place
Time

The above may be forwarded as now corrected. (Z)

Censor. Signature of Addressor or person authorised to telegraph in his name.
* This line should be erased if not required.

"A" Form.
MESSAGES AND SIGNALS.
Army Form C.2121 (in pads of 100).

TO: Savage

Sender's Number: G.956
Day of Month: 14/5

AAA

My G.946 is cancelled aaa Fresh orders will be issued aaa ACKNOWLEDGE aaa Addsd SAVAGE SCHOOL SENIOR rptd all concerned

From / Place / Time: Adv Strong 12/50 pm

"A" Form.
MESSAGES AND SIGNALS.

Army Form C.2121 (in pads of 100).

TO STRONG 6

Sender's Number: S.V.986
Day of Month: 14
A A A

SATIN has relieved SASH both Hqrs now in CADIZ aaa SASH Hqrs and one company move back to GREEN LINE when C.Os are satisfied that front is properly taken over aaa SANE has relieved SWAP aaa SWAP reorganised to form one by holds CHAPLIN and CASH and SANE holds CUBA aaa SANE Hqrs in CUBA aaa 2 of 4 reserve M. guns moved up to railway and now in position about I 14 a. 0 3.

From: SAVAGE
Time: 10am

(Sd) W.F. Simson Capt

"A" Form.
MESSAGES AND SIGNALS.

Army Form C.2121 (in pads of 100).

Guns of SATISFY and SANDAL South of line. CUT CLYDE aaa Guns south of this line will be relieved by SCHOOL aaa acknowledge

From SAVAGE 5pm

(Z) H.J. Simson Capt

CONFIDENTIAL

50ᵀᴴ M.G. COY.

Sepᵀ 1916.

Army Form C. 2118.

WAR DIARY
or
INTELLIGENCE SUMMARY
(Erase heading not required.)

50 M.G. Coy
September 1916

Instructions regarding War Diaries and Intelligence Summaries are contained in F.S. Regs, Part II. and the Staff Manual respectively. Title Pages will be prepared in manuscript.

Place	Date	Hour	Summary of Events and Information	Remarks and references to Appendices
# EAUTERNE	1		Shrapnel over the village during the morning. Intersection relief carried out. "B" Section refused at "B" Section. "B" Section retired relief. "C" Section returned to Position at CEYNEUX. Relief received from "B" Section as follows:- A Section Guns in action. Nil. Casualties Nil. Work done. Shelter at WARWICK, rounded off corner of trench leading to emplacement and revetted square, cleaned and oiled at emplacement, all ammunition in Store at CROSS ST. B Section Guns in action Nil. Casualties Nil. Work done at lighted up round. B Section Guns in action Nil. Changing position at 4.45 PM have gun teams proceeded five positions have been altered. Changing position at 4.15 PM have gun teams proceeded to take up position at YIDDISH No 1 and SHRINE POST, remained there during the night and returned to 1/7 position in the morning. B Section Guns in action Nil. Can watches Nil. Work at their emplacements being carried on. Co-andged co-operation with southern group of artillery.	Clear.
	2		Relief from Section as follows:- A Section Guns in action Nil. Work done at CROSS ST. Repair four sections of trench rounded off and widened. Fired Scarabbyaing along side of trench. Work done on camouflet his traverse. B Section Guns in action Nil. Casualties Nil. Work done lot of work done at emplacement for both guns & men. B Section Guns in action at 1/7 position Improving both at covered and concealment for both guns & men. B Section guns in action at position Nil. Casualties Nil. Emplacement at WOMAN Emplacement and YANKEE were improved. Guns of night Section vacated by the C.O. by night & F.	Clear.
	3		Heavy bombardment heard in the region of THIEPVAL. 2 wills vacated guns of left Sector by night. A Section Guns in action Nil. M.G's were active at night. Relief received from Section. A Section Guns in action Nil. Casualties Nil. Work done at WARWICK, trench widened in alternative position, emplacement German sandbagged, duck boards taken up to the trench, and guttered made in same. B Section Guns in action Nil. Casualties Nil. Work done in directing fire position fired at German aeroplane. 750 rounds expended. Casualties Nil. B Section Guns in action Nil. Revetting trenches round the emplacement of the 1/7 position. "B" Section Guns in action Nil. Casualties Nil.	Clear.
	4		Visited by the Brigadier in the morning. Gas discharged successfully at night. Reports from Section 2. Rounds expended 1280. Casualties Nil. Shots & no guns fired between 8.15 PM and 9.20 PM on the following points. (1) Rossignol Wood. From K12 B98 to K12 D47. (2) Road then K12 A and D to point K12 D28. CROSS ST. Gun in action 1. Every aeroplane fired at in the early morning, when he returned to our lines. Working duck boards put down in trench leading to alternative position. Trench cleared up. Casualties Nil. B Section Guns in action Nil. Casualties Nil. Work done 1/7 position was completely duck-boarded and cleaned. One emplacement cemented. B Section Guns in action 2 at 8.45 PM. 2 guns at WOMAN silenced fire on enemy working parties in trenches. 500 rounds expended. Casualties Nil. Work done Gun emplacement at WOMAN duck boarded. New emplacement at YANKEE completed and gun gear transferred to it. ELBE and EPTE communication trenches revetted.	Clear.
	5		Two officers and 60/12 leave for BAYENCOURT. "C" Section claim to be subject. Intersection relief carried out. C.O. detained on M.G. work at BAYENCOURT. "B" Section retired "A" Section. Enemy's shelled village with virulence by arm. "C" Section retired "B" Section. "B" Section retired Co-operated with the artillery. 4 P.M. discharged at 8 P.M.	Nil.

WAR DIARY or INTELLIGENCE SUMMARY

Army Form C.2118.

50 M.G. Coy.

September 1916.

Place	Date	Hour	Summary of Events and Information	Remarks and references to Appendices
HÉBUTERNE	5		Reports from Sections as follows:- B Section fired on Enemy working parties and Enemy Co-operation with the artillery. and fired for about 2½ hours. 2100 rounds expended. Casualties at SONIS. 1 wounded during two bursts unasked out. C Section Guns in action. Casualties Nil. at Stand to one gun took up position at YICKLES H.No.2 and another gun at SHRINE POST. B Section all guns in action. WOMAN. M.G.gun opened fire at 5.33 PM. ELBF Communication trench. Rounds fired 1000. WOMAN Left gun Searched FPTE Communication trench. Rounds fired 750. YANKEE gun Searched ETC H.Road, and 3rd gun was also fired on Rounds expended 500. YVONNE gun fired at CEMETRY EXE Communication trench. Fired 500 rounds. Casualties Nil wounded. 2 guns had their Emplacement at YANKEE also improved and steps were Heavy Bombardment heard on our right. Some Germans who shewed themselves in the enemy were fired on with good effect. Enemy M.G.s very active during the night, some Britishers chopping trenches at the Refuts from Section "B" Section gun fired at enemy aeroplane on tour occasion. 450 rounds expended Casualties Nil. SAA expended. 5A amount at SONIS. "C" Section at CROSS S.P. one gun fired with 5 Wagon of German amm'y party 400 rounds expended Casualties Nil. worked General clean up of gun gear and ammunition. B Section Guns in action. Casualties Nil.	Chu.
	6		Casualties Nil. Some H.E. dropped again H.E.M the morning and evening. Reports from Sections. "B" Section Guns in action Nil. Casualties Nil. watched New road fm. 147 Jackson Lookout Dug out enlarged and 2nd roof taken off. D Section Guns in action. one gun from old house position using BIG WOMAN fired on working parties about 500 N.E. of CEMETRY. Rod fired on enemy Occupied. Seen target slept 8.20 & 11.30 AM and 5.30 PM, each time with Success. Rounds expended 500. Casualties Nil. Worked & sweeping position close in WOOD S.E. and run an ar/peroration Ray. Rodes. made Hand at YANKEE steps leading to gun emplacement. went united, also fire steps at altered line position. E.B. HQ YANKEE. Co. united Transport lines at COYNEUX. and gave a Rather at BAYENCOURT. "A" Section ourated German and B. half aeroplane very active. Heavy Bombardment heard on our right. Refuts from Section. "B" Section Guns in action. Casualties Nil. Aeroplane gun fired at 3 enemy aeroplanes at 11-5 PM 500 rounds expended Casualties Nil. Welcome Dug out 117 position worked on. The urgent for the roof, some expended in front of the position. D Section Guns in action. one gun was unmounted & new spring put in. Wood St. at 9.30 AM working party formed Emplacement to hold Range 2020 hoshow in WOOD ST. and during the day with success. Casualties Nil. Casualties Nil. Worked on Emplacement. Wood St. was formed	Chu.
	7			Chu.
	8		In the Section Relief carried on C. E. "A" Section relieved "C" Section "C" Section returned to reserve at COYNEUX. Heavy Embardment on their Sand on left. not really heavy about the evening Refuts from Sections A Section Guns in action two of 6 PM. Aeroplane action during the evening Refuts from Sections A Section Guns in action two of 117 position. Rounds expended 2500. Casualties Nil. worked on improved Emplacement made on augmts. Tag't ft. B Section Gun in action NY	Chu.
	9		Gun fired from 117 Lookout. Enemy Gun team extinguish to YANKEE, YVONNE and WOMAN from the 117 positions. Last guns fired at Bosch party at YANKEE, in forward trench ray gun at WOMAN and YVONNE	Chu.

WAR DIARY or INTELLIGENCE SUMMARY

Army Form C. 2118.

50 M.G. Coy.

September 1916

Place	Date	Hour	Summary of Events and Information	Remarks and references to Appendices
HEBUTERNE	10		CO toured round defences of HEBUTERNE and visited each gun by night. 117 shots exchanged. Reports from sections as follows. A Section Guns in action. Nil Casualties. Nil. workdone daily. Nil informed. B Section Guns in action. Gun at No 2 position at CROSSt. fired a few bursts during the night on Enzelis at working parties. Casualties Nil. Chargon position at Right hand gun of SONIS rgtn enfeeble CROSSt new position fired. before by enemy indirect. Enemy shelled out front line trench enemy rifle grenade and shell fired. C Section Guns in action one gun at WOMAN tr action at night against enemy working party 1750 rounds expended. Casualties Nil. workdone. Improvements made to dug outs in WOMAN YANKEE and YVONNE.	Ccc..
	11		Several Lewy Halls fell in to HEBUTE + NE about 8.30 AM. searching for our Battery 117 shots exchanged. Report from sections. A Section Guns in action 2. Rounds expended 2,500. Casualties Nil. Target Right flank to trench from of 9.15 PM and 11.55 PM. K11 a 27 to K5 c 9.5. and on line + K11 a 18. workdone steps made to houses below H.a.1/3 position. Gun in action Nil. Casualties Nil. Chargon Position B Section Guns in action Nil. Chargon workdone New emplacement made + made to WOOD St. Newgun position at WOMAN backs fitted and ammunition carried. C Section Gun in action Nil. Casualties not. Workdone completely finished, trimmings of stand continued.	clean
	12		Safut, at YVONNE duck boards finished, trimmings of stand continued. A Section Guns in action 2 on K11 a 27 N. Covered 99 no. Log. more indirect fire shots unranged, one gun in enemy were in EPTE direction 229/c. marked at gun the line by left. Report from Section A Section 11 to position Guns in action 2 at K11 a 27 N. K5 a 95 and K12 a 03 from 9PM-10PM, and on K4 d 8½ 7½ and K11 a 03 from 10PM-12MN. Rounds expended 2,500. off CROSSt Nol gun stopped firing at 9 PM E2 rg mounted fired at whole position need to CM B Section Guns in action. Casualties Nil. workdone woodSt new position. C Section Gun in action one gun at WOMAN fired at a working party to the right right 1250 rounds expended. C Section Guns in action 2 empted working party at right. Rounds expended 1250 Casualties Nil	clean
	13		or the emount and dug out GommeBourt WOOD. saving gun emptied unopposed made in Aug on 1s. before at YVONNE. Steps used and improvement made in Aug on 1s. interaction of the B Section returned. A Section went into action Nil. before at YVONNE. Steps used Camed out B Section Reports from Sections. C Section Gun in action 1 at CROSSt. firing at battalion at COYNORE. H.Q. visited by Brigadier. A Section Gun in action 1/17 both in reserved at COYNORE. H.Q. visited by Brigadier. B Section Guns in action day interred Casualties Nil. workdone on K 5 a 65. Rounds expended 1500. Casualties Nil. workdone on K 5 a 65. Rounds expended 1500 rounds expended	clean
	14		in trade during the light at 8 PM Target EPTE trench battery at light on detailed by Ga Courts. Report from Sections. A Section in trench 2. Covered by officer detailed by Ga Courts. one of the Bole front fire noted known authority in our vicinity. Report from sections. A Section Go Coy was not the Bole front fire noted known authority Rounds expended 2000. Fired at interval during the right Communication CROSSt one gun Target Rossy. At wood 1500. Casualties Nil Casualties Nil. C Section CROSSt one gun Target P 4 a 67. Rounds expended 1500. Casualties Nil Casualties Nil. C Section Gun in action 1 at WOMAN. Target Sunken at YVONNE. D Section workdone at WOMAN, owing to turn out and churned elevation fixed K11 a 84 and EPTE 2500 rounds expended. Casualties Gun in action 2 a 11 9 a.m. Target trenches K11 a 84 and EPTE 2500 rounds expended. Casualties	clean
	15		Nil and other active during the morning. H.Q visited by the Brigadier. Orders received or relief by 51m G coy and active dummy ammunition made to B Coy H.Q. in the event of a attack.	clean

Army Form C. 2118.

WAR DIARY
or
INTELLIGENCE SUMMARY
(Erase heading not required.)

50 M G Coy
September 1916.

Instructions regarding War Diaries and Intelligence Summaries are contained in F.S. Regs., Part II. and the Staff Manual respectively. Title Pages will be prepared in manuscript.

Place	Date	Hour	Summary of Events and Information	Remarks and references to Appendices
HÉBUTERNE	15		Report from Section. Guns in action 2. at Crosser Target Rossignol Wood at WARWICK Target German Communication trenches. Rounds expended 2500 Jimmy Holt flare up irregular on hourly during the night. Changes from Cann at Wood St answer to Gr 21 St No 3 position. Excellent Gun in action. St. Jacques from WOMAN fired on Germans working party to the right of Pigeon Wood Count them nil Workers Riddled Air Drew atter train to dig in at Frome.	Clear.
	16		Company returned by SIMG Coy Relief completed 5 PM. Company moved off. Looked at CUTNG u.k. followed. Then moved round to CAUMES, L. where we were billetted arriving about 11 PM. Before leaving HÉBUTERNE one Sergeant and one O/R were wounded by shell which nearly fell on our cook house.	Clean
CAUMESIL	17		Company handed for Inspection all officers summoned to Batt. Hd. and from there notice was to ground near AUTREBISE FARM where we watched trenches of positive HÉBUTERNE & MEZEROLLES. Weather in favour CO summoned to Brigade	Clean
	18		Company shoots by 18 Rifleman attack discussed	Clean
	19		Company took part in Co attack on Model Trenches in conjunction with the 6th Dorset. Company/no on the Qt of Rennen. Observation without received to move to direction of MEZEROLLES	Clean
MEZEROLLES	20		Company moved off at 8.15 A.M. and and travelled via Anxi. B. CHATEAU.	Clean
BERNATRE	21		Company travelled at 9.10 A.M. And proceeded to the sleeping front FROHEN LE GRAND and marched to BERNATRE. Travelled vice Anxi B. CHATEAU	Clean
	22		Company moved off at 8.55 A.M. and marched via ST RIQUIER, ON Q x 2 x NEUFMOULIN to NEUILLY L'HÔPITAL	Clean
NEUILLY L'HÔPITAL	23		Company arriving about 1.30 P.M. and of Company finally settled in Billet	Clean
	24		Company handed at 9.30 A.M. for checking and cleaning gun gear. Co. cadre to programme work to Bde for 16 days Inter train training	Clean
	25		Church Parade. Companies also handed for Inspection. Musketry and Reading instruction. Ones Indicators. Recognising Bren Sniper.	Clean
			Programme of work. Exercises. Clean Rifles - later then the examination of Rifle.	Clean
	26		Immediate Indication John Martin able to written demonstration in the use of the Bayonet. Henceforth on course. Company attended about off as and one 12 detailed for Gas Course.	Clean
	27		Programme of work Ranging and luncheonc in action. Stopper Range Taking and action to Mechanism and chatting about.	Clean
			Programme of work advanced D. net. 13 and 2 w stages. Stopper Range Taking Field in the afternoon.	Clean
	28		Programme of work advanced D. net 3rd and 4th stages. Indirect Fire. Point Before ducy. Stopping.	Clean
	29		Rifle Meeting won 10.	Clean
			Programme of work Rifle Exercises Clean Indoor Bull Care and Cleaning Stripping. Slow Bolts	Clean
	30		Programme of do Tactical Exercise. Advance, Rear guard. Occupation of positions. Firing in the Range	Clean

Vol 8

War Diary
of
50" Machine Gun Company
Machine Gun Corps.

October 1916.

Army Form C. 2118.

WAR DIARY
or
INTELLIGENCE SUMMARY

(Erase heading not required.)

October 1916 — 50 M.G. Coy

Place	Date	Hour	Summary of Events and Information	Remarks and references to Appendices
NEUILLY L'HOPITAL	1		Company paraded for Church Parade. In the afternoon training in Signals for observation of fire, Lachrymatory Gunkers, and Stand Fast was carried out.	Open
	2		Company carried on tactical defence scheme. CO and Coy attended a lecture on administration by a Staff Major at Bde HQ.	Open
	3		Company trained in Drill until armoury tripod and gas lecture were given by officers who have attended Gas Course. In the afternoon Tech of Elementary Training carried out. Officers attended a lecture on Communication given by a Staff Colonel at Bde HQ.	Open
	4		Company trained in snow with the armoury tripod, and drill with the arms and Signal drill. CO attended a conference of CO's at Div.around HB. 2/21 SN Rouwetron attended to Hospital and evacuated.	Open
	5		Company paraded for Run to march. Route CANCHY, DOMVAST, ARGONVILLERS, MILLENCOURT, NEUILLY L'HOPITAL. Officer instructed a lecture on Sanitation at Bde HQ. Operation orders received.	Open
	6		Company paraded 5.50AM and marched on ARGONVILLERS, GAPENNES, YVRENCH and arrived at MAISON PONTHIEU when 6.12.30 PM where we were billeted. Warm Bouillabaisse admitted to Hospital and evacuated.	Open
MAISON PONTHIEU	7		Company paraded at 8.20 AM and marched via HIERMONT, BERNATRE, MAICOURT, FROHEN & GRAND to REMAISNIL where we were billeted. Operation orders received.	Open
REMAISNIL	8	6.00AM	Move cancelled at 6.00AM. Company stood by all day. CO attended a conference at CO's at Bde HQ.	Open
	9		Company paraded for Rifle and Gun Inspection. CO and 2nd i/c attended a Bde Conference to arrange a rehearsal for future operations. Operation orders received.	Open
	10		Company paraded at 8.15 AM and marched via MEZEROLLES, outre BOIS, OCCOCHES, DOULLENS to GRENAS, where we were billeted. 8 men of Battalion attached to us as reserve garrison. Operation orders received.	Open
GRENAS	11		Company paraded at 9.00 AM and marched via PAS, HENU, to SOUASTRE where we were billeted in huts.	Open
SOUASTRE	12		Company paraded for rifle and section training. CO and Coy rode to HEBUTERNE to see the ground allotted for defence scheme. Company found on tic the afternoon.	Open
	13		Company paraded for Rifle Drill and gun cleaning. CO and Coy rode to HEBUTERNE to interview OC SIM Coy, the relief opn two orders received.	Open
HEB-I-TERNE	14		Company handed at 9.00 AM for the trenches. And moved off Rif Section. "B" and "A" Section remained in reserve at SAILLY au BOIS. HQ installed at HEBUTERNE. "B and C Sections relieved two sections of SIM Coy in the line. B section at WOMAN 2 guns, YANKEE & CROSS ST No 3. "C" Section at CROSS ST No1 and 2 guns. Everything fitted 11.15 pm them. HEBUTERNE. Relief complete 1pm. All guns inspected by CO in the afternoon. Enemy shelled HEB outskirts of and the town occasionally during the day and night.	Open

Army Form C. 2118.

WAR DIARY or INTELLIGENCE SUMMARY

October 1916.

Place	Date	Hour	Summary of Events and Information	Remarks and references to Appendices
HEBUTERNE	Oct 14		Reports from Sections as below. "C" Section at CROSS ST. Guns in action Nil. Casualties Nil. Work done. Dugouts cleaned up at 1/17 position. Guns in action 2 Targets K14d75.20, K14cl52.10, K11a15.75, K11a20.05, K11a12. Rounds expended 1100. "B" Section Guns in action Nil. Casualties Nil. Work done. Dugouts cleaned up at YANKEE and putting up a post at WOOD ST for night limit of gun. Relaying of running posts at YANKEE.	Chn
	15		Our H.Q. visited by Divisional Staff Officers and OC 51 MG Coy. Plans of future of works arranged and gun positions inspected. Enemy guns again active. Reports from Sections. "B" Section. Guns in action Nil. Casualties Nil. Work done at WOMAN, work was carried on for 4 1/2 hours during the night on two Jam placements. To night and 50 + 60ft of WOMAN shaft emplacement. "C" Section Guns in action at CROSS ST. Nil. Casualties Nil. 6 gun shields mounted at CROSS ST No 2. one gun in action at 1/17 position. Same targets as night before. Rounds expended 2000 rounds.	Chn
	16		The General and CO visited all gun positions by day. Reports from Section "B" Section Guns in action Nil. Casualties Nil. A direct hit on WOMAN shaft emplacement, causing fall of it to fall in. Work done cleared out to defend at CROSS ST. Nil Casualties Nil. Work done CROSS ST finished. "C" Section. Guns in action at CROSS ST. No 4. in proved and side of trench No 1. emplacement 1 in 1/17 Commenced. No 3 dug out commenced. No 4 emplacement 1 in 1/17 position. Targets. K14cl75.20, K14d82.10, K11a15.75, Sap sandbagged. Guns in action at 1/17 position two. Rounds expended 500.	Chn
	17		K11a20.05, K11a12, K11a12. Rounds expended 500. One gun "A" Section in reserve relieved one gun of 19 MG Coy at WARWICK. Reliefs complete 1PM. "A" Coy fitted 7 Fps and informed them of the disposition of our guns. Carrying party supplied by Section in reserve, carried up 36,000 rounds SAA to WOMAN. Several shrapnel fell in the Coy. Sections at CROSS ST. Guns in action by the crews ready at night. Reports from Sections "C" Section No 1 emplacement finished. No 3 dug out made Cross ST. No 4 emplacement sandbagged on top. A 1/17 position at 12.50. Action Nil. Casualties Nil. Work done at ANNA Rounds expended 2250.	Chn
	18		ready for action the roof supports. No 4 emplacement at WOMAN night open emplacement "B" Section guns in action Nil. Casualties Nil. Work done. FARM yard and C.T. left open emplacement & finished. Each 13 were knocked out cavity finished and ready for concreting left open emplacement hit by shell. cleared away. From shaft emplacement between guns. Visited by OC and 2nd i/c. erected section on night to arrange communication. Company completed by 11 PM. Company OC 14 MG Coy received operation orders which we relied received. Reliefs completed by 11 PM. Company marched back by Sections to BAYENCOURT where we are billeted. One two orders received HENN, PAS, GRENAS to Billets in HALLOY operation orders.	Chn
BAYENCOURT	19		Company paraded at 1PM and marched via ORVILLE, BEAUQUESNE, VALDEMAISON, to TALMAS. Company paraded at 9.30AM and marched via officer proceeded on leave. Name informed that Lt. R.J. Gibbin is appointed	Chn
HALLOY	20		Company were billeted. One officer proceeded on leave.	Chn
TALMAS	21		2nd in Command of 95 MG Coy. Operation order received and marched via RUBEMPRE, Beaucourt to FRANVILLERS where we are Company paraded at 10.00 AM and marched via Lua 5449 Wt. W14957/M90 750,000 1/16 J.B.C. & A. Forms/C.2118/12.	Chn

WAR DIARY or INTELLIGENCE SUMMARY

Army Form C. 2118.

October 1916.

Place	Date	Hour	Summary of Events and Information	Remarks and references to Appendices
FRANVILLERS	22		Lt R.J. Gueriro taken at 9.6 m.t. by Company paraded at 11.00 A.M. and marched via HEILLY, TREUX, VILLE to MEAULTE when we are billeted.	—
MEAULTE	23		Company paraded for gun cleaning and checking gear etc. one officer made to CITADEL CAMP to reconnoitre ground of man. Orders received.	—
	24		Company stood by all day. CE went on a staff ride and reconnoitred ground around Mt CANCHET, CONTOUR, GINCHY, GUILLEMONT and Les BOEUFS.	—
	25		Company paraded for physical training and the new gun and tripod slings arranged on pack mules. and were briefed by officers and NCO's. Company paraded for battle in the afternoon. Very heavy bombardment heard of enemy the night.	—
	26		Company paraded for instruction in packing gun tripod and ammunition on pack mules. Melbourne and instruction in stoppages. Orders received.	—
	27		Company paraded at 7.45 AM and marched shortly for CORBIE and MAMETZ to MANSEL CAMP. where we got lodged in tents. work done on returning the camp and transport.	—
	28		Company paraded for Rifle Exercise and a fair about of work done on returning the camp and transport lines.	—
MANSEL CAMP	29		Some of the Coy paraded for church parade. warning order for the trenches received.	—
	30		at 2.00 AM order for reconnoitring party to trench to H.Q. 23 MC Oy in the line received. CO and two officers left at 7.00 AM. CE sent out order for A and B sections to proceed to the trenches. Message received 2.30 PM A and B Section left at 3.10 PM but owing to delay in traffic C.O and B.O. and B.O. Section left about 11.30 PM and were then ordered back to Camp. On return bad state of the roads & they arrived at Camp about 12 M.	—
	31		Pack mules used to carry the gun gear. Two gun teams of B and one gun team of A got separated and remained at Pozée H.Q. Remainder of Section arrived back at Camp at 11.00 AM and in a bad condition. at 9.00 A.M B and C Sections moved off and marched in the line and relieved 23 M.C Oy. The remainder moved up and D Section left at 11.30 AM and proceeded to camp at A and B Trench feet and failed was the same camp. Weather conditions very bad. CO rejoined our latter and Co. on the night in the line Henry of Stubbs Controlled one O/R wounded. one O/R missing. J.	—

Vol 9

50ᵀᴴ MACHINE GUN COMPANY.

WAR DIARY or INTELLIGENCE SUMMARY

Army Form C. 2118.

50. M.G. Coy.
November 1916.

Place	Date	Hour	Summary of Events and Information	Remarks and references to Appendices
LES BOEUFS and vicinity	1		Company in the line. Situation 6 guns in front line at ZENITH TRENCH. 2 guns in reserve at SUNKEN Rd Dugouts. Rations and water sent up from Tpt Camp situated on the road as EARNEY Rd, roughly one & half miles. One officer in charge of front line guns, one officer at SUNKEN Rd Dugouts. These dug outs acted as advanced H.Q. C.O. at Coy H.Q. System worked on the men per team relieved every 48 hours, followed by 48 hours rest at MANSEL CAMP. Officers tour of duty one day in SUNKEN Rd Dugout, one day in front line, 48 hours rest in camp. Enemy shelled Suffolt Run heavily. Casualties 10/R wounded, 1 O/R wounded.	Clean
	2		Two new Brevet Officers arrive 2/Lt. H. Wilson and 2/Lt E. Mills. Heavy shelling of our support line. Casualties Nil. Guns in action Nil. Guns fired slightly, by single shots & firing. Trench in very bad condition, almost impossible to keep guns clean.	Clean
	3		2 officers and 24 O/R go up to the line to relieve all men in the line. Return convoy of Lt & MANSEL CAMP. Reports from officers concerned "Guns in action Nil. Situation considerable enemy artillery activity throughout the day. Support line lightly bombarded. Very few shells fell in the front line. Officer commander reports 4 alarm of attack were stood to and one in front of our line caused No 3 gun to a temporary new position on F.L. gun year during the day". All gun teams were shaken considerably. 36 Belt-boxes of ammunition sent up from Tpt Camp.	Clean
	4		Heavy shelling again. Rations water and ammunition successfully taken up to the front line. Casualties Nil.	Clean
	5		One officer and 12 O/R go up to the line. Reports "advance Hits in the dug out in the front line caused our patrol two of water to be blown. No casualties. Main entrance to the dug out was blown in. Communication arranged with two battalions in the line and gun hauled at disposal of the OC. Communication with two battalions to the all out of the Eastern works. Every Lt up, our intense barrage all day. One guns in front line put out barrage behind every front line in hopes of catching the enemy when retiring. Casualties 3 O/R wounded.	Clean
	6		One officer and 12 O/R go up to the line. Heavy shelling Tpt road, Buse sunken Rd Dug out. Heavy shelling in vicinity of the line. Enemy forward position of the mere. CO summoned to Bde H.Q. re redistribution of guns. Casualties 1 O/R killed.	Clean
	7		2nd machine CO & CoyHQ. Posting of guns now as follows. 4 guns in ZENITH TRENCH. 4 guns in THISTLE TRENCH. 4 guns in COW TRENCH. 4 gun grand contact set up to cover trench on part of and Notes are of one activity at night. One a.s. gun teams now have 6 gun team in corfor their guns and all officer and bath Holt all night, simply 4 gun stretcher... and sick	Clean

Army Form C. 2118.

WAR DIARY
or
INTELLIGENCE SUMMARY

(Erase heading not required.)

5 M.G. Coy.
November 1916.

Instructions regarding War Diaries and Intelligence Summaries are contained in F.S. Regs., Part II. and the Staff Manual respectively. Title Pages will be prepared in manuscript.

Place	Date	Hour	Summary of Events and Information	Remarks and references to Appendices
LES BOEUFS	8		C.O. returns. T/t Camp. Officers and 120/R go out to the line. Reports enemy gun in front line beat off & hostile bombing attack with success. Heavy shelling started rather. Casualties Nil.	—
"	9		One officer and 120/R go out to the line. Guns in action Nil. Enemy barry quiet. Few shells drop in neighbourhood of T/t camp. Guns weather advent very active.	—
"	10		One officer and 120/R go out to the line. Carried two N.L. Guns in action Nil.	—
"	11		C.O. summoned to Bde H.Q. to witness Co. 1st Guards M.G. Coy. re relief and took them to Coy H.Q. arrangements made to hand over all guns except gun co attached by Div G.S.O.1 who spoke well of our guns. One officer and 120/R go out to the line. Relief party leaving Coy camp at Casualties 10/12. It was 30/R wounded.	—
	12		Orders for relief received. New form transport to escort to "C" Camp for relief. Men at MANSEL CAMP to march to CITADEL CAMP. Relief carried out without casualties. Completed 11 P.M. All guns from Cow trench brought back the guards only taking over guns from MANSEL CAMP and FLAUCOURT.	—
	13		Return sent to "C" Camp and MANSEL CAMP and FLAUCOURT. Left brought back from MANSEL CAMP. The T/t Camp at 3.30 p.m. The T/t move off at 7 p.m. and arch to DE No 3 Cy C.ASC. and parks at SAND PITS Camp for the night. COY H/Q. Moves to CITADEL CAMP ordered for northern front received.	—
EDGEHILL	14		Party of CITADEL CAMP went to SAND PITS Camp and MEAULTE TO BOGNAL. Party at MANSEL CAMP Coy bought up Heavy arr. there. T/t moves off by road under O/O of 2/Lt No 3 Cy ASC. Coy entrains at 12 noon. & arrives at HANGEST at 3.30 p.m. waited for 2 hour Thence Marc Convey up to our billets in MOLIENS VIDAME	—
MOLIENS VIDAME	15 16		Company rested. 2/Lt W. Bower back reports Coy over fifty sections to billets in CAMPS en AMIENOIS. orders received to move. Company moves off by sections to billets in CAMPS en AMIENOIS. T/t arrives at night.	—
CAMPS EN AMIENOIS	17		Day spent in inspecting and overhauling of guns and kit. Some stores drawn from ordnance C.O. goes on leave.	—
	18		Guns gas cleared all day.	—
	19		Muster Parade Inspection of equipment etc. Church Parade and cen limbers cleaned Company hard at it in the afternoon	—
	20		Company carried out programme of Work. Anecdote Drew. Physical Training General Beg/Sn. Commanders Brut for N.C.O.s.	—
	21		Company paraded for Baths and did Mechanism and stoppages in the afternoon. Rain frequent Officers 2/Lt J. lockest arrives.	—

2449 Wt. W14957/Mgo 750,000 1/16 J.B.C. & A. Forms/C.2118/12.

Army Form C. 2118.

50 M.G. Coy
November 1916.

WAR DIARY
or
INTELLIGENCE SUMMARY

(Erase heading not required.)

Instructions regarding War Diaries and Intelligence Summaries are contained in F. S. Regs., Part II. and the Staff Manual respectively. Title Pages will be prepared in manuscript.

Place	Date	Hour	Summary of Events and Information	Remarks and references to Appendices
CAMPS en AMIENOIS	22		Early morning parade by order of G.O.C. Bde. to be cleaning up billets etc for the future. Company paraded for a route march. Route HALLIVILLERS, SELINCOURT, AUMONT, HALLIVILLERS, CAMPS en AMIENOIS. Football match in the afternoon.	Chu
	23		Company paraded for drill out of doors in the morning. In the afternoon close order drill. Range finding. Mechanism stoppages.	Chu
	24		Company tested guns and took part in Sectional Training. In the afternoon all Coy. labour was instructed in Mechanism stoppages. Co. and adjt. attended a Bde. Tactical Scheme.	Chu
	25		Company trained in Sectional training all day. C O rode to CAVILLON to meet M.G.C representative at Corps H.Q.	Chu
	26		Company cleaned guns and attended church parade. In the afternoon Football match between Officers and the Coy.	Chu
	27		Company paraded for Gun Drill, Combined Drill. T.O.E.T. Close order Drill. Mechanism Staff Parts. We are informed that our 2 and 2nd /4s have been ordered to GRANTHAM. Two new permanent officers 2/Lt R.O. Ellis and 2/Lt C.S. Tennant arrive.	Chu
	28		Company paraded for close order drill. Gun drill. Overhead Fire. Visual Training. Judging distance.	Chu
	29		Company went on a route march. Route HALLIVILLERS, AUMONT, MAISONT and then round and back to CAMPS en AMIENOIS. In the afternoon the Coy was ford in a Bde Field a bit.	Chu
	30		The Coy paraded for Baths in the morning and played football against the 50 T/M Battery in the Bde Football League in the afternoon.	Chu

Vol 10

WAR DIARY
FOR
THE MONTH
OF
DECEMBER 1916
FOR
50TH MACHINE GUN COY.

Army Form C. 2118.

WAR DIARY
or
INTELLIGENCE SUMMARY

50 M.G. Coy.
December

Place	Date	Hour	Summary of Events and Information	Remarks and references to Appendices
CAMPS les AMIENOIS	1		The Company cleaned and tested guns. and carried out a tactical scheme in conjunction with the 10th & West Yorks. In the afternoon Range Firing Fire orders. Visual Training overland fire.	Chu
	2		Section officers lectured their sections on Tactical Handling of Machine Guns, and of a tactical scheme in conjunction with the 10th West Yorks. In the afternoon an inter-section football match was played.	Chu
	3		Company cleaned guns and attended church Parade. Inter-section Football match in the afternoon.	Chu
	4		Company paraded for Trench Feet Drill, Close order Drill, and Gun Drill, in the afternoon. Use of Pack saddling. Supply of Ammunition. Concealment of Guns and Liaison. Transport inspected by OC 17th Divisional Train.	Chu
	5		Company paraded for Trench Feet Drill. Tactical Scheme. in the afternoon guns were fired on the range and introduced Stoppages.	Chu
	6		G.O.C. Bde inspected the Company and transport. In the afternoon football match at Les Boeufs.	Chu
	7		Company. Court of enquiry held on Vickers gun lost at Les Boeufs.	Chu
	8		Company paraded for Baths and Pay. the afternoon was spent on cleaning the Harness. Company paraded for Trench Feet Drill. Musketry. Tactical Handling and Bombing. In the afternoon Parade for fitting Equipment and "Foot Drill". Lt H.C. Gay appointed O.C. No. 6 section vice Capt. H.W. Button to Home Establishment.	Chu
	9		Company cleaned and tested guns. and did Mechanism and Stoppages and Bombing. Gun wagon were painted. Warning order received, attached were transferred to MG Corps order thus.	Chu
	10		Company paraded for Church Parade and Bombing.	Chu
	11		Company paraded for tactical scheme and Bombing. and Trench Feet Drill. Operation orders for Tpt to move to unknown received.	Chu
	12		Company paraded for Trench Feet and Packing Limber. Transport moved off at 1.30 pm in the pickets to proceed to FOURDRINOY. We learn that Sgt Raymer and Sgt Sturgeon are awarded the Military Medal. Operation order received.	Chu
	13		Company paraded 8.30 AM. (Billeting party sent in advance to VILLE) and marched to Ville in LONG-PRÉ. officers kit & c sent by motor lorry to VILLE.	Chu
LONG-PRÉ	14		Company paraded at 6.45 AM and entrained at 7.10AM arrived at EDGEHILL at 12.30 pm and marched to billets in TREUX.	Chu
TREUX	15		Company cleaned and tested guns, and worked on making a range. G.O.C Bde inspected and we think of firing at new ranges, and not satisfied. New ranges made by our officers and then ten.	Chu
	16		Company cleaned and tested guns, and worked on the range and cleaning Harness. We learn that Lt Lowther from No. 20 M.G. Coy, Lt as been a/H/12 2nd i/c of this Coy.	Chu

WAR DIARY or INTELLIGENCE SUMMARY

Army Form C. 2118.

50 M.G. Coy
December

Place	Date	Hour	Summary of Events and Information	Remarks and references to Appendices
TREUX	17		Company paraded for Church Parade and rested from parade.	
	18		Company went on a route march. Route MERIcOURT L'ABBÉ, HEILLY, RIBEMONT, MERICOURT-L'ABBÉ, TREUX. In the afternoon working party supplied for the R.E.'s. Remainder of Coy employed on the range.	
	19		Some officers attended a lecture at CORBIE on instruction. One Coy did nothing. Party supplied for the R.E's and the Company paraded for various inspections. 2nd & 3rd Lt's NI and Nos 3 & 4/3 arrived returning after instruction on the new M.G. Guns tested and cleaned, and an Powers Class under 2nd Lt. Section officer lecture their Sections on Machines.	
	20		Operation orders received.	
	21		Working party supplied for the R.E's. Company paraded for instruction in Mechanism and SMLE Hotchkiss Bomb party cleaned and tested guns, overhauled belts, Class notes drill. Section officer lecture their Sections on Tactical Handling, Co-operation, a confirmed Co's at Bde HQ. E.O and some officers visit HEBECOURT Coy at rest.	
	22		2nd Section Lewis Bullets at 10.00 AM Order was to the BRIQUETERIE and remain there for the night.	
	23		C Coy goes to H.Q Bomb Coy, near WATERLOT FARM. And carries out gun firing in the line and remainder at Coy HQ. B Section relieved A gun teams of BOMB Coy in ZENITH P.2 and returns to Remainder of Coy Rest Billets H.Q 1.D.O AM and move back to camp 18 on the Montauban-CARNOY Rd.	
	24		1/2 C and 1/3 D Section leave camp at 9.15 AM. and relieve gun teams of Bomb Coy in the FLERS line, O.K. Coy THISTLE. Position of Guns as follows: ZENITH two guns, FALL and gun, A.21.a.MN one gun, THISTLE two guns, Cow two guns, Oz one gun, FLERS line. HQs Guns, 4 guns in reserve at CARNOY. Camp Coy HQ. at WATERLOT FARM. Relief not until 1PM. No casualties. Lt's LITTLE as orderly, 2nd Lt H. WILSON, 2/Lt M.S FITZRONG Officer attached 2/Lt S.W DAVIS. 2/Lt R.D EDIS. Reports from front line guns all correct, everything very quiet. Report from the same	
			all remaining guns.	
			arranged system of relief carried out as follows: Subaltern Supt: Each gun manned by 8 men, gun team do one day in Flag line and Ox, one day in THISTLE and C.OW. one day in ZENITH, FALL and A.21.a.MN. OR 16.0/R front line, 16.OIR Support line 16.O/R reserve line at FLERS and OX. Officers in follows:	
			Officer in ZENITH. 1 officer in FALL, I officer in Cow. 1 officer in FLERS. I officer in FLERS line. Lost officer tour of duty 2 days in the front line and two days in entire Cow & FLERS. Co went to THISTLE line. Report to be from C.O. and THISTLE all carried guns tested Casualties 10/R added General Situation quiet. Report from Cow and THISTLE Casualties NIL. Guns tested one gun hit by shrapnel and put out of action. Replaced from FLERS line. Gun from Carry Complete to FLERS line. Front line tested in Good condition and Emplacement.	
LES BOEUFS vicinity	25		Special Coy Sheel fired in the vicinity of Coy HQ during the early hour of the morning. 2nd/Lt. was in position in the said. Daily relief carried out. Guns of action. One gun at THISTLE I find evidence on 1010 TRANSLOY, and vicinity Bethuin. The hour of 10.00AM and 2.30 N.M at unequal intervals. 1000 rounds expended. Report from line, all correct. Casualties 10/R shot stock. Guns take woodworm one new proof bench and emplacement support line, all correct. Guns tested for position in front, less. cleaned. Relieve Company. Gun testing New enfranment commenced. Can ceased to unaltered Casualties NIL.	
	26			

WAR DIARY
or
INTELLIGENCE SUMMARY

50 M.G. Coy.
December.

Army Form C. 2118.

(Erase heading not required.)

Place	Date	Hour	Summary of Events and Information	Remarks and references to Appendices
Les Boeufs	27		C.O. visits guns in the line. 2/Lt _____ returned, admitted to hospital. Report from reserve knoll 2 in-one emplacement made. Guns tested. Casualties Nil. R range target small for eff on placement. One gun mounted on a tripod. Not a very long burst under 12. 6 of test gun and turn-pod-off the trench to allow it to get away. It could be blocked. Isn't mounting ltd of (L) way to damage to either gun in trench. Supporting also tested. Guns tested with clamp on. No firing tried tried. Casualties Nil. 3 out fin_ sector offices reported that our Lewis started FALL lastly constantly damaging barrel and emplacement. Barraging gun was reserved and got into working order. Casualties Nil Zenith guns all complete. 8 MGs kept lively fire in vicinity of Cy. H.Q. at night.	Clear.
	28		2Vicker M/C gun in the Line. Report from front line. Guns tested and all correct. Casualties nil. Most dond or trenches and emplacements conditions very heavy rain. Subject to an Placements and meet more shoots at night. Reserve and Guns tested. Dug only occupied up. All correct. Guns tested this afternoon for out. Casualties Nil a few very large emplacements on present more shots at night in vicinity of Cy HQ.	Clear.
	29		C.O. visits FLERS line. Reports front line. Guns. Tested all Correct. Cast nil. A few very large emplacements. FALL & autumn in recent y of L. Bull in ZENITH in the early a.m. The incoming welcome. Left enhanced / dug out. Lots of water about from trench. Enemy also shelled vicinity of C2 on his twice 11.50 am and 1.30 pm. Support line all correct. Guns tested. Reserve line dry in' cleared. On hour dock loaded gun recovered. Guns tested. Casualties Nil	Open.
	30		C.O. today our {SIM/A round round the line from to relief to remove Enemy artillery active by day and night. From line on top that trenches and in very bad condition and enemy fire at often turn to ZENITH without delay. With the morning. THISTLE left gun first reliance on 1st TRANS 46 Y and Sunken Rd at 16 gulled intervals from 11pm. 2 am M.Gs. was expected. Gun in past and Enemy working fairly at dawn. At C2 w_ new emplacement and ammunition stone hand board and Enemy Flers emplacement wanted. Duckboards or standings made for second dog in to shelter left Casualties Nil. All flank off dawn and men in Camp _____ for C.A.D NOY Camp.	
	31		Coy MG Coy Cuvalnos 10/P kueld 6/p2 wounded.	Clear.
		8 pm	Remainder of Coy in use to MANSEL CAMP Company relived by 51 MG Coy Casualties 10/P M A N S E L C A M P Relief complete	Clear.

Vol XI

WAR DIARY
FOR
JANUARY
OF
50ᵀᴴ MACHINE GUN
COMPANY

WAR DIARY or INTELLIGENCE SUMMARY

Army Form C. 2118

50 M.G. Coy.

January 1917

Place	Date	Hour	Summary of Events and Information	Remarks and references to Appendices
MANSEL CAMP	1		Company had a pruden parade. Cleaned guns Rd.	—
	2		Company paraded for kit inspection. Close order drill + route march out in the afternoon.	—
	3		Company paraded for kit inspection, close order drill, cleaned guns + much inspection Paraded C.O. + Adjt. roll. W/o Bdr Adams at the Briquetterie for adviso.	—
	4		The hew. that Major H.N. Britton + 2/Lt Packard as mentioned in despatches + that L/C L. Sirrow + C.S.M. Breso are awarded the M. Many Cross. Company paraded for inch fly drill. Much inspection parade + cleaned + oiled guns. Section Officers retained their sections in the afternoon. 2/Lt N.A. Maclean proceeded on leave.	—
	5		Coy paraded for tryunch, fly drill + cleaning up and made improvements to Company canteen built in the evening. 2/Lt S.A. Nilson + 2/Lt N.S. Tarpin retained to kit bags. 2/Lt J. Parks + required pitch of England struck Off Ky. strength.	—
	6		Company paraded for tryunch, fly drill, cleany + Oil guns + celb-transp. C.O. + Adjt. Adjts. to he. BDE. HQ. the relief of 52 M.G. Coy. 2/Lt M. Brown 8 mg. admitted to hospital + left the Offen posts HQ of 59 M.G. Coy. as relief of 2 guns in the line. Arrangements for relief made by C.O.	—
	7			—
	8		Company bus stunt are notes Off Rates camp at 9 am + moved to 52 M.G. Coy. H.Q. at GUILLEMONT. Relief of 52 M.G. Coy Off the line completed by 3 am 9/1/17; 9 guns	—
MORVAL SECTOR XV CORPS	9		2 guns being relieved, three guns of 59 M.G. Coy. in the line. Position of officers + gun teams as follows:— HAIE WOOD 2 Officers CICET March 1 Officer. Gun positions FRONT LINE No. 5. T6b94. No.4. U1C99. No.3. U1D56. No.2. U2C23 SUPPORT LINE S3. U7a39. S11. T6D7b0. R2. T11 Central. CICET. T11a 7½.3½. SP8 T11a.13. Sn. Rd. T5D55 Total 11 guns 3 guns in reserve Coy H.Q.	—
			Reports received all carried guns at work done in improving trenches + positions by Standing orders + range cards sent up to all positions. Casualties NIL. All guns hold spare men from MANSEL CAMP. These are employed by Company dugouts at GUILLEMONT. transport remains at MANSEL CAMP. Pack mules at the BRIQUETERIE.	—

WAR DIARY or INTELLIGENCE SUMMARY

Army Form C. 2118.

50 M G Coy

January 1917

Place	Date	Hour	Summary of Events and Information	Remarks and references to Appendices
MORVAL SECTOR XIV Corps	10		4 gun teams in front line relieved by 4 teams in Sailly sub sector town of thirty days. Gun teams in support line teams thirty 4 days. Hit men to both gun. Officers, NCOs and guns in. Support line reliefs by night. Reports received from all guns. Guns in action. NIL. Casualties NIL. Spent hours in cleaning + renewing hutches + emplacements. Each gun team fired 1 belt of SAA fire in ambush for unknown positions per gun.	Ceu
	11		C.O. proposed plans of dug outs for unknown positions. 1st Bde. Gun team in S.T. relieved by gun team in nature. Owing to bad condition of the trench. Roberts CICET one gun fired indirect. Jingles Dugouts at u.17.69. Period of firing 11 P.M.	Ceu
		2:00 AM	at irregular intervals. Rounds expended 750. R2 one gun fired indirect Target u.16.91.92 Twin string 11 pm — 2 am Rounds expended 750. Work done in beginning cleaning of trenches dugouts + laid in some trenches + emplacements. Casualties NIL.	
	12		Roberts Bde relieved. Casualties NIL. Knees in action. 1 R2 dugout. Work continued in improving trenches + dugouts. Casualties NIL. Some snow to fall. Ammunition in No 5. Fried on German carrying party + scattered them. All guns tried. The are pioneered by an average 4 umbrella in dugouts. Cpl CICET + SPB Carrying party	ceu
			cleared of the hostility Coy R.E. proposed deep dugouts + support line guns by night. officer of the hostility Coy. That's time Gun team relieved U.S.T. relieved.	ceu
	13		Roberts Ned down in improving general conditions. Trenches revetted + dugouts improved. Casualties NIL. Guns in action. NIL. Guns in action CICET	ceu
	14		hostile work an unknown in trenches continued. Casualties 1 OR killed. Guns in action. Tangle dugouts at u.17.69. Time of firing 11 pm — 2 am Rounds expended 600. R2 Jingle u.18.9/29.2. Time of firing 11 pm — 2 am and Rounds expended 500. All other guns tested relieved by C.O. of 86 M.G. Coy. All reliefs known.	ceu
	15		Company relieved by night by 86 M.G.Coy. Relief completed aug 16/1/17. 6 O. overseas in leave to UK. Company moved to travelling coy dugouts for the night.	ceu
GUILLEMONT	16		Company leave dugouts at 11 am + proceed to P.L. Platoon + entrain for CORBIE trains move in dependently they arrive at CORBIE at 8 p.m. + get comfortably settled in billets. Transport arrive at 6 p.m.	ceu
CORBIE	17		Company spend the day in general cleaning up of kit.	ceu
	18		C.O. summoned to Bde H.Q. Company parade for kit inspection clean guns + harness. Ammunition numbers check. Company paid out.	ceu

WAR DIARY or INTELLIGENCE SUMMARY

Army Form C. 2118.

50 M.G. Coy

January 1917

(Erase heading not required.)

Place	Date	Hour	Summary of Events and Information	Remarks and references to Appendices
CORBIE	19		Company parade for baths. Fitted out with kid. object clean gun gear & ammunition. D/Coy instructed in the use of the belt filling machine. Harness cleaned. Run-of-range officer 2/Lt P.E. Mitchell joining.	Clm.
	20		Company parade for physical training. Mechanical action studies. Range filling. Belt filling machines fired & clean harness. Reinforcement officer 2/Lt M.S. Tatham arrived.	Clm.
	21		Company parade for church parade. Clean wagons & a football match in the afternoon v 25th King's Battery Amm. Clm. Subs. Officers + Sgts. attend a lecture at MERICOURT on the identification of aeroplanes.	Clm.
	22		Company paraded for advanced training. Range finishing. Cleaning ? gun and am" and close of drill.	Clm.
	23		Company paraded for advanced training, introducing indication & recognition. Fire orders. One Sub Offr, close order drill. Lectures on Gas. Morale. Recognition of Aeroplanes, etc. Duties. 0 men on sick returned.	Clm.
	24		1/2 Company move to MALTZ HORN camp, also transport, arriving about 11 P.M. remainder of Coy remain at CORBIE. OC with Sqn. G. Coy at HAIEWOOD at relief.	Clm.
SAILLISEL FREGICOURT Sect of	25		1/2 Coy of MALTZ HORN camp. move to HAIE Wood. Arriving at 3.30 P.M. and relieve 59 M.G. Coy in the line. Remainder of Coy arrive at HAIE Wood at nightfall remain there in reserve. Tpt. move to MARICOURT. Coy H.Qs at HAIE Wood. Position of guns and officers as follows:— N1 U142 71 N2 U142 82 N3 U142 58 N4 U146 23 P1 U196 8585 P2 U146 1045 Total 13 guns. 3 guns in reserve at HAIE Wood P3 U14a83 P4 U13a72 Looked after by one offr at the Shaft	Clm.
	26		4 No a gun teams. 2 days in each group of guns, working on a 6 days in each gun in reserve. Relief of 59 M.G Coy complete 7.50 P.M. 2 drums and 4 mules killed by shell at MARICOURT. CO inspected all guns in the line activity on Bell side very active. Guns in action R.E. Camouflets NIL all gun tested. Workdone determined. Repair from officers. P.2. Trench and clay ones cleaned in all punts. Q1 T24 c 5590 Q2 T24 c 1075 Q3 T15 c 82 Looked after by one offr at Morlow Copse	Clm.

2449 Wt. W14957/Mgo 750,000 1/16 J.B.C. & A. Forms/C.2118/12

WAR DIARY or INTELLIGENCE SUMMARY

50 M.G.Coy. Army Form C. 2118

January 1917

Place	Date	Hour	Summary of Events and Information	Remarks and references to Appendices
Front System	27		German aeroplanes very active. Report from officer. Guns in action P4(ii) one gun fired indirect from 12 MN - 4.00 AM at irregular intervals. Target Stad X Rds at U.10.d.14 ammn. fire expended 2000 rounds. Anti air craft gun at P.14.ii. brought down a German aeroplane about midday. All guns tested. Casualties Nil. Work done on improving and improvement and trenches. Intel Company relief successfully carried out	C.H.H.
SAILLISEL Sector	28		Officer relief carried out. Report from Officer. Guns in action. P4(ii) gun fired indirect between 12 MN and 4.00 AM at irregular intervals. Target U.21.b.15. 1500 rounds expended. P.1. gun indirect between 12 MN and 4.00 AM at irregular intervals. Target W16.c.70 traversing from front to Govt Farm. 1500 rounds expended. Casualties Nil. All gun tested. Work done. Trench boards improved. Enfilement for Q1 commenced	C.H.H.
	29		Report from Officer. Guns in action Nil. Casualties Nil. All guns tested. Work done in deepening and widening trenches and improving emplacements and dug out. recces made in red bay. Relief successfully carried out	C.H.H.
	30		C.O. summoned to Bde HQ to explain fall of fire of guns etc. Report from Officers. Guns in action Nil. Casualties Nil. Wounded O/R one all guns tested. Work done. Maintenance of ground repaired to trenches and emplacements. Preparation for Indirect Fire shoot made	C.H.H.
	31		Indirect Fire practised in Batt. 150g Trench. Report from Officer. Guns in action Nil. Casualties Nil. All guns tested. Work done. Dug outs and emplacements to strengthened. C.O. summoned to Bde H.Q. One improved position of two m/c guns in the line	C.H.H.

Vol 12

War Diary

for

February 1917.

50th Machine Gun Company.

WAR DIARY
or
INTELLIGENCE SUMMARY.

Army Form C. 2118.

50 M.G. Coy.

- February -

Place	Date	Hour	Summary of Events and Information	Remarks and references to Appendices
SAILISEL Sector	1		Reports from all positions. Guns in action N.L. Carried on N.L. work slow on wire front line placements and trenches.	Opos
	2		Four of our guns fire indirect on communication and artillery formation trenches. Rounds expended 5000. Position of Guns. Built Doc trench. Targets. U.14 B.9 & B.3, U.15 a.8.5. no1, U.15 c.4.9.7.4, U.15 a.9.9. 8.5, U.15 a.7.0.9.5, U.15 a.2.6.5.5, U.15 B.6.0.10, U.15 a.7.0.9.0, U.15 B.7.0.2.0, U.9 c.4.0 05. Tunes of firing 2 pm-3 pm. Workdone at the line Trench. Commenced a/c to emplacement at P1, afternoon the emplacement commenced and dug out at P2, one gun at the slope faced at Lewis aeroplane. 150 rounds expended. Emplacement at Q1 emptied. Two gun position charged out reserve gun over to 01, and our reserve gun at P was move N 02 B.2 position in BETTY trench.	Opos
	3		Reports. 3 guns fired indirect targets and position as before. Rds expected 7000 rounds. Times of firing 12 noon to 4pm. One gun at the SHAFT fired at enemy aeroplane. Rds expended 200. Casualties NIL. Workdone General maintenance and repair of trenches. Emplacement made a/c head of Sap, head of 02 position. Shelter for gun team made in trench. Emplacement made 8x left of 02 position.	Opos
			Company returned by 52 M.G. Coy. Relief complete. 9 pm. Coy on relief proceed to BRONFAY camp. Company faired full musters rolls call, clean Kit guns and gungear. Coy. fair out in the evening	Opos
BRONFAY CAMP	4		and 6 gun teams leave HAIE WOOD and relieve 8 guns of 52 M.G. Coy in NI N2 N3 01 02 P3. 2 officers and CO walks out to position order for the coy for the attack of the 7 of John on Feb 8.	Opos
	5			
	6		— Operation Orders —	
			General Idea. The 16 guns of the Coy will cover the 7 of York Rept on its attack on the enemy front line from U.14 B.8.5.25 to U.15 20 5 90, early on the morning of the 8 inst. with 3 guns in support line, 3 guns in reserve line, 10 defensive guns and 10 guns firing indirect on to enemy communication and points of App[.] 14 guns of the 52nd M.G. Coy, 4 guns of 6/5 M.G. Coy and 18 guns of the 3rd Y Brigade Bde, will also assist by machine gun fire on similar targets.	
			Detail 2/Lt W.S. Tanner, "A" Section has one gun covered on for one gun, will relieve the gun of 52nd M.G. Coy, in the Support line position N1 N2 N3 on the night of the 6/7 inst. 2 under from these positions will be at HAIE WOOD at 5.30 pm. 6 12. 2 days water and rations to be taken. The positions covered	

Army Form C. 2118.

WAR DIARY
or
INTELLIGENCE SUMMARY.
(Erase heading not required.)

50 M.G. Coy.

February 1917

Place	Date	Hour	Summary of Events and Information	Remarks and references to Appendices
BRON FAY CAMP	6		and in defensive positions, and in fire and only be opened in the event of enemy attack and at targets which present themselves during the course of enemy attack on the Zonnebeke attack and be notified later.	
	2/Lt. J.C. Mitchell		"C" Section knowing commanded as far margin, will relieve the guns of 52 M.G. Coy in the reserve positions P.3.a.01.02. on the night of the 6/7 inst. Guides from these positions to lead HAIEWOOD at 5.30 p.m. 6th inst. 2 of guns will and return to be taken. The positions been held are defensive positions with the reserve line. Fire will only be opened in the event of enemy breaking thro' our front and sup/port lines. Zero hour which is the hour of attack will be notified later, all reports on situation to Coy H.Q. HAIEWOOD.	
	2/Lt N.O. Mortram Lt H.B. Mummer Williams		"A" Section commanded as far margin, will occupy gun positions in SOUTH COPSE, during the afternoon of the 7th inst, and lay out lines of fire in enemy communication trenches. 3 guns to fire at U.15.a.6.1 - U.15.b.4.6. Particular attention being paid to the following points. Road junction U.15.a.6.1. to junction BEYRATH trench, Corpse road U.15.a.80.35. U14 b.40.60. Point where COBURG trench crossed at U.15.b.40.60. Fire to be obtain but not along the whole of the target. 1 gun on Sunken Rd NW of ST PIERRE VAAST wood U.15.d.0.0 - U.21.b.1.5.	
	2/Lt N. A. Maclean		"B" Section commanded as for margin, will occupy gun positions in the vicinity of the Strong Point South COPSE, during the afternoon of the 7th inst. and lay out lines of fire on to enemy communications. 3 guns to fire on U.14.b.95.85. - U.9.c.27. on guns to pay particular attention to road junction U.14.b.95.85. The final of the O2 Regiment, to be obtained along the whole of the target. 1 gun to fire Sunken Rd NW of ST PIERRE VAAST WOOD from U.15.c.74 - U.15.c.80.	
	Lt. R.P.E. Ell		Remaining guns of B and C Sections [5 guns] Commanded as for margin, will occupy positions in enemy W.13 central during the afternoon of the 7th inst, and lay out lines of fire on to enemy assembly trenches U.15.d.96 - U.15.b.4., destroying the fire of the 3 guns along the whole of the target. Particular attention being paid to the corpse U.15.d. No 18.	

Army Form C. 2118.

WAR DIARY
or
INTELLIGENCE SUMMARY.
(Erase heading not required.)

50 M G Coy
February 1917

Instructions regarding War Diaries and Intelligence Summaries are contained in F.S. Regs., Part II. and the Staff Manual respectively. Title pages will be prepared in manuscript.

Place	Date	Hour	Summary of Events and Information	Remarks and references to Appendices
BRONFAY CAMP	6		Zero hour when is the hour of attack will be notified later. Rapid fire will be opened at Zero, and maintained until Zero + 6, after which it will be used for maintaining the cessation of hostile barrage. The lines of fire laid will also be the SOS lines. In the event of an hostile attack rapid fire will be opened on those lines. Ammunition 14 belts per gun. will be taken into position, and 4000 rounds S.A.A. Further supplies of S.A.A. will be sent up on application to Coy H.Q. Rations, water 2 days supply to be taken. Report to Coy H.Q. HAIEWOOD on situation, demands. Battle order.	Clear
SAILISEL SECTOR	7		3 officers and ten gun teams leave BRONFAY Camp at 11.00 A.M. and arrive at HAIEWOOD about 2 P.M. all gun gear and ammunition taken to pack mules to SOUTH COPSE other Lewis guns are to fire indirect from hides of 4 respectively. Coy H.Q. moves to HAIEWOOD co vol. H/17 gun when in position. Report received from off. cmt. Enemy Huy correct. Casualties Nil. Zero hour of attack 7.30 A.M. attack made by the 7th York, & Lanc. & Lincolns. & Tyneside Garrison. Our indirect fire guns fired as ordered, and co-operated with the artillery. 20ff in 73/12 two over heads. Report from off.cmd. SOUTH COPSE.	Yes.
	8		Gun in action 10. Rounds expended 19 500 rounds. Targets as ordered. Situation 9.5 A.M. No shelling. Rare enemy sad 5.9" mortar landed around fr.t.by dug outs, the neiod SAILLY SAILISEL and its surroundings being found particular attention to Barrage of the enemy supported our infantry advance and in the village. Our guns fired rapid from 7.30 A.M. - 8.00 A.M. slackened down to every other gun from 8.00 A.M. - 8.45 A.M. Ceased fire 9.00 A.M. work done. Filling belts and carrying up more S.A.A. Situation 1 P.M. Guns in action 10. Targets as ordered Rounds expended 6350. Firing of shelling heavy around the line severe in CHATSAU WOOD. 5.15 P.M. - 8 P.M. during from Bouchavesnes. Report from O.2. 4.00 A.M. Guns in action Nil. Guns tested and cleaned. 6.00 P.M. Have been recently firing low but that deficiency lost. Two enemy aeroplanes flying low, very evidently warehaled spent a good many infantry in the near clash at this time.	

A.5834. Wt.W4973/M687 750,000 8/16 U.D.&L.Ltd Forms/C.2118/13.

Army Form C. 2118.

WAR DIARY
or
INTELLIGENCE SUMMARY.
(Erase heading not required.)

50 M.G. Coy.

February 1917.

Instructions regarding War Diaries and Intelligence Summaries are contained in F.S. Regs., Part II. and the Staff Manual respectively. Title pages will be prepared in manuscript.

Place	Date	Hour	Summary of Events and Information	Remarks and references to Appendices
SALISEL SECTOR	8		Our guns kept a continuous target all day. Both fr. artillery and machine gun fire. The targets at O1 [position] was destroyed. P3 position and the wood had been noted a heavy barrage all day. Casualties Nil. Report from BEAN TRENCH. Guns in action. N2 and N3 fired at 5.00 [time]. Our targets out gun was a complete success except that our barrage was short, causing several casualties as I had to get my guns back to rest, though going. [The report was sent in by 2/Lieut TANNER, who has been recommended for the M/C for good position control and elevation tactics.] Enemy shelled out our support position, trans and duck-board track heavily all day but worked and everything found correct. Reports. BEAN TRENCH used OK.	Chis.
	9		O2. Guns in action Nil. Casualties Nil. Previous heavily shelled throughout the day and woods of BETTY trench destroyed. Engineers sheltered in the new S.A.P. being made by the R.E's. The following report was sent in by 2/Lt F.C. MITCHELL from O2.
		7.25 AM	Field battery fired about 3 shots.
		7.27 AM	Some Machine guns [not from SOUTH COPSE] opened fire
		7.28 AM	Infantry observed to be leaving trenches immediately to our front. Slight haze on target to be observed, and advance started at slow pace with men about 4 yards one another.
		7.28.5 AM	Artillery barrage opened. Several shots observed to be falling short, clouds of smoke risen the night [?]. Which were presumably covering bursts. Shells put before reaching the top of the ridge, the face was gunboomed, and the infantry disappeared over the ridge.
		7.40 AM	Men observed to be running back down lines. Few in number probably wounded or runners. Enemy trench mortars opened fire. Enemy put up a weak counter bombardment. Out of our aeroplanes noticed flying low, and slowly over trenches encountering.
		8.30 AM	Aeroplane flew a good distance back and dropped a white light.
		9.3 AM.	Two enemy fast [?] machines [?] low was out over Suw far the same turning over the ridge

WAR DIARY
INTELLIGENCE SUMMARY

Army Form C. 2118.

50. M.G. Coy.
- February -

Place	Date	Hour	Summary of Events and Information	Remarks and references to Appendices
SAILLISEL Sector	9	9.15 AM	Enemy infantry moved and it is stated they were asleep when the attack commenced	
		10.00 AM	Enemy fire became very intense, and BETTY trench, and the wire in front were registered perfectly, and heavy shells fell there throughout the day. Enemy barrage seemed to be about 200 x in front of the PERONNE – BAPAUME Rd, which is sunken at this point.	
			Report from B4.	
			Guns in action 10. Casualties Nil. Turns of firing 9 PM – 9.35 PM. Targets as before. Rounds expended 11,000 rounds. Heavy bombardment started and suspicions when it got into action at 9 PM and fired SOS lines. Red rockets were observed from either side of the attack from enemy's lines.	Chu
			Report from O2.	
			Guns in action. Nil Casualties Nil. All guns tested, work done. Q1 new shelters improved and strengthened. O2 Revetment of emplacement improved. P3 Trench cleaned, shelters and dug out cleaned.	
			Arranged to get in touch with BEAN trench by night.	
			Bean Trench	
			Guns in action Nil. Casualties Nil. There was a bombing attack on our new front line. Attack repulsed. Some of our lewis wounded/hrs shot today.	
	10		Q4	
			Guns in action Nil. Casualties Nil. Situation. Enemy opened up heavy barrage this morning at 1.45 AM. Sent up red and white rockets. Weded not open fire but stood to until it quieted down at 2.20 AM. Reason probably infantry seen relieving. East of enemy guns fired 15 rounds every 10 seconds, during the night.	
			10 Indirect fire guns were in the harrow from B4 position in the afternoon. Teams proved to BRONFA by cars. Guns in N1 N2 N3 O1 O2 P3 relieved by 52 M.G. Coy. Relief complete 1.00 AM 11/2/17. During relief casualties wounded O/R 1. Enemy sent over several gas shells in vicinity of HAIE WOOD about 11 PM. Six teams and Coy H.Q. on relief proceed to BRONFA camp on relief.	Chu
BRONFA CAMP	11			Chu
	12		Coy parade for Church Parade. Kit, guns and gun gear cleaned during the day. 2 officers and 8 gun teams leaving count for the 5th in and relieve 8 guns of the 51 MG Coy in the line at the following positions.	Chu

Army Form C. 2118.

50 M.G. Coy.

– February 1917 –

WAR DIARY
or
INTELLIGENCE SUMMARY.
(Erase heading not required.)

Instructions regarding War Diaries and Intelligence Summaries are contained in F.S. Regs., Part II. and the Staff Manual respectively. Title pages will be prepared in manuscript.

Place	Date	Hour	Summary of Events and Information	Remarks and references to Appendices
BRONFAY Camp.	12		W 1 Maf Ref W 14 a 9.8, W 2 Maf Ref W B C 6.0, W 3 Maf Ref W B C 9.5, W 4 Maf Ref W B C B 9. V 1 do W 8 a 9.2, V 2 do W 8 a 7.2½.½/3 do W 8 a 5.5, V M do W B C W 9½. Relief complete 1.00 A.M.	Chu
	13		Remainder of Coy. parade for an hours physical training, and cleaned and tested guns.	Chu
	14		1/2 Coy paraded at 9.30 A.M. for fitting of new Sweet Loc respirators at 11.00 A.M. 2 officers and 8 gun teams left for HAIE WOOD and relieve the remaining 8 guns of 51 M G Coy in the at the following position:	
NORTH COPSE Sector.			W 1 Maf Ref W 14 a ½2.8, W 2 Maf Ref W 7 d 7.9, W 3 Maf Ref W 7 d 7.9½, W4 Maf Ref W 7 B 9.8 X 1 do T 17 B 9.7 X 2 do T 18 C 9.4. 2 guns Reserve Coy H.Q. Coy HQ dug out at HAIE WOOD. 2.30 P.M. Co W H Q. gun in the line with Co. 51 M G Coy	Chu
	15		Enemy shelled our support line very heavily, and HAIEWOOD. Report from officer that everything is O.K. and relief carried out completely.	
	16		During the afternoon enemy shelled our 60 pounder heavy gun & hellen retaliated at 5.30 P.M. the enemy again attacked the 1 of John in the newly captured trench. aeroplanes of both sides very active forwarding their own lines. Report X 1 X 2 W 4	Chu
			Gun in action 3 Target hostile aeroplane. Rounds expended 150. no observations. Our new positions in other positions. X 1 continued enemy machine gun action in other positions. Report W 1 W 3	
			Gun in action Nil. Casualties Nil. Target Hostile aeroplane. Rounds expended 550. Report from front line guns.	
	17		Gun in action Nil. Casualties Nil. Working on sandbagging and revetting emplacements. Co W H Bte H R and left Battalion H Q. Relief of officers and teams carried out by night.	Chu
			Very quiet day on the front. Report from officer that relief was carried out successfully all gun in action Co W H Right Batt H Q in the line. and that quiet day on the front.	Chu
	18		Report from officer: Gun in action Nil. Casualties Nil. Enemy movement & refill of enemy x 1 emplacement reverted and trench at these positions. a statement emulated W.	Chu
	19		Co W H Btl H Q. 70 to Inc his trench. Report from officer: Gun in action Nil. Casualties Nil. W dldon, general maintenance x 1 emplacement completed. x 2 emplacement being worked on	Chu

A.5834. Wt.W4973/M637. 750,000. 8/16. D.D.&L.Ltd. Forms/C.2118/13.

Army Form C. 2118.

WAR DIARY
or
INTELLIGENCE SUMMARY.
(Erase heading not required.)

February 1917

Place	Date	Hour	Summary of Events and Information	Remarks and references to Appendices
NORTH COPSE Sector	20		Relief which should have taken place to-night cancelled till to-morrow night. Transport and men start move from BRONFAY to MONTAUBAN. Reliefs for the line. Guns in action NIL. Casualties NIL at X1 and X2 emplacements. NIL work done. Emplacement at X1 and X2 carried on with, and finished, and gun teams in one pit, to send parties/rations/shelters at W1 completed. Remainder of teams kept in general mountencies and repair of trenches.	Chen
			Coy relieved by 86 M.G. Coy. Relief complete 11·30 P.M. Casualties NIL. Coy on relief proceeds to MONTAUBAN, and stay there for the night	Chen
Montauban	21		Coy move to huts in MEAULTE. arriving about 4 P.M.	Chen
MEAULTE	22		Coy parade for a minutes inspection parade, and clean equipment, guns and gun gear. Coy had to go out in the afternoon	Chen
	23		Coy parade for squad drill in the A.M. Cleaning and testing guns etc. Cleaning Harness and fitting on of Kit. Transport inspected by O.C. Divisional Train. C.O. attends conference of C.O.s at Bde H.Q.	Chen
	24		Coy parade for Church Parade and baths	Chen
	25		Coy parade for foot friction drill. Final check up and cleaning up of gun gear, testing guns. Wagons packed ready for moving. In the afternoon Coy parade to have box respirators tested in gas chamber. C.O. admitted to hospital	Chen
	26		Coy parade for foot friction drill. Physical Training and work under section officers. In the afternoon an Inter Coy football match played	Chen
	27		Coy parade for foot friction drill. Physical Training and work under section officers. In the afternoon a Muster inspection parade is held and squad drill in afternoon	Chen
	28		Operation orders for Coy are to be in readiness reserved. Billeting party sent to ahead to WALLOY	Chen

War Diary.

58th Machine Gun Coy.

March - 1917.

Army Form C. 2118.

WAR DIARY
or
INTELLIGENCE SUMMARY.
(Erase heading not required.)

50 M.G. Coy.

March 1917

Place	Date	Hour	Summary of Events and Information	Remarks and references to Appendices
MEAULTE	1		Coy paraded at 8:30 A.M. and march via VILLE, BUIRE, LAVIEVILLE, HENENCOURT to WARLOY arriving about 3 P.M. where men were billeted	Chev
WARLOY	2		Coy parade for foot inspection and friction drill, cleaning equipment and harness. Close order drill and rifle exercises. Officers paraded for Reconnaissance and Respection.	Chev
	3		Coy parade for a defense scheme, in the neighbourhood of CONTAY. Football match in the afternoon against Brigade Signals. Co Lectures, officers and Sergeants on "Orders and Messages".	Chev
	4		Coy parade for voluntary Church service	Chev
	5		Coy parade for a tactical scheme the morning, lecture of HENENCOURT. Baths in the afternoon Lecture in range cards in the evening to officers and Sergeants.	Chev
	6		Coy parade for foot inspection, close order drill, cleaning and testing guns, wagons & football scheme arranged by the Bde Major carried out in the afternoon	Chev
	7		Coy carry out same tactical scheme as yesterday. Lecture on bandaging in the afternoon by an officer of the 53 Field Ambulance. Lecture by "Smithers" in the evening to officers and Sergeants.	Chev
	8		Coy parade for foot inspection and Physical Training. Cleaning and testing guns. Mechanism.	Chev
	9		Officers camp out to Reconnaissance. Coy had training in use of Pack saddlery, Mechanism and stoppages. In the afternoon a tactical scheme is carried out in conjunction with the 10 West Yorkshire Regt.	Chev
	10		Coy have training in Lewis, taking up defensive positions. In the afternoon Football match against the ?sc	Chev
	11		Coy parade for Church Parade, and were fitted out with clothing & necessaries. Bath in the afternoon Conference of O.C.'s at Bde H.Q.	Chev
	12		Coy parade for tactical scheme in neighbourhood of CONTAY. Bandaging Lecture in the afternoon.	Chev
	13		Coy parade for Physical training. Revolver and Musketry. Cleaning guns and packing wagons. Officers schemes resumed.	Chev
	14		Coy paraded at 7:50 A.M. and march via CONTAY, RUBEMPRÉ, HERRISART, CANDAS to BEAUVAL arriving about 2 P.M. and billeted for the night. Officers schemes resumed	Chev
BEAUVAL	15		Coy paraded at 8:30 A.M. and march via DOULLENS to BOUQUEMAISON arriving about 1 P.M. and billeted for the night. Officers schemes resumed.	Chev
BOUQUE-MAISON	16		Coy paraded at 7:45 A.M. and march via FREVENT, FILLIEVRE, LINCHEUX to OEUF, arriving about 2:30 P.M. when we are billeted	????
OEUF	17		One officer and 20/a proceed on M.G. course. Coy parade for Foot inspection and cleaning clothing, gym front. Rugby football in the afternoon. C.O. rejoin the Coy.	Chev

WAR DIARY
or
INTELLIGENCE SUMMARY.

Army Form C. 2118.

50 M.G. Coy.

March. 1917.

(Erase heading not required.)

Place	Date	Hour	Summary of Events and Information	Remarks and references to Appendices
DEULF	18		Coy parade for church parade. Football match. Officers in Coy in the afternoon.	Clear
	19		Coy parade for cleaning guns and gun gear and washing wagons. Mechanism. Stoppages. Cleaning. Signalling. Henram.	Clear
	20		Coy parade for Mechanism. Stoppages. Gun densention. Lecture on allocation of clothes. Classification of ammunition & Recognition. Signalling.	Clear
	21		Coy parade for Mechanism, stripping, assembling of lock, points before cleaning and oils for firing. Stoppages. Lecture on Range Cards. Fire orders. Signalling.	Clear
	22		Coy parade for repair + adjustment. Revolver instruction. Gun signals. Gun drill. Close order. Close Lecture on Fire Direction. Fire Control. Open Order.	Clear
	23		Coy parade at 9.15 AM and marched to BLANGERMONT HAUTE COTE. PREVENT, to REBREUVETTE where we are billeted in huts. Arrived about 4 PM.	Clear
REBREU VETTE	24		Coy parade for close order drill. Gun drill. Combined drill. Lecture on Recognition. Use of Packs + saddlery. Signalling. Officers instruction in Saddling up horses.	Clear
	25		Coy parade for R.t and Equipment inspection. Football match. Officers in Coy in the afternoon.	Clear
	26		Coy parade for Mechanism. Stoppages. Lectures in Mc's & new Quick. Building. Rafeyth Majarathing	Open
	27		"B" Section do a tactical scheme in conjunction with 7 Bt. Yorks. "A" Section do a tactical scheme in conjunction with the 6th Dorsets. Remainder of Coy parade for Close order drill. Combination of Guns taking up positions. Musketry. Cleaning gun's lost fitting.	Clear
	28		C and D Sections do a tactical scheme in conjunction with 10 worcesters Regt. coy of E. York. A and B Section parade from Outpost scheme by brigade.	Clear
	29		Coy parade at 7.00 AM. and moved for Brigade Tactical scheme. Lorry arrived at LUCHEUR. the scheme was carried owing to the rain. Coy marched back independently.	Clear
	30		Coy parade at 11.50 PM. for a Brigade Tactical scheme which was successfully carried out.	Clear
	31		Coy parade for between to holiday scheme, Gun lecture and machine Gun in outfork. Cleaning gun's gun gear. Revolver. Lust & Musketry. Rangefinding. Officers instruction in Rangefinding on a Bryant Stuff Ride.	Clear

1917

Confidential

JB/14

WAR DIARY

FOR APRIL

50th MACHINE GUN COY

Army Form C. 2118.

WAR DIARY
or
INTELLIGENCE SUMMARY

(Erase heading not required.)

50. M.G. Coy.
a.u.e.
May 1917

Place	Date	Hour	Summary of Events and Information	Remarks and references to Appendices
REBREUVETTE	1		Coy/Coy parade for Church Services.	Coy
	2		Coy/Coy parade for a Brigade tactical scheme in the vicinity of SUS ST LEGER. Visited by XVIII Corps MGO & advised.	Coy
	3		C.O. had a conference of officers with reference to forthcoming event H. Coy cleaned guns and gear.	Coy
	4		and fixed diagrams ready for the line. Lecture given by Divnl G.S.O.1 on forthcoming operations C.O. attended. Coy paraded for a tactical scheme and lectures on open warfare. Instruction and Recognition.	Coy
	5		Coy paraded from wash palace. Instruction given to Recognition. Training not parade for a Divisional Bn. Recon Scheme. Operations order received for move to AMBRINES.	Coy
			Coy paraded at 10 a.m. and marched via WAMIN, BERLENCOURT, DENVIER, to AMBRINES. Arriving at 1.P.M. Billetted for the night. Warning order sent to send cancelled.	Coy
AMBRINES	6		Coy cleaned guns gear and wagons. and parade for clean order called.	Coy
	7		Coy paraded at 9.4.S A.M. and marched via VILLERS-SU-SIMON, IZEL-les-HAMEAU to LE HAMEAU arriving at 11.30 A.M. billetted there for the night. O/O received from known AGNEZ	Coy
LE HAMEAU	8		Coy paraded at 7.30 A.M. and marched to TALAYER CAMP AGNEZ arriving at about 1.30 p.m Coy to huts. 2 Officers n.c. & men Rations carried on off. 20 men left and Bde. depot.	Coy
AGNEZ	9		Coy stand bay and await orders. Cavalry observed going up towards ARRAS. O/O received at 3.30 p.m. to move towards ARRAS. "B" Section paraded at 4 p.m. and for the scheduled guard on 7 H.C.R Yorks Line Regt. Coy moved off at 4.30 p.m. Several Bricks for the road when the cavalry and artillery moving up. At 5 p.m. the Brigade Column arrived at a Blockade to Reconnoitre for ARRAS. Orders received to Bivouac in the line for the night. It was caused at	Coy
Vicinity of ARRAS	10		ARRAS orders received at 9 a.m. to send billetting party to ARRAS. Cavalry and artillery noted returning from ARRAS. Coy received orders to move to ARRAS at 10 a.m. On arrival when the GRAND PLACE and Billets found by the	Coy
		12 noon	and an Advanced Billetting Officer received. So carried the warning order.	
ARRAS	11		Coy clear guns and transport to the satisfaction of Summer to Bde. H.Q. and informed that we were to assist the Cavalry Corp. in the L D Corps and would work in Conjunction with the Bde. Sc4gan. Coy paraded at 4.10 p.m. and for to the GRAND PLACE accompanied by Coy Truck. There now very slow owing to traffic and sleeping of the main ARRAS, CAMBRAI Rd. We eventually arrive at about a billion front TILLOY, and the Brigade Column in front of the church and FRENCH.Y. C O Summoned to Bn. H.Q. with an order to gl the Rood, "A" and "B" sections ordered to operations area 44 MG Coy. Culham wing orgs us to when MG Coy un to relieve	Coy

Army Form C. 2118.

WAR DIARY
or
INTELLIGENCE SUMMARY.

(Erase heading not required.)

50 M.G. Coy.
April 1917.

Place	Date	Hour	Summary of Events and Information	Remarks and references to Appendices
ARRAS	11		A section receives orders to relieve 4 guns of 44 M.G. Coy. "C" Section is ordered to relieve 4 guns of West Yorkshire Regt. B Section in reserve in the BROWN Line and "D" Section remains in reserve at Coy. HQ at FEUCHY. Both relief positions in the BROWN Line. Coy H.Q. at FEUCHY.	Cler.
FEUCHY	12		Covered by XVII Corp. M.G. Corps advice, acted by the 9th Divn. in own left sector, attack by 4 of our guns, the 6th Bomb attack on our front succeeded. "D" Section ordered to report to the Rgt. Battalion by it. 10th West Yorkshire Rgt and successfully came into the line well supported. A Section reports received for officer. A Section with Rgt Battalion relieved 4 of 4 M.G. Coy. guns. "D" Section moved up to same position plan gun in support 2 rifle coys. Of "D" Section. Ended the enemy beat though. A Section relieved a gun of 44 M.C. by in Lt. left battalion the gun in the front line. Gun in steel plate. B Section HQ at H.23 d.7.0. facing H 33 c 4.4. Gun attached also the left battalion front from H.23 central to H.33 c 4.4. "C" Section returns "B" section returned to the Brown Line. On gun of "D" Section wound found to achieved for L. 1.31.c. approximate references to gun position as follows:- BROWN Line 4 guns between R 9 & H.28 a 6.9 and H.34 Central. 4 Left Battalion gun at H.23 d.6.2, H.29 d.7.7, H.29 B 8.1, H.29 a.8.8. 2 guns commanding valley and roadway running I.31 a.8, a.6. H.36 d.5.5 and I.31.c.r.l. One gun in strong point I.31.c. 5 guns in support positions between H.29 c.6.o and H.35 a.9.5.	Clear.
	13		Enemy makes an attack on MONCHY te PREUX about 5.30 A.M. one gun in strong point I.31.c, mainly instrumental in repelling the attack Sgt Tyldesley and L/Cpl. Slaters was all the gun recommended by Lt. Dc.M. L/H.B Mories Williams with Lt. Left Battalion gun succeeded in keeping every M.Gs. at I.25 c.1.9 and H.30 d.84. He observed on every Gun firing from I.28 c.7.8.8. All gun in front line short of ammunition of any in any target observed. Gun keeping Coy. referenced by 52 M.G. Coy. all gun, held the location of 3 relieved. Gun keen in battalion in a field at FEUCHY for the night.	(No entry)
	14			

Army Form C. 2118.

WAR DIARY
or
INTELLIGENCE SUMMARY.
(Erase heading not required.)

50 M.G. Coy.
April 1917

Instructions regarding War Diaries and Intelligence Summaries are contained in F.S. Regs., Part II. and the Staff Manual respectively. Title pages will be prepared in manuscript.

Place	Date	Hour	Summary of Events and Information	Remarks and references to Appendices
FEUCHY	15		One of the enemy teams arrived in the early dawn of the by name is Lt Ry Truagle and Bivouac. Men for a couple of hours then move on to billets in ARRAS.	Clear
	16		The remaining 2 guns arrive in safe and move to ARRAS. Total casualties O/R, 1 killed, 4 wounded.	Clear
ARRAS	17		Coy Parade for Muster Parade and general clean up. Five men from Base Depot report to the Coy.	
	18		Orders received to relieve 52 M.G. Coy. D and B Sections move off at 3 P.M. and take up positions in the BROWN LINE about A.28.c.9.3. A and C Sections move off at 5 P.M. and relieve D of 52 M.G.Y. gun about H.29.d. Coy H.Q. Open at FEUCHY at 6 P.M. Relief complete 12 MN	Clear
FEUCHY	19		Divisional Machine Gun Officer visits Coy H.Q. re Machine gun Barrage in forthcoming operation. Cons- to all gun's the officer in conjunction with a representative of Gunners for forward. During the night 80/m enfiladed our west by our gun about H.29d.	Clear
	20		A and C Sections move up to gun bn. H.at H.35 b.4.3. Men old position being taken over by some my 12 men to best alone and attacked to the Coy for carrying purposes. A relay of 12 Section very active on the Blue left	Clear
	21		30 men in each team successfully carried to A and C Sections. Report from officer in the Blue left all guns in the placement and ready for following operation.	Clear
	22		Operation orders received. B and C Sections move to from the BROWN LINE to H.29.B.5.6. 2 of B Sections gun's move along to forward position about H.24 and 74 hrs. to hunt a scout lookout for enemy	Clear
			M.G.S. - Following operation orders issued by the O.C.	

A Section 4 guns C Section 4 guns

Phase I.
Capture of First objective i.e BLUE LINE [running thro I.26 a and c, I.32 a and c,
and Hente south 7.

A N° of Guns 8
  Gun Positions H.35.6.6.2.
  I.32.d.33 to I.32.B.3.3.
  Target H.35.b.6.2. I.32.d.33 to I.32.B.3.3.
  Time Zero to Zero + 16 minutes
  Rate of Fire Barrage Fire [1 belt per gun per 4 minutes].
  The BLUELINE should be reached at ZERO + 60 minutes

B/ at or about this time the 8 guns will move forward to occupy front
  line at I.31.a.

C on arrival there they will take of defensive positions, and be prepared to engage
  any moving target objects of guns defensive in case of counter attack on BLUE LINE

WAR DIARY or INTELLIGENCE SUMMARY

Army Form C. 2118.

50 M.G. Coy
April 1917

Place	Date	Hour	Summary of Events and Information	Remarks and references to Appendices
FEUCHY	22		Phase II.	

Capture of second objective = RED LINE running thro' I.27.a and D.I.33.C and d, round eastern edge of BOIS du SART.]

A) Attack timed to leave BLUE LINE at ZERO + 7 hours.
B) Attack timed to arrive at RED LINE at ZERO + 8 hours.
C) at about ZERO + 7 hours the guns will start moving forward to vicinity of I.32.a.6.0.
D) at ZERO + 8 hours indirect fire of 7 guns if possible will be applied to area of JIGSAW WOOD.
E) Object to cover occupation and digging in of RED LINE.
F) SOS lines will be laid at JIGSAW WOOD. from the position for night firing on indirect day.

Notes
(i) Rapidity of manoeuvre & accuracy of fire is safest way of getting there.
(ii) Take forward ammunition SAA in Cov'd Vickers as possible.
(iii) Leave great coats to be picked later, as you cannot position.
(iv) Leave 2 men in every position on guns to mark position for communication and that you push forward from H.35.c.6.2.
(v) Coy HQ will be at present position FEUCHY, until the BLUE LINE is reached of the above a reference true
(vi) During the occupation of the BLUE LINE i.e ZERO to ZERO + 7 hours. Enemy aeroplanes will be dealt with by gun
(vii) 2 day on the 23rd April Zero hour will be notified later.
(viii) There orders to be destroyed when unclean travelled & [illegible]
(ix) Davis B section. Gun 2 guns will be firing at Zero. From front line H.23.d and H.19.c. They will move forward to present enemy front line I.25.c at ZERO + Zero + 60 minutes.
(x) They will move forward from line to vicinity of I.32 Central at 2 + 7 hours.
(xi) You will see that your target in the front line is slightly altered to about 300 x also NORTH
(xii) When in your second position i.e I.31.a. you must enfilade indirect fire on present enemy scheme
(xiii) & thicket fire.
(xiv) Do not unclutch traverse to firing work, as they will have no doubt chauffeur Putin during work when you have fixed guns.
(xv) Zero hour will be before dawn. So gun lines will have to be laid for night firing
(xvi) Night firing will be carried out during the night Zero/Zero + on barrier gun supply ammunition
(xvii) All section command power SOS Signal and SOS lines on which guns are laid
(xviii) All crews his suffer from H.35.c.6.2.

Army Form C. 2118.

WAR DIARY
or
INTELLIGENCE SUMMARY.

(Erase heading not required.)

50 M.G. Coy
— April 1917 —

Place	Date	Hour	Summary of Events and Information	Remarks and references to Appendices
FEUCHY.	22		Operation orders "B" Section 4 guns. D Section 4 guns.	
			Phase I.	
			Capture of first objective at Blue Line running thro' I.26.a and c, I.32.b and c, O.2.a and c, O.2.b and 2. due south.	
			A. B Section	
			No y Guns 2.	
			Gun Position H.30.G.9.9 CANAL BANK.	
			Targets Any enemy in overcoat.	
			Zone on wards, any gun's target offer themselves. Special look out to be	
			kept for enemy M.G's in canal bank I.25.G.	
			Kind of fire Direct.	
			Note Covering party and guides will report to O.C. "B" Section to right in front of	
			line [Rgt] H.236. to thule place this gun forward to position during the night	
			and to be in position before Zero.	
			Later orders issued to O.C. "B" section.	
			(A) 16th 7/B of the 6 L Borders regt are forming to right with this message.	
			(B) This party is the covering party for the 2 guns to go along canal bank.	
			(C) They have not been along this area so know nothing.	
			(D) You will take the 2 guns in question will covering party in front along Ry to where Ry	
			crosses canal at H.24 a 5.7.	
			(E) The covering party will then proceed along south bank keeping 100x in front of gun	
			teams, until touch by contacting flees.	
			(F) They are to push on to a point where canal bends to the south at H.24 d 6.7 realm	
			700x from bridge.	
			(G) The covering party will then push on ahead about 100x and form a sentry guard.	
			(H) The guns will dig in to have protection from all sides.	
			Object of guard.	
			(1) fire on enemy M.G's which can be seen by flashes in the dark or seen in the	
			day light. Enemy M.G's are known to be in the wood ground south east of canal in	
			I.25.a and c, ie between the flank of the attacking Division.	
			(11) any hostile troops in vicinity of canal bank and southern edge of Roeux.	

WAR DIARY or INTELLIGENCE SUMMARY

Army Form C. 2118.

50 M.G. Coy.

April 1917.

Place	Date	Hour	Summary of Events and Information	Remarks and references to Appendices
FEUCHY	2 2		K. After Zero the guns are to push forward for the purpose of covering the along canal bank turning & behind alignment of out-flanking troops and front feeling MG's. I have enforced as this is the NCO i/c layout of the covering party. To gain this about order yourself.	
			M Zero hour must be judged from the opening of the barrage.	
			N There is a very important task and it's doubt extremely valuable and will be done if carried out correctly.	
			O 2 men who go with the guns are to come back to you and report when you are in position.	
			P And return known.	
			You do not push forward beyond Ry X.	
			Otherwise –	
			A1. B Section 2 guns.	
			D Section 4 guns	
			Gun Position Present Bn to front line vicinity of H 29 c 7.5.	
			I 25 c and outskirts of Roeux.	
			Target Zero to Zero + 5 minutes	
			Rate of fire Barrage fire. Either 1 or gun (or in minute J).	
			Direct Overhead.	
			B. Blue line should be reached at Zero + 60 minutes, at or about this time the 8 guns will in co operation to vicinity of present enemy front line I 25 c. Objective for these guns will be pretend baggage on arrival, they may well take up defensive icicles on attack on Bullet W.E.	
			C any enemy target of guns.	
			Plan ′y	
			Capture of second objective i.e. RED LINE running this I 27 a and cl, I 33 b and cl round Eastern edge of Bois du SART.	
			A Attack turned to leave Blue line at Zero + 7 hours	
			B attack timed to arrive at RED LINE at Zero + 8 hours	
			C at or about Zero + 7 hours the 8 guns will move forward to vicinity of I 32 central	
			D at Zero + 8 hours to Zero + 8½ hours will act on direct or I direct if possible will be affixed to.	
			I 34 d 3 7. vicinity	

Army Form C. 2118.

WAR DIARY
or
INTELLIGENCE SUMMARY.
(Erase heading not required.)

50. M.G. Coy.
April 1917

Place	Date	Hour	Summary of Events and Information	Remarks and references to Appendices
FEUCHY	22		Z object to cover occupation and digging in of RED LINE. F. S.O.S. lines will be laid on I.34.d.3.7 areas for night firing as well as day from this position.	Clear.
			Note	
			(i) Night firing will be carried out during night of Zero/Zero+1. An ammunition supply party from
			(ii) Ammunition Supply Party SAA Gun. / H 35 G.6.2.
			(iii) All Sentries must know S.O.S. Signals, and the S.O.S. lines on which the guns are laid.
			(iv) Rapidity of movement over the open is the safest way of getting there.
			(v) Take forward on mule SAA. Limbers on limbers.
			(vi) Collect as much SAA ammunition from front & British front line.
			(vii) Leave 2 men in every limber on guide to lead forward for communications.
			(viii) HQ will be at Front Post No. in FEUCHY, on the BLUE LINE is reached after which a rendezvous will be at H 35 G.6.2.
			(ix) During occupation of BLUE LINE i.e. ZERO to ZERO + 7 hours enemy aeroplanes will be dealt with by (x).
			(x) H 35 G.62 will probably be the spot his aircraft watch on Z night for Z+1 day. They can be destroyed when undertook and caught.
			(xi) A and C Sections will be firing at Zero from H 35 G.62, they will move forward to front enemy front line I.31.a. at or about Zero + 60 minutes.
			(xii) They will move forward from this place to vicinity of I.32.d.6.0 at Zero + 7 hours.
			(xiii) Zero day will be 23rd afternoon Zero hour will be notified later between midnight & before dawn.
	23 to 25		Report on operation of our guns from 6th 23rd - 25th.
			A Section Lt E W Davis. 23rd.
			Barrage Fire from H 35 G.6.2. on to I 32 B 33 to I 32 d 3 8 from Zero to Zero + 16 minutes at 5.35am the Section moved forward to northern end of BAYONET TRENCH H 36 d and took up defensive positions. During the day odd bursts of the enemy were fired on an enemy MG I 26 c and effect at 6pm when an aircraft was made on BAYONET trench raid fire was applied to Western slope of valley in I 31 c and a, but no targets were seen. About midnight Section moved back and took up defensive positions in front

WAR DIARY OR INTELLIGENCE SUMMARY

Army Form C. 2118.

50 M.G. Coy.
April 1917

Place	Date	Hour	Summary of Events and Information	Remarks and references to Appendices
Fampoux	23 to 25		**A Section Cont'd 23rd**	

A Section cont'd
An original front line in H.29.b.6.5. one gun, three guns in barrage position H.35.c.6.2 and SOS lines on I.25.d Central, during 24th and 25th.

During the day of the 24th the section remained in place. Position about 8 p.m. the 24th the one gun of the section in H.29.b.6.5 moved to barrage position in H.35.c.6.2 and fired barrage I.23.a.& c. and X Roads I.25.c.7.9. During the night 24/25 intermittent fire was carried out in this vicinity at 3.50 A.M. 16 Zero+20 when 52nd Bde attached Rifle and BAYONET trench, for MONCHY. A mostly demonstrative barrage fire was maintained till daybreak.
Section was relieved at 10.30 pm 25th by a section of 35 M.G. Coy.

C Section Lt H.B.Mones. Wellaing 23rd
Barrage fire from H.35.c.6.2.0 to I.32.d.38 from Zero to Zero+16 about 5.30 a.m.
Section moved forward to the old German trench in H.36.d and took up defensive position during the day and fired on east slope of the valley I.31.a & C.6.t on BAYONET trench and road to eastern slope of the valley H.29.b & to H.23.d and took up defensive positions and renewed in plan for harassing the day 24th & 25th.
no targets presented themselves.

At about 8 pm 24th section moved to barrage positions H.35.c.6.2 and laid lines on to vicinity of X Rds I.25.d and were found intermittent fire during the night 24/25

Barrage fire was opened on the same points at 3.50 a.m. when 52nd Bde attached RIFLE and BAYONET trenches from MONCHY. At daybreak fire ceased. It's attack was fairly successful at the N end of BAYONET trench and a small part of RIFLE was obtained the rear of the enemy. No further attack was made by one of the section and took to its defensive position in old front line H.29.b.6.5 vicinity.
At 9.30 p.m. 25th section was relieved by a section of 35 M.G. Coy.

D Section 2/Lt N.A. Maclean 23
Section covered with one gun the 22/23rd and took up position in front line H.29.b. at Zero to Zero 4th barrage. Fire was maintained on southern outskirts of Roeux and at S.P. Valley as BAYONET trench would not at fired. Targets available in want of original position. No targets were seen during the day. During exchanged barrage fire was maintained at 2 am. At 6.10 pm. Lt Silver was ordered to take up 3 machine guns to BAYONET trench and push forward to BLUE LINE for consolidation. At 8.30 p.m. Lt Silver sent back for orders as this section was held up on Silver trench and unable to advance. We were comd to take up and fire on BAYONET trench and
N.A. Maclean 2/Lt

WAR DIARY or INTELLIGENCE SUMMARY

Army Form C. 2118.

50 M G Coy
April 1917

Place	Date	Hour	Summary of Events and Information	Remarks and references to Appendices
FEUCHY	23 to 25		B Section cont'd 23rd in H 36 had act to cover 7 of East York attacking a new line on the N side of MONCHY. That gun consisted of the line 24.2 some was taught were obtained at 3.30 pm 7 of E York made a bombing attack on frontage of BAYONET and RIFLE trench. The gun opened rapid fire and swept the parade & wife of RIFLE trench. The attack was not successful. 25th at 3.30 AM 5th E Yorks launched an attack against BAYONET and RIFLE trenches from MONCHY northwards. Fire could not be opened owing to attacking troops masking our fire from day break onwards. Plenty of victory enemy good targets were found in vicinity of BOHAIN T25d. attacking the enemy party leaving attack in the front trench BAYONET held station the ? lane. MOVING RIFLE trench during barrage. Relief by 15 MGC at 10.30 pm. Section was relieved by a section of 35 M G Coy. B Section 2/4 W S Tunnel 23rd at 2.30 pm 23rd B section moved to the front line in vicinity of H 29 C 7.5 and rest of Cruer for 2 guns on W of the matter ROEUX and RGaux Wood at Bombing 2 gun and be the officer in ? front until coming park of the 60 South along of ? bank of canal to about H 2485 67 guns and hold by in old ? but sent by? ? MG left ? in this amounts in the vicinity by 5.15 Bde. Gun Zeen onwards in enemy MGs could be located. So fire was opened on likely places T25c.10 Pond, along River Rutus wood etc a 10 am the offices to locate the gun to get thru H 29 6.75 and were in ? at 5.00 Bde. ? enemy guns of the section were as follows. 19 ? N.1 at H 30 6.05, 2 gun to part of H 30 6.17 company west bank of ?, 12 guns were hold up by the offices ? there in H 30 6.99.99 & day would cover ? part of SP ? ? but 72 offices established? the had MT of 515 Brin was kept at small ? of ? but ? MGs were heard along the 2nd day. Then two guns intact ? on ? for the ? ? by enemy ? in vicinity of Roeux Wood and along the SCARPE. at 3.30 pm 25 was ? by the two guns in ? bank to vicinity of Roeux and ? in T25 c.7.9 and 5120 Bdeattack. During the day the entire mag/maj. the enemy with ? by m.gun fire along the bank T25 c.7.9 enabling trying to open fire BAYONET trench W.Eun. at 10.30 pm Section was relieved by a section of 35 M G Coy. Coy HQ was established at H 27 6.75 and Bn. HQ of 7 Battn and Rear Coy HQ in FENCHY. Casualties 1 Killed 80/R wounded. out of line B/R ? 90/R wounded 20/R missing. Return was sent to Rear Coy HQ to advance Coy HQ and from ? is usually to ? Bde ? S.A.A carried at H 35 C 62 and H 29 C 7.5 as total went ? to Landeken Cy ammun. Communication this ? was not let out by the guns.	
ARRAS	26		Section in reking proceeded to ARRAS and stayed there for the night. Coy paraded at 9.45 AM. proceeded in to Depot. While Coy Capt F. into private residence Rue Bapt. Ambulanced 2 pm	Cler
SOMBRIN	27		Arrived at SOMBRIN about 4 pm. were under billets	Cen
	28		Coy had part of Musketry Cause passed clean guns guns and part of ? instructed ? for M Garnet & FOSSEN Brink	Cen
			one officer & 1 NCO Instead in MG Course. Instructor Capt MAgnall & FOSSEN Brink	Cen
	29		Coy Parade for checking & cleaning weapons. Gun Drill Squad Drill	Clen
	30		Coy handed Gun section Ammunition on trip to checked. ? for move to LARISET are required warning notes to move to ST NICHOLAS area ?	Cen

WG ? Capt
Commanding 50 M G Coy

Vol/15

War Diary
May-1917.

50th Machine Gun Company M.G. Corps.

WAR DIARY
or
INTELLIGENCE SUMMARY.
(Erase heading not required.)

50 M.G. Coy   Army Form C. 2118.

aug. 1917

Place	Date	Hour	Summary of Events and Information	Remarks and references to Appendices
SOMBRIN	1		Coy parade under Section Arrangement to cover Pay Day. Men went in the afternoon. O/c returned from leave.	
			to ARRAS by bus in aftn.	Ctre
	2		Coy paraded at 7.15 AM marched to BARLY then entrained to ARRAS. Army chit room when	
			we arr. attached wagons failed ready for going up to the line. Warning 2 hours notice received.	
			32 men out to the Coy from the battalions.	Ctre
ARRAS	3		Coy stood by all day. ARRAS fairly heavily shelled all day.	Ctre
	4		Coy stood by all day. Calm and after dinner. Two extra 1 ok shell entered 3 forward	
			and the Coy billeted. Ammunition dump alongside the shed caught fire and the 6	
			LeWB Martin LRP. Ltts. acc. out for fatigue in salvaging for food of the equipments. the	
			Coy returned to the Coy alone first and the wounds are awaited orders. The casualties Segt.	
			Succeeded in getting out the boy animals away safely. The enemy was also shelling ARRAS	
			with his long range gun. Total casualties 1E.H.M. Lowling M.C. expired. Killed 3 O/R	
			wounded 6 O/R. O/c returned to resume duty to Y Huts L.I. 13	Ctre
Y Huts L.I. 13	5		The Coy came back by sections to Y Huts. Arriving about 12 noon. Another we pation	
			parade held and deficiencies in equipment ascertained for -	Ctre
	6		Court of enquiry on the fire held. evidence of fame to Brig. was of command of equipment round on	en

WAR DIARY
or
INTELLIGENCE SUMMARY.

Army Form C. 2118.

50 M G Coy
May 1917

Place	Date	Hour	Summary of Events and Information	Remarks and references to Appendices
YH & H 4.18	7		Section parade with the battalions where to bring at. Lecture between battalions & M G Coys	
			C.O and one officer goes to meet O.C 26 M.G. Corps. the time at which Mor equipment received from	
			Dedges. O/o orders for relief of 12 M G Coy. and 26 M G Coy. received	Clen
	8		Coy completed unit equipment. B section parade at 4 P.M. and goes to the line and relieve 11	
			guns of 12 M G Coy. Relief complete 12 M.N. A section under the orders of O.C 12th Btn.	Clen
	9		Coy on own section move to St NICHOLAS by day and relieve 12 guns of 26 M G Coy in the	
			line by night, coming under the orders of G.O.C. 26th Btn. on the night of the 10th all guns	Clen
			reverted to command of G.O.C. 50th Btn.	
			Dispositions of Sections.	
XVII Corps	9-13		A section 4 guns 2/11 W.S. Tower	
Left Div Sector			Relieved 4 guns of 26 M G Coy on the right of the 9th in position for positions at E.11.29.95	
			Night of the 10th. these four guns were moved to Habby trench HUE and replacements	
			made. relieved five S.O.S. lines were laid 6 - 2.36 guns one covered T.I.d.9.3 2 night guns	
			on vicinity of CUPID trench I.14.a. During the day of the 11th incessant fire firewas	
			laid first at guns on the vicinity of T.2.d.0.0 at 7.30.P.M & 2am of the 6th Corps to	
			attack on the strong point I.13.6. barrage fire was maintained on the above until relief	

WAR DIARY
or
INTELLIGENCE SUMMARY.

(Erase heading not required.)

Army Form C. 2118.

Place	Date	Hour	Summary of Events and Information	Remarks and references to Appendices
Kn Corps	9-13		A Section cont'd	
			target in conformity with the artillery barrage and a slow rate of fire thro'out	
Left Div Sector			Throughout the night. At 6.30 a.m. we opened fire & emptied out 7 yards cable on CHARLIE	
			CURLY & CUPID barrage had an gun opposed to the target on before on CHARLIE	
			trench was not captured lines were laid on the trench from I.7.6.8.9 to CUPID	
			and WHIP and a slow rate of fire kept up throughout the day and night	
			Night of th 12th B section took over the four w'chest positions and 2 guns of A	
			Section sent forward to take up defensive positions in CUSHION. The other two guns	
			remained in reserve. Night of the 13th 2 guns were moved forward & in reserve in	
			in Aus. I.D. under the section officer to positions in the Rg ew trenches at I.13.b.	
			Section RE attached and endeavours made so as to bring about employment to	
			CHARLIE trench from I.7.8.5.0 eastwards	
			B section 4 guns Lt R P Elly	
			Relieved A guns 12 M.G. Coy. night of 8th in defensive positions at H.12.c.4.2, H.12.d.7.3.	
			H.18.b.6.9, H.18.b.5.5. at about midnight night of 10/11th the 4 guns were moved forward	
			to cover track 2 guns took up forward about I.7.c.85 to find dug'outs in rear	
			of enemy strong point in I.13.b. The other 2 guns were kept in readiness to consolidate	

Army Form C. 2118.

WAR DIARY
or
INTELLIGENCE SUMMARY.
(Erase heading not required.)

5 o M G Coy
May 1917

Place	Date	Hour	Summary of Events and Information	Remarks and references to Appendices
XVII Corps Left Bde Sector	9-13		Enemy Strongpoint before mentioned when captured by 6th Dorsets. At Zero + 7.30 pm 11 other 6th Dorsets attacked the Strongpoint and C.P.O. trench. The Huns gun in CLOVER opened fire line and secured a large ? of enemy retiring. They then renumed on reaching tunnel any enemy counter attack from the N.E. Liason was arranged between the Siego Office and O.C. Assaulting troop for consolidation of strongpoint also on one barrage formed over the southern portion of CLOVER, the 2 guns in ord about to south end of CLOVER where arranger for 6th Dorsets was to meet them. At Zero + 10 messenger arrived for 6th Bomb and gun went forward to the strong point and fort w/defences for more runners enemy counter attack for Railway in the east. The 6th Bomb looked out as enemy M.G. captured, which was at once removed and placed in a defensive position. At Zero + 15 the Captured gun opened for on enemy aeroplanes 37 feet below of the enemy were collected in this trench. The 4 guns Strong fort in their positions and at 6.30 am at zero for the attack on CUPID CURLY CHARLIE, covering fire was opened on enemy parapet until the 1st wave of attack reached the gun positions. In accordance with o/o the 4 guns then moved to the 13 tent as before and during the evening this section took over the 4 Indirect fire guns from A section in HOLLY B	

WAR DIARY
or
INTELLIGENCE SUMMARY.
(Erase heading not required.)

Army Form C. 2118.

50 M.G. Coy

May 1917.

Place	Date	Hour	Summary of Events and Information	Remarks and references to Appendices
XVth Corps			Carried on slow fire enfilading CHARLIE trough out the night of the 13th and day of the 13th.	
Left Bn Sector	9-13	At 10 pm 13th when barrage started men near CURLY Range fire was opened on the same target. Casualties to date 10/0 wounded 10/0 missing. No doubt the casualties of the section were so small owing to the guns being placed the far side of the place where the enemy barrage was expected to fall and did fall.	
			C Section 4 guns 2/Lt F.C. Mitchell	
			Relieved 4 guns of 26th M.G. Coy on night 9/10 in defensive positions in H.6.c.8.1.2 guns H.12.c. 4.8 2 guns on the night of the 11th after the capture of the 6th Dorsets the 4 guns were ordered to CLOVER trench to defensive positions and held in readiness to consolidate the objective [CUPID trench] of the 7th york on the morning of the 12th. Unfortunately on the night of the 11th two of the guns and their teams were buried in the trench on the way up to CLOVER trench being killed and 4 men wounded, others note dug out were severely shaken and the guns could not be found. The other two teams went forward with their officer to CLOVER in extended waves was arranged with 7th yorks and on the morning of the 12th when the objective of this Battalion was gained, the guns proceeded forward to consolidate.	

Army Form C. 2118.

WAR DIARY
or
INTELLIGENCE SUMMARY.
(Erase heading not required.)

50 M.G. Coy

January 1917

Place	Date	Hour	Summary of Events and Information	Remarks and references to Appendices
XVII Corps	9-13		They got as far as CROOK trench and found it impossible to proceed further owing to wire from CARRY which had not been captured. 2/Lt F.C. Mitchell was killed at this point.	
Left Bde			The Sergeant took charge of the guns & immediately sent back word of the position to	
Section			Consolidation with Brigade. It was decided to keep these guns in their position to protect the gap between CUPID and CUBA, and to cover the higher ground in front of CUPID, also to form 2 more guns in defensive position in CUSHION for support of the right front. In the evening Lt H.B. Morris Williams took forward 2 guns of 'A' Section and hostile defensive position in CROOK. The two guns in CUSHION taking overhead covering on advance of the 2 guns in CROOK. The two guns slightly further back the team of which had been killed by the crater of barrage. The gun could not be made use of as a bullet had struck with the barrel and was spare barrel was available. The gun was later back to CUSHION by the officer who endeavoured to put it into working order. On the night of the 13th the two teams the CROOK were relieved by the 2 teams in CUSHION. Casualties 1 officer 2% killed 5% wounded.	
			B Section. 2 guns. 2/Lt N.G. Maclean.	
			Night of the 9th relieved 4 guns 26 M.G. Coy in defensive position in CLASP trench.	

WAR DIARY or INTELLIGENCE SUMMARY

Army Form C. 2118.

50 MGC Coy

May, 1917

Place	Date	Hour	Summary of Events and Information	Remarks and references to Appendices
XVII Corps Left Div. Sector	9-13		2 o't I.7.a.6.5. 2 o't I.7.a.6.2. Night of the 10/11th 2 guns were moved forward to cu B4 trench, to a position of readiness to consolidate objective of 7th East Yorks. should attack gained. In consultation with OC 7th East Yorks. it was arranged that 2 guns would go forward to consolidate and the other 2 guns left in CuA5P to move forward to defensive positions in CuB4, should the attack on the 12th succeed. The objective was not gained. So the guns did not move forward. Night of the 12th/13th OC 7th East Yorks. ordered the 2 guns in CuA5P forward to CuB4, on account of probable heavy shelling of CuA5P. Defensive positions for guns were taken up in CuB4. 2 guns about I.7.d.1.4. Evening of the 13th one of the latter 2 guns was moved to CuA5.4 at I.7.a.5.4 to enfilade CHARLIE trench during enemy attack by 7th East Yorks and 7th Yorks. on CURLY at 10 P.M. Report from our left m/g gun and the other guns on to CHARLIE during the attack. Casualties 10/2 killed 20/2 wounded. Enemy very active shelling back areas. Aimed hit on Coy H.Q. hut, two warning guns out of action. Report received from 2 guns on Ry. embankment that they were subjected to heavy shell fire. Hostile batteries between Gun + CUSHION. Hat CAM. CLYDE, CADIZ indicated on to CHARLIE all night. Reports from Guns at CUSHION. Hat CAM. CLYDE, CADIZ	
	14			Clear

A6945 Wt. W14421/M1160 350,000 12/16 D. D. & L. Forms/C. 2118/14.

Army Form C. 2118.

WAR DIARY
or
INTELLIGENCE SUMMARY.
(Erase heading not required.)

50 M G Coy   July 1917

Instructions regarding War Diaries and Intelligence
Summaries are contained in F. S. Regs. Part II.
and the Staff Manual respectively. Title pages
will be prepared in manuscript.

Place	Date	Hour	Summary of Events and Information	Remarks and references to Appendices
H.Q. Camp	14		O/o on relief received	Cpln
Left Bns	15		Enemy shell heavily shelling back areas. O/c 153 M Coy and 51 M Bn m/c to E Coy H.Q to	
Sector		relief.	Relieving teams started about 10 P.M. 153 M G Coy taking our guns in CROOK and	
			CUSH.10N. 51M G Coy taking our guns in HOLLY. CUSH. CASH. Our 2 guns on the Ry embankment	
			han orders to withdraw.	Cpln
	16		Relieving teams arrived under heavy shell fire and relief a complete one.	
			Long before the enemy attack our forebed and got back through before CUSH.N".	
			Teams relied proceed back to the tent camp ST NICHOLAS. Minto Rd and	
			forced in Red and Th Coy sect.	
			Total Casualties of the Coy. 1 Officer Killed. 20/12 killed. 7 O/R wounded 2 O/R missing	
			6 O/R shell shock attached arms. 10/R killed. 1 O/R missing. 3 O/R shellshock.	Cpln
St NICHOLAS	17		Coy paraded at 10.00 AM for a service Clean parade. Clean guns Jungan and Clark	Cpln
			Same also fitted out with successores. 2 hour warning Notice received	
	18		Day spent under section arrangements to their guns and gun gear	
	19		Coy paraded for Close order Drill. Gun Drill. Indirect Fire and Baths. Coy paraded	
			in the evening	Cpln

WAR DIARY
or
INTELLIGENCE SUMMARY.
(Erase heading not required.)

Army Form C. 2118.

January 1917

Place	Date	Hour	Summary of Events and Information	Remarks and references to Appendices
ST NICHOLAS	20		Coy paraded for church parade. O/c received formally of 52 M.G. Coy and 2 guns of 51 M.G. Coy	
			C.O. gave an advance warning of intended relief. Gun team reconnoct. about 8 P.M. at intervals. Relief successfully carried out and complete by 1.00 A.M. Guns were under the orders of 52nd Bde.	Cen
XVII Corps Left Sub Sec N.1	21		Dispositions of guns in the line as follows:- Bracke Map.	
			3 guns in CONRAD at I.1.b.99, I.1.b.27, I.1.b.35. 2 guns in CORK at I.1.a.63, I.1.a.97.	
			under one officer; 2 guns in CORK support at I.1.c.65, I.1.c.82, under one officer;	
			4 guns in HOLLY trench at H.11637. Furthest forward barrage. So shwn on X R. trn I. 22635.	
			Runners post and Ration dump at H.5.d.84. Coy H.Q. at H.10.6.7.6.	
			Report for the time that shelling fairly incurred and above normal Counter N.d.	Cen
	22		Bde Major went to the C.O. re dispositions of our guns. Enemy shells back area fairly continuously.	
			Orders issued in the event of the enemy and our officer on our sent up to the	
			line. Two guns to accompany left Battalion, 2 guns to accompany Right Battalion	
			N.I.'s did a bombing raid at night in which 2 of our guns in CONRAD co-operated.	
			Wet day an infantry subjected to and deepening trenches.	
	23		B.W. M.G.O and C.O. viz guns in the line and arrange positions for the defence of the left	Cen
			Flank of the Division. One new received. Flew 1 - H.E. Shell H Corner. Report of leaving	

WAR DIARY
or
INTELLIGENCE SUMMARY

Army Form C. 2118.

(Erase heading not required.)

May 1917

Place	Date	Hour	Summary of Events and Information	Remarks and references to Appendices
XIII Corps Left Sub Section	23		of COR K and CONRAD and bad areas. 2 guns in conjunction with N19's bombing attack fired from 1.30 AM - 1.40 AM Target I.16.85.35 - I.16.10½. Ranges respectively 750. Casualties wounded O/R 5.	Claim
	24		We obtain an R/E party and with the half of our own Coy in an emplacement in HERD with one gun from HOLLY to be moved. One gun from CONRAD moved to I.16.35.10. Fire for the defence of the left flank of the Division. CONRAD heavily shelled, due to firing by the T.M. Battery. Intel Company relief carried out on fatigue men were available. We learn that 35+3 L/Cpl Sharpe W. awarded the 2nd Military Medal for gallantry at	
			MONCHY.	Cut
	25		R/E's complete emplacement and trench in HERD and gun moved for HOLLY to that position. Both areas constantly shelled. CONRAD again heavily shelled.	Claim
	26		O/O for relief by 52 M.G. Coy received. Relief starts at 9.30 PM and relief complete by 12.30 AM. Troops on relief make their way back to Tent Camp S.1 N.10.21.31.	
ST NICHOLAS	27		Usual Cuthey heavily shelled. Total Casualties of the Coy 20-26 2 wounded of wounds O/R 1. Wounded O/R 6. Coy rest and found for baths in the afternoon. Guns cleaned and wagons getting ready for moving off tomorrow to GREENSareas.	

Army Form C. 2118.

WAR DIARY
or
INTELLIGENCE SUMMARY.
(Erase heading not required.)

May 1917

Place	Date	Hour	Summary of Events and Information	Remarks and references to Appendices
St NICHOLAS	27		One new frame to Officer 2/Lt F.S. FORD and detail from Brigade Depot reports. an officer of 10.3m.G.Coy arrived to take over one team. Some officers attend a lecture on "how to distinguish hostile aircraft".	
	28		Transport worked under orders of the T/O at 6.55 A.M. and arrive at CRENASAfor 4 P.M. Coy paraded 1 P.M. and march to the Goods yard station ARRAS entrain there at 3 P.M. Arrive MONDICOURT at 4.30 P.M. and march to GREENAS where we are in CAMP.	Cun
	29		Coy parade as for Muster Clean Parade and attend by the C.O. Clean order drill cleaning guns gun gear and wagons and kit inspection at night march past throwing against Brigade Signals. We have Hat Colt H.O. GAY. who leave us today in dispatches.	Cun
	30		Coy parade for Muster Clean parade and general cleaning wagons march to HALLOY for inoculation purposes.	Clea
	31		Coy rest all day as per Brigade orders	Cun

[signature]
Capt
OC 50 M.G. Coy

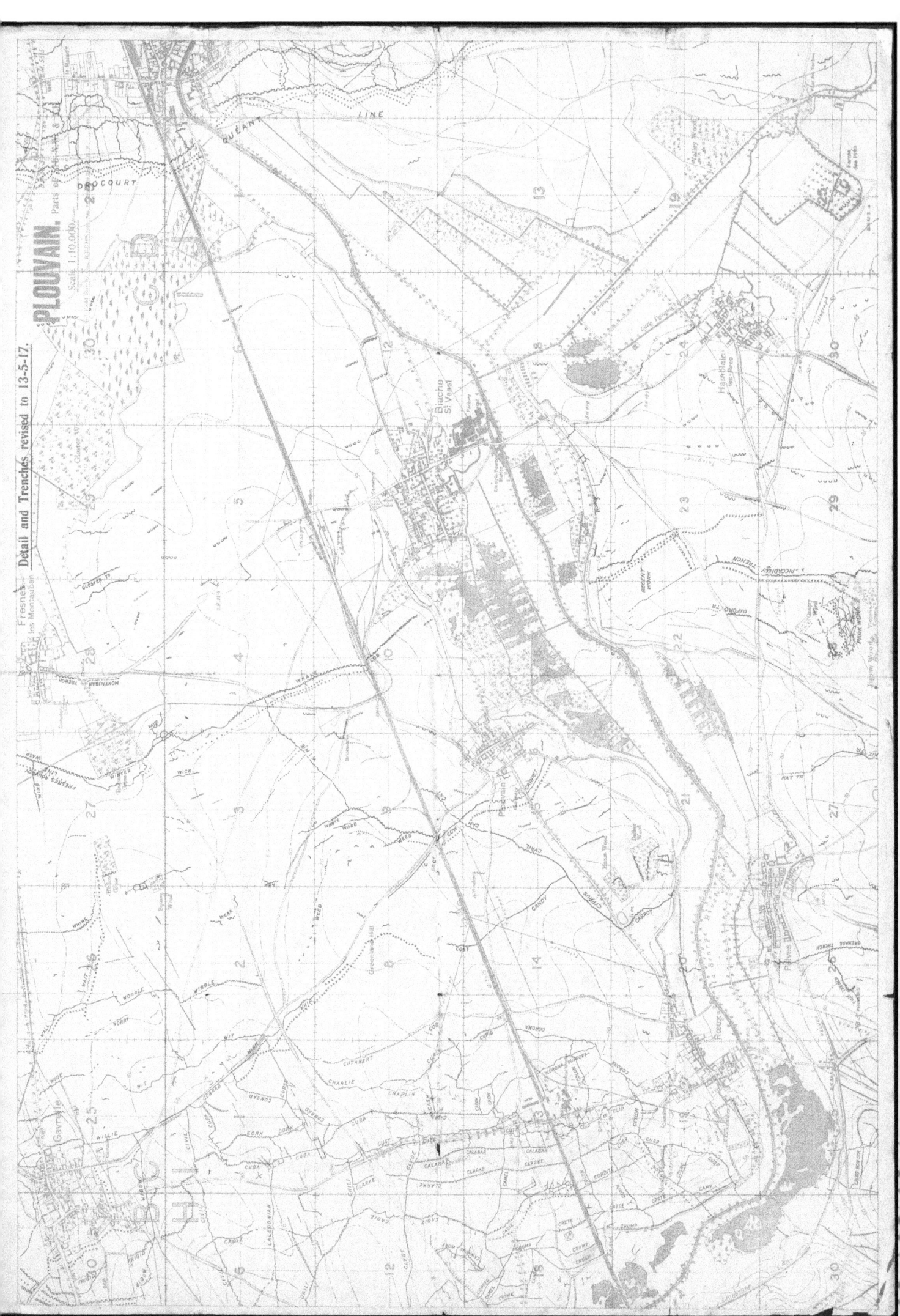

MISCELLANEOUS ORDERS

"A" Form.
MESSAGES AND SIGNALS.
Army Form C.2121

Prefix......Code......m	Words	Charge	This message is on a/c of:	Recd. at......m
Office of Origin and Service Instructions		Sent	......Service.	Date......
SECRET	At......m			From......
	To		(Signature of "Franking Officer.")	By......
	By			

TO { W Yorks E Yorks Yorks Dorsets
     MG TM 78 Field Coy 58 Field Amb
     Nº 2 Coy Train

Sender's Number: SV 522
Day of Month: 2
In reply to Number:
A A A

All units of 50 Bde Group will be at 2 hours notice from a Zero hour probably early tomorrow which will be notified later.

From: 50 Bde
Place:
Time: 4.30 p

"A" Form.
MESSAGES AND SIGNALS.

Army Form C.2121
(in pads of 100).
No. of Message

| Prefix | Code | m. | Words | Charge | This message is on a/c of: | Recd. at _____ m. |

Office of Origin and Service Instructions.

Sent
At _____ m.
To 7th East York, 7th York, 8th
By .....

10th West Yorks, Dorset, 90th ...
B.J., FA Amb, 90th Coy Train.

TO K.224.

AAA All units of the 90th Brigade will be ready to move at 2 hours notice after 8 A.M. AAA Acknowledge

90th Bde
7/4D F.M.

From _____ Lieut.
Place _____ for OC Maj. 90th Bde.
Time

Vol 16

WAR
DIARY
JUNE

50th
MACHINE GUN
COY.

Army Form C. 2118.

50. M.G. Coy.

WAR DIARY
or
INTELLIGENCE SUMMARY.
(Erase heading not required.)

June 1917.

Instructions regarding War Diaries and Intelligence Summaries are contained in F.S. Regs., Part II and the Staff Manual respectively. Title pages will be prepared in manuscript.

Place	Date	Hour	Summary of Events and Information	Remarks and references to Appendices
GRENAS.	1		Light Duty after inoculation. Range Firing all morning.	(Plus)
	2.	7.15am	Muster Clean Parade	(Plus)
		9-12.30pm	Close order Drill. General Description. Stripping. Gun Drill.	
		2-4pm	Mechanism. Immediate Action & Lecture on Firing at Aeroplanes.	(Plus)
	3.	Sunday	Church Parade Service	
		7.15am	Muster Clean Parade	(Plus)
	4.	9-12pm	Company Drill. General Description. Stripping Mechanism.	
		2-4	Battles	
	5.	9-10am	Physical Training	(Plus)
		11-12	Care and Cleaning. Points when Driving and after Firing. Lecture on Alteration of Sights. Instruction in B.F. Traversing.	
	6.	2-4.30pm	Continuing Stoppages on Range. Ch. Blue Pattern. (C.) Becoming Bon Responsators.	(Plus)
	7.	7-9am	Muster Parade	
		9-10am	Close order Drill. Gun Drill. 3rd stage. Lewis Gun instruction. Tests of Elementary Training.	
		2-4	Includes & Recognition of Targets. Lewis Gun instruction.	(Plus)
		7am	Muster Parade	
		9-10.30am	Physical Training. Pack Animal Drill. Instruction in Lewis Gun.	
		2-4pm	Spare Parts. Lewis Gun.	(Plus)
	8.	7-am	Muster Parade	
		9-12pm	Close order Drill. Lecture on Range Cards. Concealment of Guns and Crew. Taking up position.	
		2-4	Fire orders. Fire Direction. Overhead Fire.	(Plus)
	9.	1-am	Muster Parade	
		9-12	Gun Drill. Fire orders. Fire Direction.	
		2-	Brigade Sports. Winners. ½ mile. 1st Capt HALL. A.M. Team consisted of. 2×L.T.E. ralli 1st 50. M.G. Coy. Cpl. HALL A.M. Pte Walker. PG Currier. Relay Race. 1st 50 M.G. Coy. ½ mile. 220. Ran 220. ¼ mile. 220 respectively.	

Army Form C. 2118.

WAR DIARY
or
INTELLIGENCE SUMMARY.
(Erase heading not required.)

50 M.G. Coy.
June, 1917

Instructions regarding War Diaries and Intelligence Summaries are contained in F. S. Regs., Part II. and the Staff Manual respectively. Title pages will be prepared in manuscript.

Place	Date	Hour	Summary of Events and Information	Remarks and references to Appendices
GRENAS	10		Events were as follows 10% 220x ¼ mile. Relay Race. Obstacle Race. Tug of War (New Style) Tug of War (Old Style) Boot Race. Mule Race.	Rhw.
			Sunday. Church Parade. 10.50 am. C.T.E. Amusements. 3.45 am. Cricket match. Coy. v. III Army water Supply Column. Litterly. Tremendous Thunder storm all night.	Rhw.
	11.	7. am	Muster Parade.	Rhw.
		9-12.30 pm	Indirect Fire. Overhead Fire. Pack Animal Drill.	
	12.	9-12.45	Firing on the Range.	Rhw.
		2-4.	Combined Sights. Instruction in German Machine Gun.	
	13.	7 am	Muster Parade.	Rhw.
		9-12.30 pm	Pack Mule Drill. Lecture on M.G.S in Attack. Trench & Trench, Open & semi open Warfare.	
		1-4.	Judging Distance. German. M.G.	
	14.	7- am	Muster Parade.	Rhw.
		9-12.30	Ball.	
		2-4.	M.G. Tactics. Practical Demonstration of Indirect Fire.	
	15.	8 ac	Field Firing Competition. Two Teams of 20. inclusive 1 Offr & 1 Sgt. '19 OR M.V. Maclean & J.K. Spence started at 10.30 am. M. Rifles 48 Sgt. Center. 7.30 am. he did 48 min.	Rhw.
		9-12.30	Remainder of Company. Pack Animal Drill.	
		2-4.	Mechanism. Gun Drill & Stoppages.	
	16.	7 am	Officers Staff ride to arrange Tactical Scheme	Rhw.
		9-11.30 pm	Tactical Scheme. Taking up a position to consolidation, supervise fascines, cover fire, & Field of fire brought out.	
		2-4.	Cleaning up Gun Gear. Pack in Limbers. 5 men sent to 197 M.G. Coy.	

Army Form C. 2118.

50. M.G. Coy

WAR DIARY
or
INTELLIGENCE SUMMARY.
(Erase heading not required.)

June 1917.

Summary of Events and Information

Place	Date	Hour	Summary of Events and Information	Remarks and references to Appendices
GRENAS	17		Sunday. Church Parade.	Blw.
			Honours & Awards. Under authority granted by His Majesty the King. The Corps Commander has awarded the MILITARY MEDAL to the following. 26489. A/Cpl. HALL. A.M. 50. M.G. Coy. 15.6.17.	
	18.	5. a.m.	Reveille.	Blw.
		5.30	Breakfast.	
		6. a.m.	Parade for Tactical Scheme. Consolidating Position on arranged Tactical Scheme on the 16th. Attack carried out.	
		9. a.m.	Rest of Day devoted to Cleaning up Pasture Kitchen ready for Move up the Line. Billeting Party go on in advance to St Nicholas. 2/Lt MacLean. Cpl Hall. Batmen.	Blw.
	19.	5.30 a.m.	Reveille.	
		6.15 "	Breakfast.	
		7.4"	Parade. Dress Full Marching order. Company March to SMMETA and Embus for ARRAS.	
		7.15 a.m.	Transport per Starting Point. GNEVAR CHATEAU.	
		10.30 a.m.	Company Arrive at ST NICHOLAS. Take over Camp of 101 Coy.	
		3 p.m.	Transport arrive and take over Transport Lines of 101 Coy. No. 12 & Found guns & out Kitchens &guns Franklin.	
			2 " Gandelaine	
			4 " Alley/Whitton	
			4 " Shilway & Cutting. (Reserve)	
ST NICHOLAS	20	7 a.m.	Reveille.	Blw.
		7.45	Muster Parade.	

Army Form C. 2118.

WAR DIARY
or
INTELLIGENCE SUMMARY.
(Erase heading not required.)

50. M.G. Coy.
June 1917.

Instructions regarding War Diaries and Intelligence Summaries are contained in F.S. Regs., Part II. and the Staff Manual respectively. Title pages will be prepared in manuscript.

Place	Date	Hour	Summary of Events and Information	Remarks and references to Appendices
St NICHOLAS	20	9 am	Breakfast.	(B.W.)
		12.30pm	Dinner	
		4.30 "	Tea.	
		9.30 am	Company Parade to packing kitchen, not guns to festing. Each gun team tournament of 4 men.	
		2.30pm	"A" Section under Lieut. E.W. Davis. parades togo up and relieve 162 Coy. Guns in No 1. I.1.B.30.55.	
			– 2. E.1.B.05.86. Camrai	
			– 3. I.1.A.10.45 Cork.	
			– 4. I.1.C.70.70.	
		8 pm	"B" Section under Lieut. H.E. Swift. parades togo up and relieve 102 Coy. Guns in 4. guns HOLLY. I.12.A.50.80. 1. A.A. gun.	
			"C" Section under 2nd Lieut. I.E. Mills. togo up to GAVRELLE LINE relieve 102 Coy.	
			No 5. gun. H.6.c.86.20. CHILL.	
			– 6 – H.6.c.50.50.	
			– 7 – H.6.c.50.90.	
			– 8 – H.6.A.40.10. HELI[F]ON.D. and A.A.gun. N.A.	
		5.45pm	"D" Section under 2nd Lieut. McPherson and 2nd Lt. E.S. Told. group b to Pearkeys Cutting and relieve 4 guns. 102 Coy in Reserve. Will order Knuckle 2. A.A. Emplacements.	
		5.45pm	Coy. H.Q. group to take over from 102 M.G. Coy.	
		5.45pm	Adv. Depot consisting of 20 O/R. parade to go to Rue Court [at] N.C.O's except 1 Sgt. 1 CPL parade Remainder of Company, which will be 50 to transport lines.	

Army Form C. 2118.

WAR DIARY
or
INTELLIGENCE SUMMARY.
(Erase heading not required.)

50. M. G. Coy.
June 1917

Place	Date	Hour	Summary of Events and Information	Remarks and references to Appendices
In the Line	20.	3.45 am	Belt Boxes + Tripods taken over. Guns meet Coy at Rouling Bridge. Relief Complete. Company H.Q. is Granville Line No 14. Dugout. Occupants are Capt. H.C.Gunn. Lieut. H.B.Morris-Wilson and H.E.Smith. Site 7.5 mille. Signallers + Men. Sgt Major Lyness stays at Dump with Reserve Ammn. 2 from each Section. Daily Report later. Casualties. 9 to 3 Pt Bruting. G. Gun thin ration. nil. Change in Position. nil.	[signature]
	21		Work Done. No 2 gun. Conrad Alternative Emp made. again Holey. No 10 Emp. repaired. S.O.S. Lines checked gun when necessary fresh ammn. belts put out. New A.A. Emp Sighted. No 8. Emp. improved. No 6. Dug out sighted tank returned. No 7. No 5. Intends to be moved to Stoney Point. C.S. Emplacement so no work done. General Situation quiet. Guns in Action. nil. Casualties nil. Change in Position. nil.	[signature]
	22		Work Done. Alternative Emps of Nos 1.2. To 6 guns. Made. French Scheme. Hosey, Trench. Inclin. Timothy + Honey. cleaned. S.O.S Lines full checked. by Swift Angle + Bed S.O.S Lines - Elevation were given.	[signature]

A5834 Wt. W 4973/M 687 750,000 8/16 D.D.&L. Ltd. Forms/C 2118/13

Army Form C. 2118.

WAR DIARY
or
INTELLIGENCE SUMMARY.
(Erase heading not required.)

50. M.G. Coy.
June. 1917.

Place	Date	Hour	Summary of Events and Information	Remarks and references to Appendices
In the Trenches			No 8 gun. A.A. position Commenced. 6 & 7. Guns. Small splinter proof Gun pits Completed. Trench cleaned up.	
			Railway Cutting Guns. 2. A.A. Emps. made.	
			A.A. Report. No. Enemy Aeroplanes came within Range.	
			Work to Pce Done. General improvement everywhere.	
			General Situation Quiet. The Enemy shelled trenchline with gas shells between 12. midnight & 2 am. 2.2" inst. also bombarded French with Trench Mortars.	H/Shm
	2&3		Targets. Guns & action 6	
			Time. Number of gun. Rounds Fired.	
			Enemy Aeroplane dawn. No. 1 ⎫	
			" No. 3 ⎬ 300	
			T2. a. 6.9 11 pm - 2 am. No. 11 ⎭	
			Do Do " 12 ⎫	
			T2. d. 25. 87. Do No. 10 ⎬ 2,350	
			Do Do " 9 ⎭	
			Enemy Aeroplane 4.30 am. No. 12. 250.	
			Enemy Aeroplanes were active during the day, but were kept to time at	
			Casualties nil.	

WAR DIARY or INTELLIGENCE SUMMARY

Army Form C. 2118.

50. 19. 6. Coy.

June 19. 17.

Place	Date	Hour	Summary of Events and Information	Remarks and references to Appendices

Change in Position.
1 Gun from Cutting into No.5 sent up to New Position in CORK at I.1.a.6.2. firing South E.

No.1 Gun. Position at I.1.B.3.5. CONRAD. abandoned.

Work Done. — Emplacement Gun "Attenuation Emplt. completed.
HOLLY GUNS. No.9.10.11.12. General improvement of Position.
No.8. Gun. Work carried on at A.A. Emplt.
No.6 - 7. Guns. Firing Step made & Trench improved.
No.5. Trench cleaned up & improved.

Watch to Done. New position for 2 guns in I.1.a.6.2. & the communication
by O.E.8. General improvement of Emplt. Trenches in Vicinity.

General Situation. At about 1.30 am a German Raiding Party made some
of dead ground in front of No.1 gun I.1.6.3.5. And the High Explosive went out.
Succeeded in capturing the Gun + Tripod.
The Matter is being inquired into & full report will be presented as possible.

Operations. In view of the prospective operation entailing the capture of the gun pits in I.1.6. I have been in consultation with O.C. 1st West Yorks and have arranged to place a gun on each flank of the attacking party & keep up a Barrage left of the South horn and firing to attack also the 4 Guns in HOLLY. Programme of firing in accordance with the arrangements has been arranged by "D" O.C. 15 Bn
Times of firing by A. Sutch with greentime.

A. Sutch
by "D"

A. Sutch

WAR DIARY or INTELLIGENCE SUMMARY

Army Form C. 2118.

50th M.G. Coy.
June 1917.

Place	Date	Hour	Summary of Events and Information	Remarks and references to Appendices
In the Trenches	24th		50th Brigade. I have given orders to withdraw gun in cover at I.6.05.9.0 & have moved to I.1.a.6.2. when it will have practically normal field of fire. At I.1.a.6.2. an emp. is being made by the R.E.'s for this gun & it was hoped to accommodate its alternative machine gun & also items that was at I.1.6.3.6. as soon as completed. R.E.'s have got on fairly well with the work, & think it advisable before we are now. The gun I sent up to replace the captured one has been put in the new position firing S.E. I am making arrangements to leave guns & separate to its defence if the trenches & a plan of their loopholes. I understand that the enemy attempted a raid on this gun on last night, but it did not succeed, and a new of the S.E. ground running off to the right of this gun there being no cover to enemy has a splendid covered approach & it. In its new position it will cover 250 yds of our own trenches towards C.W.L. & will also protect on flank where it.'s the position it covers altogether I.16.D.1.2 on the left.	(B.R.)
			Guns in action. 3.	
			Targets. Time. Nº of rounds. Remarks.	
			I.2.a.6.9. 11.p.m. Nº.9.	
			" 1.10	
			I.D.25.8.7. 1.30pm. " 11. 1566	
			Casualties.	
			2nd Lieut. N.A. MacLean wounded. and 1 O/R. wounded.	
			Work Done.	
			Two new Emp. made at I.1.a.6.2. A.A. Emp. [strikethrough] made at Nº.8.	
			Travel Drained at Nº.6 & 7. Splinter Proof Shelters made in H.2.L.Y.	
			Work to be Done. Dug outs to be carried on by R.E's. at I.1.a.6.2.	

WAR DIARY or INTELLIGENCE SUMMARY

50th M.G. Coy.

Jan. 1917.

Army Form C. 2118.

Place	Date	Hour	Summary of Events and Information	Remarks and references to Appendices
In the Trenches	25.		Change of Position. No 1 Gun at I.16.35 moved to I.1.a.6.2. } Fields of fire same position as before. " 2 " I.1.b.05.90 " I.1.a.6.2 } 1 Gun team Rainbow Cutting was sent up to relieve No 1 Gun whose team was lost. Situation Quiet. Enemy shells heavy on HUDNUM last night work 4.2". 5.9s. between 12.30am and 3.30am. Enemy Aeroplane about 6fts over any Targets. Guns in Action. 6. Targets. Time. No of Gun. Rounds Fired. I.8.a. } Cooperation 3pm 3.10 No 9 I.8.c. } with 3 " " - 10 500 I.8.c. } Artillery " " - 11 Harrd Fire on Enemy Trenches 11pm-2.30am. No 9 2,250. I.2.c. - 10 - 11 Enemy wire infront } during of WIT TRENCH. } Night. No 3. 500. This gun was moved up into Conrad for this purpose.	CRK

WAR DIARY or INTELLIGENCE SUMMARY

Army Form C. 2118.

50. M.G. Coy.

June.

Place	Date	Hour	Summary of Events and Information	Remarks and references to Appendices
			Enemy Aeroplanes. During week No 8. 1,250	
			— Do — — Do — — 12 250	(Photo)
			— Do — — Do — — 14 250	
			Casualties. nil.	
			Work Done. All reserve S.A.A. & Front line moved to new position 5 CORK LINE 10,000 per gun. Emp. made for No 2 gun. on being up to back to CORK line at I.1.a.5.5.	
			General improvement of all positions & Trenches in vicinity.	
			Culmination of Dug outs in I.1.a.6.3 by R.E's.	
			Work this Div.	
			Culmination of Dug outs — I.1.a.6.3. by R.E's	
			Ammunition Emplacement made to all gun positions.	
			Present position to be wired and sandbagged.	
			Changes in Position.	
			4. guns from Cutting relieved 52 M.G. Coy.	
			3 — CHARLIE.	
			1 — CORK near Bricquettri.	
			No 3. Gun from I.1.6.12.6. moved to I.1.5.7.2. & relieved 1. gun of 52. Coy.	
			Relief complete about 2.30 am.	

Army Form C. 2118.

WAR DIARY
or
INTELLIGENCE SUMMARY.

50. M.G. Coy. June 1917.

(Erase heading not required.)

Place	Date	Hour	Summary of Events and Information	Remarks and references to Appendices
In Trenches	26		Guns in Action. 6 Casualties. 1 Or. Wounded at Duty. Gun. Target. Rough Trend. No 13-14. I 22 d 25.87. ⎫ 3,250. " 15-16. I 2 a 5.8. ⎭ " 12. Enemy. 400 " 16. Aeroplanes. 320 Change i Position. Nil. Work Done. New A.A. Emp. started in HOLLY & in HAWTHORNS. shelter under strengthened Emp. Sandbagged. S.A.A. Reserves shifted from Emp. & Bombs carried up. Deepening Trenches near gun, making mule reserve, splicing in gear, etc. Work carried on at Dugouts Cnk I 6 a 63. Wrk Trench. Deepening Trenches, etc. Casualties. Nil Guns in Action. 5. Targets. Training & Firing. Gun. Rounds Fired. Enemy Aircraft. 2.30 p.m. No 10. 450 - do - 8.40 p.m. - 12 - 250.	ABW ABW
	27			

Army Form C. 2118.

WAR DIARY
or
INTELLIGENCE SUMMARY.

(Erase heading not required.)

70. M.G.Coy
June.

Place	Date	Hour	Summary of Events and Information	Remarks and references to Appendices
	28		Enemy Approach.) pm No. 13 ——— 4,500 Rounds. to pstn. & I.2.D. } 11.15 – 2.15 .14 + I.2.A .15	(Sd)
			In Conjunction with T.M.B. Rapid & Barrage fire } 2 am – 2.15am No. 13 was brought to bear on .14 2,500 behind target engaged by T.M.B. .15	
			Change in Postion. Nil	
			Work Done. No. 1, 2&3 & CHARLIE. Emplacement being dug. 4.5.6.7.8. C.nh. Deepened. Building up " at all positions. No. 10. Aust Air craft Emp. finished. 13.14.15.16. General improvement & repair. Austrain Aircraft Emp finished.	(Sd)
			Casualties. Nil.	
			Guns in Action. 8.	
			Targets. Nil. No. 9 Gun. Road Fixed.	
			Both Vicker's) During Night. No. 8 Gun taken 500. infantry M.G. } Gun Dismantled.	
			E.A. raining day. No. 12.10.6. 800.	
			Harrich Fire) 10.20 pm 4 Gun 2,600. on E Track. } 11.30 pm. nightly. I.2.A. I.2.D.)	

Army Form C. 2118.

56. M.G. Coy.

WAR DIARY
or
INTELLIGENCE SUMMARY.
(Erase heading not required.)

June 1917.

Place	Date	Hour	Summary of Events and Information	Remarks and references to Appendices
In Trenches.			Work Done. General improvement of positions at Nos 4, 5, 6, 7 & 8. CORK. Emplacements rewritted + Aux. Store Made. at 1, 2 & 3. CHARLIE. 13,000 Rounds S.A.A. taken up to these positions giving its supply. Work Started. Dug out & the entrances by R.E.S. as under in Divn Defences Scheme.	
	29.		Company was relieved by 51. M.G. Coy. A completion of Relief Company returns to R.T. Nicholas Ek Men 5 y Coys camp. Relief complete 3 am.	
S.T. Nicholas	30	9.30	Mens Parade	

War Diary
July
1917.

50th
M.G. Coy

Army Form C. 2118.

50 M.G. Coy.
July 1917.

WAR DIARY
or
INTELLIGENCE SUMMARY.
(Erase heading not required.)

Place	Date	Hour	Summary of Events and Information	Remarks and references to Appendices
ST NICHOLAS	July 1st	7.0 a.m.	Muster Parade	
		8.30 a.m.	Checking & Cleaning Gun Reel	
		2 p.m.	Bathing Parade	
-do-	2nd	7.0 a.m.	Muster Parade	
		8.30	Checking & Cleaning Gun Reel	
		2.30 p.m.	Below over river	
-do-	3rd	7.0 a.m.	Muster Parade	
		8.30 a.m.	Physical training	
		9.30 a.m.	Saddles fin	
		10.45 a.m.	Instruction	
		2.0 p.m.	Below over hills	
		3.0 p.m.	R.S. Inspection	
-do-	4th	7.0 a.m.	Muster Parade	
		8.30 a.m.	Cleaning & Eating Guns	
		8.30 a.m.	Jumpers Inspection	
-do-	5th	7.0 a.m.	Muster Parade	
		8.30 a.m.	Physical training	
		9.30 a.m.	Park saddles fin	
		11.0 a.m.	Scaffolds Instruction in A.A. work - Instruction for members in I.F.	
		2.30 p.m.	Clave after Relief	
		3.0 p.m.	Bathing Parade	
-do-	6th	7.0 a.m.	Muster Parade	
		8.30 a.m.	Physical training	
		9.30 a.m.	Gun Drill	
		10.45	Gun Drill	
		2.0 p.m.	Coin order Drill	

Army Form C. 2118.

WAR DIARY
or
INTELLIGENCE SUMMARY.
(Erase heading not required.)

50. M.G. Coy.

July, 1917

Instructions regarding War Diaries and Intelligence Summaries are contained in F. S. Regs., Part II. and the Staff Manual respectively. Title pages will be prepared in manuscript.

Place	Date	Hour	Summary of Events and Information	Remarks and references to Appendices
St NICHOLAS	July 7th	7.00 am	Aurile Parade	
		6.00 pm	Preparations for moving to the line	
		12.30 pm	A Section moved and Tups forward to relieve 51 Coy.	(Blue)
	8/5		Guns as follows:-	
			No 3 I 14c 2060	
			4 I 8c 0008	
			5 = I 7D 9525	
			6 I 7D 0040	
		1.30 pm	C Section under 2/Lt Bourne	do
			Guns as follows:-	(Blue)
			No 1 I 14c 0540	
			2 I 14c 0393	
			9 I 13B 5165	
			10 I 13B 4090	
		2.30 pm	A Section under Lieut Savin	do
			Guns as follows:-	
			No 17 I 19A 3095	
			18 I 13c 1535	
			19 I 13c 2565	
			20 I 13A 0030	
		3.30 pm	D Section under 2/Lieut C.S Boyd	do
			Guns as follows:-	(Blue)
			No 21 H12 D 7540	
			22 H12 D 8050	
			31 H 18 A 8050	
			32 H 18 A 7575	
			Coy. Headquarters at H 17 C 2055	
		6.0 p.m	Relief of 51 Coy Complete	(Blue)

A 5834. Wt. W4973/M687. 730,000. 8/16. D. D. & L., Ltd. Forms/C.2113/13.

WAR DIARY or INTELLIGENCE SUMMARY

Army Form C. 2118.

50. M.G. Coy
July 1917

Place	Date	Hour	Summary of Events and Information	Remarks and references to Appendices
In the Trenches	July 9		Daily Report to Bde. Guns in Action: 8 Rounds expended: 12,000 Targets: 17 g.m. on I 15a 3939 18 I 15a 2345 19 I 9c 2519 20 I 15a 2506 21 I 14b 8207 22 I 14b 3979 51 I 14b 5755 32 I 14b 4565 Special attention being paid to CLIFF Trench and the new work being done in the vicinity. Times of firing: 12.111 a.m. to 12.15 a.m. and 12.12.10 m to 12.12.25 a.m. Rounds expended: 12,000 Casualties: Nil Work done: Numerous alterations, improvements etc. and S.A.A. dumps inspected. At Redoubt trench positions worked for Tripod legs fitted & Safety Braces put in. & improvements carried out - Repairs done where necessary. Work to include Continuation of work under the heading as given in previous report. General: Enemy machine gun reports to be firing bursts from direction about NE of 6.22 gun being fire. Retaliating the French between Line 314 & gun	[illegible]
do-	10th		Daily Report to Bde. Guns in Action: 7 Rounds expended: 6,000 Casualties: Nil Guns Tested & found correct Work done: All safety frames fitted at Redoubt. New Positions Surveyed for and for tripod legs. New	[illegible]

Army Form C. 2118.

WAR DIARY
or
INTELLIGENCE SUMMARY.
(Erase heading not required.)

30 M.C. Coy.

July. 917.

Place	Date	Hour	Summary of Events and Information	Remarks and references to Appendices
In the Trenches	July 10		Emplacement ready for No 20 emplacement. Dannert reverted to No 11 position. General maintenance of repairs & condition of guns during the day. Work to be done. Improvements of emplacements. Revising aegiress in front. General maintenance of repairs & condition. Inclination of plates. Revetting. Dis-construction of A.A. emplacement for No 11 gun. (additional) in new construction. Change in Position No 22 gun to No 3 position to replace gun damaged by shell fire. General indirect gun fired on area between I.1400s - I.5510 - I.1205 I.9400. 3 runs fired 11:35 - 11:35 P.M. Rounds fired 12:20.12.21 AM. Special attention being paid to Gipouy behind Shrewsbury in I & D. WDFA Trench and dugout along communication in I & D - Conjunction with artillery.	N/a
			Daily Report to Base	
			Guns in Action 4	
			Rounds expended 4500	
			Casualties nil	
			Work done	
—do—	July 11		Improvements of emplacements. Creating safety frames. Revising maintenance of repair. Revetting where necessary. Alternative emplacements to be made. General maintenance of repair & condition. Improvising of sanitary arrangements. Extra where necessary. Continuation of extension & improvement of planking around at two platoons about 5:30 am.	N/a
			Work to be done.	
			Anti Aircraft work. No. 14 to 20 gun fired 500 rounds assisting 1000 shrapnel airplanes. Rounds expended 1500	
			Guns fired as follows	
			Shrapnel 2nd Guns No 31 12.35AM - 1.35AM; I.20 B 8165; I.20 B 3276; M2 I.9 C 2343	
			No 21 12.35AM - 1.35AM 1.25 - 2.50 AM	
			No 20 1.5AM - 2.5AM 1.0 - 3.0 AM	
			Rounds expended 3500 2.15 - 3.0 AM	
—do—	July 12		Daily Report to Base	PMcK
			Guns in action 5	
			Rounds expended 9400	
			Guns fired nil	
			Casualties all and found over Wounded 39373 Pt. McKay	
			Work done Slight attacks. Gun emplacements & minor additions. Dannert where necessary. Revetting in place. General maintenance of guns where necessary by No 11 alters.	
			Work to be done Continuation of general maintenance & repair. Revising rifle mechanism & improvements to No 11 gun.	

Army Form C. 2118.

50. M.G. Coy.
July 1917.

WAR DIARY
or
INTELLIGENCE SUMMARY.
(Erase heading not required.)

Instructions regarding War Diaries and Intelligence Summaries are contained in F. S. Regs., Part II and the Staff Manual respectively. Title pages will be prepared in manuscript.

Place	Date	Hour	Summary of Events and Information	Remarks and references to Appendices

In the line	cont. July 12		Machine Gunnery
			Change in Position nil
			General
			Anti-Aircraft: No 4 gun fired 4 patterns:-
			70.7 250 rounds at 4 AM
			60.20 200
			60.31 } 350
			60.32
			Total 800
			Indirect harassing gunnery
			Barrage Rounds fired
			17 I.19.6.87 10.50 PM 2250
			18 I.15.0.46.b 2.20 AM 1800
			31 I.9.c.31.2.6 1.10 AM
			32 I.14.13.79.71 2.50 AM 2275
			                10.15 PM
			                11.20 PM 2275
			                12.30
			                 2.25
			                       Total 8600
			Six machine guns in HAUSA WOOD & vicinity reported to be very active against an enemy during day
				W

do.	July 13		Aeroplane Report to Bde.- Guns in Action 6 Rounds expended 9800 Casualties nil North Shore AA emplacement for No. 11 gun made. Dugouts commenced & improved in tea gun positions. 17,000 40. rounds & equipments expended to collaborate. Guns taken & cleaned. maintenance of repair and condition. At emplacement B. Battery a smoke - Dugout intended to serve as an emplacement. Store to be arranged. Begun noon to be finished. Not to be done	Blue

Army Form C. 2118.

WAR DIARY
or
INTELLIGENCE SUMMARY.
(Erase heading not required.)

50. M.G. Coy
July 1917.

Instructions regarding War Diaries and Intelligence Summaries are contained in F. S. Regs., Part II. and the Staff Manual respectively. Title pages will be prepared in manuscript.

Place	Date	Hour	Summary of Events and Information	Remarks and references to Appendices
In the line	July 13 (cont)		Changes in Position Guns at I14A 2050 moved to I14A 1186 Guides assumed up to new guns posts as follows: No 17 6.10 7.30 pm 20 3.00 7.30 pm 31 4.15 9.10 pm 32 5.00 9.30 pm The future posts of No 17, 20 guns, this awaited reports on [?] but devoid not receive the enemy on [?]. Report Quin. No of Guns Damage Rounds of firing Rates 31 I14B A893 (Order M.G.) 12noon–3pm 700 17 I91894909 (during morning) 11.00pm–2am SAM 4750 18 —do— 19 20 31 I14D4050 32 I14D7050 } 12.30–1am 1300 A hostile machine gun was firing against No 19 gun at I130 1575 at intervals during ring throughout mounted prevents [?].	W
do—	July 14		Duty Report to Bde. Guns in Action 10 Rounds in 24 hrs 8,500 Casualties D/R 2 New dem [?] New improvements to No 5 gun at I14A 1186 completed. AA position constructed at I14C 1835. Work continued on dugout at I7D 0040, General improvement & [?] Guns Posts. Maintenance of dispersion & reconstruction from water to be finished. Rifle racks to be fixed. Stair C to be enlarged. New to be down. AA explanations & dugouts to be finished.	AP [?]

A 5834 Wt. W4973/M687 730,000 8.16 D. D. & L. Ltd Forms/C.2118/13

WAR DIARY or INTELLIGENCE SUMMARY

Army Form C. 2118.

58. M.G.Coy
July 1917.

(Erase heading not required.)

Instructions regarding War Diaries and Intelligence Summaries are contained in F. S. Regs., Part II. and the Staff Manual respectively. Title pages will be prepared in manuscript.

Place	Date	Hour	Summary of Events and Information	Remarks and references to Appendices
In the field (cont.)	July 1st (cont.)		General: Anti-Aircraft Work. Guns fired in general.	
			No. of Gun — 50 rounds at 6.30 am 11 — 900 7 — 750 20 21 32 Total 1700.	
			Indirect Sit. Shoots Targets Time of Shoot. Rounds in rounds	
			CLIFFE — Sh. co-operation with Cutter WINDMILL CORNER — "Burst short" 4000 COST WORM — 11.15 – 11.30 PM Vicinity of JUNCTION COPSE + BELGAR WOOD — Sh. co-operation with butts in position 2.5 am – 2.50 am. 1200 DUMP + Railway Trench — 11.30 PM – 3.0 AM 1300	
			Daily Report to B.de Guns in action 6 Rounds Expended 11000 Casualties 4 Work done. Work continued throughout at T 14A 11.66. Salvage Wing No 15 dump. Position cleaned and repaired. Safety fence erected. General Sentrenching and maintenance of repairs in good condition – Guns oiled. NWK to be done. Dugout to be finished. Rifle racks for field stove etc to be arranged. Superimposed W/s met up where damaged by shell fire. Change in Position - Summer T 14A 11.66 moved to T 14 A 2066. General - Indirect Fire Guns. No 19, 20, 21, 22, 31 + 32. co-operation with other sections at 10.0 pm and reached new area T 8a circa to T 14D. Rounds expended = 11000.	

A534 Wt. W.4973/M687 750,000 8/16 D.D. & L. Ltd. Forms/C.2118/13

Army Form C. 2118.

5B.M.G.Coy
July 1917

WAR DIARY
or
INTELLIGENCE SUMMARY.
(Erase heading not required.)

Instructions regarding War Diaries and Intelligence Summaries are contained in F.S. Regs., Part II. and the Staff Manual respectively. Title pages will be prepared in manuscript.

Place	Date	Hour	Summary of Events and Information	Remarks and references to Appendices
La Tour / June	July 16		Daily Report to Bde. Guns in action. 8 Rounds expended. Casualties. Work done.	
		12.00	Position taken of gun relieved & emplacements. Improvements and alterations of defences & installation. Assigned to M finished. Paper reads front trenches to be constructed. Overhead cover up to emplacement. All emplacements at T.146.5.35 completed, changed up to emplacement. Supply ammo checks - start to arrange. Gate delivery message completed by 8.O.P.M.	W
			Changes in Pos: Both climate Gun fires as follows:- $h_1 31 \brace h_2 32$ 650 rounds - 7.0-9.0 P.M. 8 Barrage guns opened fire with these during which by the surprise to the enemy viz: 2 Spede main Runkels were fired by the line. Results expedited 250.	
-do-	July 17		Daily Report to Bde. Guns in action. 4 Rounds expended. 6.200 Casualties. nil Work done. Work on dugout for M.11 gun continued. Drainage channels & latrines constructed. Drainage ditches made. Supply of ammo checked. General maintenance of weapons and completion of dugouts & emplacements. All positions & emplacements to be improved & extended. Arrangement is in Infantry position. Indian ridicule. Steps to be arranged.	(File)

A 5834 Wt. W 4973/M 687 730,000 8/16 D. D. & L. Ltd. Forms/C.2118/13.

WAR DIARY or INTELLIGENCE SUMMARY

Army Form C. 2118.

56 M.G. Coy
July 1917.

Place	Date	Hour	Summary of Events and Information	Remarks and references to Appendices
Line	July 17th		Change in Position Guns in action. Over averaged, No 31 & 32 guns fired 2000 rounds at 7.30 A.M. Intense fire: 17 Vickers + Lewis Machine 18 to PLOUVAIN 31 Batn H.Q. 32 Track. 10.0 P.M — 2.0 A.M. Rounds expended £6,000	W.
	July 18		Activity Report to Bde. Guns in action 8 Rounds 2t fired 8000 nil Casualties Guns rested Work done. Attention to A.A. entanglement to 2 enforcement due to mitted. SAA Store west of B& enforcement. Question enforcement generally cleaned. Wires carrying of N.E.A.M alternative employment to be constituted. A.A. Machine injured employment in embankment pretry hill. Work to be done. Change in Position General. Guns co-operated with artillery in firing on our entanglement Rounds expended 8000	W.

Army Form C. 2118.

WAR DIARY
or
INTELLIGENCE SUMMARY
(Erase heading not required.)

56. M.G. Coy
July 1917.

Place	Date	Hour	Summary of Events and Information	Remarks and references to Appendices
Luic	July 19th		Daily Report to Batt.
Guns in Position
Routine experiences
Consolidation
Work done
12.00
hrs
Conveying Kit to FA position. Carrying supplements to kitchen in the vicinity. General maintenance, inspection & repair.
Work to be done
General
Ammunition supplements to be made up. SAA to be issued to gun position. Stored to be salvaged. General cleaning & condition maintenance.
Summary Report
709 } New Fronts in - 10.0 P.M — 2.0 A.M
18 } II.FA 37055

19 Road running through WEAK
20 Sunk behind W.H.P
21 Ground Run H.Q behind } WIGGLE   11.15 P.M to 11.20 P.M
22 Just W of WIGGLE thru WEAK   11.30 P.M - 11.40 P.M
31 Track S.W of 3 M.G Post   Defensive bursts of fire
32 Track running WEAK-WIGGLE   Burst of 50 rounds at suspicious distances | A.E.C |

Army Form C. 2118.

WAR DIARY
or
INTELLIGENCE SUMMARY.
(Erase heading not required.)

56. M.G. Coy
July 1917

Place	Date	Hour	Summary of Events and Information	Remarks and references to Appendices
In the field	July 1st		Daily Report to Bde.in. Gun in action 5. Rounds expended 6000 Casualties nil Work done: Experiments to intensified fire to be a gun Supplementary in apparent position (No. 21 again. All employed. General maintenance of material & emplacement. Improved. General maintenance of material & existing emplacement. Extermination and completion of new indirect Dire Gun. No. 21 at Dump T.98.0.2.4.5. expended 1500 rounds to 17. - I.9.8.9. B.D.O. 1500. at intermittent periods from 1 A.M. to 3.20 A.M. At 11.30 A.M. this morning an east S.O.S. signal was seen in the vicinity of Polkhoven Convoy. Charge guns fired a short Burst.	A.1
-do-	July 2	9000 13000 nil	Daily Report to Bde. Gun in Action Rounds Expended Casualties Work done General maintenance of appeal transition to emplacements and trenches in the vicinity. Emplacement for new position (No 21) to 4.22 worked upon and brought along to the emplacement. Guns aid on dummy. Continuation of new emplacement & extermination of indirect firing work. At 1 a.m. fired 200 rounds at 5.30 a.m. with 17 gun. Also 500 " - 7.10 A.M. the emplacement fired at 4 to 17 gun was harassed to an area in the direction of GAVRELLE.	A.13.a.

A.3834 Wt.W.4973/M.687 750,000 8/16 D.D.& L Ltd Forms/C.2118/13.

Army Form C. 2118.

WAR DIARY
or
INTELLIGENCE SUMMARY.
(Erase heading not required.)

50 M.G.C.
Jul 1917

Instructions regarding War Diaries and Intelligence Summaries are contained in F. S. Regs., Part II. and the Staff Manual respectively. Title pages will be prepared in manuscript.

Place	Date	Hour	Summary of Events and Information	Remarks and references to Appendices
Line	July 28 Cont'd		Indirect Fire Guns. In co-operation with the artillery in the raid carried out last night by the Y. & R.'s a W.A.R.T. Barrage of guns fired from Zero+1 to Zero+14 and managed the previous line:- I 8 B 0050 — I 8 B 9000 I 8 B 4000 — I 8 D 2606 Rounds expended = 12300 Reports from Section Officers state that it was in different to determine our S.O.S. signal from the red light put up by the Enemy.	W.S.
-do-	29		Arty. depend to B.E. 6 Guns in Action 6 Rounds expended 6000 Casualties nil Work done - Indirect Fire continued with satisfactory results. Worth drew an enemy MG in CAD,12 to new emplacement. Several direct hits registered on the trench 19 gun positions and ammunition dump discovered. M.G. 15 in down. Arty gun fire on pillbox 1 at 5.0 a.m. on 31 at 6.30 AM & 7.0 PM 19 at 6.30 P.M. + 20 mutes Rounds expended 1600 Casualties Nil Guns. Enemy MG Gun fired on Klines 1.0.14 PROVAIN N E J Do DUMP + Truck in I 9.B.00 50 } 10.30 p.m. — 1.0 a m 31 CANDY 32 Dwell in I14.45.50 (Rounds expended 1490)	W.S.

Army Form C. 2118.

WAR DIARY
or
INTELLIGENCE SUMMARY.
(Erase heading not required.)

50. M.G. Coy.
July. 1917.

Place	Date	Hour	Summary of Events and Information	Remarks and references to Appendices
In the Line.	23rd		Reports from officers on return. "A" Section. 2/Lt W. Talter. — 2/Lt D. Irwin. "B" Section	
			Guns in Action. All guns in battle positions. No. 1. AA. 150 rounds fired.	
			Casualties. Nil. nil.	
			Work Done. Trench continued to Cading. Revetting sides of N°2g. Emp. (AA)	
			Work to be done. Complete above trench. A.A position alternative Emp.	
			Change in Position. nil. nil.	
			Material Required. nil. nil.	
			General. "C" Section. A.A gun fired at 5.a.m & 7.30pm.	
			"D" Section. 2/Lt. E.S. Fold.	
			Guns in Action. 4. Rounds fired. 5000. nil.	
			Casualties. nil. nil.	
			Work Done. General Improvement. Alternative Emp. finished. Dug out trN°5 started.	
			Work to be done. " or Alternative Emp to be made.	
			Material Required. nil. nil.	
			Change in Position. nil. nil.	
			General. E.A fired at early in morning & 11.30 p.m	(H)Blake

Army Form C. 2118.

WAR DIARY
or
INTELLIGENCE SUMMARY.
(Erase heading not required.)

50. M.G. Coy.

July 1917

Place	Date	Hour	Summary of Events and Information	Remarks and references to Appendices
In the line.	23- continued.		Company relieved by 51.M.G.Coy. + returned to old Camp of St Nicholas.	(Photo)
St Nicholas Camp.	24th.		Parade for Baths.	(Photo)
			Moved Camp to new sight 200 y. nearer to Factory. Out of view of Roch.	
			Lt E.W Davis takes 3 guns + teams for A.A drill sparking ANZ IN. to LOUEZ Dumps.	
"	25.	6 am.	Reveille 6 am.	(Photo)
		6.30.	Musketry Clean Parade.	
		8-8.30	Running Drill.	
			Remainder of day spent in cleaning + checking Limbers Gun Gear Amn. etc. – Rain.	
	26th.	am. 5.30	Reveille	(Photo)
		6.30.	Interior Economy Musty Clean Parade.	
		8.845	Physical + Running Drill.	
		9.00	Box Respirator + Gas Helmet Inspection.	
		9.30 -12.30 pm.	Cleaning + Testing Guns – Amn etc.	
		2 pm	Coy Parade for Close order Drill with Arms.	

Army Form C. 2118.

56 M.G. Coy
July 1917

WAR DIARY
or
INTELLIGENCE SUMMARY.
(Erase heading not required.)

Instructions regarding War Diaries and Intelligence Summaries are contained in F.S. Regs., Part II. and the Staff Manual respectively. Title pages will be prepared in manuscript.

Place	Date	Hour	Summary of Events and Information	Remarks and references to Appendices
St Nicholas	27.		Usual Parades at 6.30am & 8am. Section Officers inspect Box respirators & Gas helmets. Rest of morning spent in cleaning guns etc.	PTS
			Baths in the afternoon	
			Lt I.W. Telfer relieves Mr Davis at the A.A. Positions.	
"	28.		Reveille mailtime. Muster Clean Parade + Physical Drill	(Plato)
			Morning spent in Gun Drill, Mechanism & Stoppages.	
			Afternoon Squad Drill with arms	
"	29.		Sunday. Reveille 6am. Muster Parade at 7. Physical Drill 8. Church Parade Cancelled after Parading owing to deteriorating.	Phl.
			Thunderstorm	
"	30.	6.30am	Muster Clean Parade.	
		8am	Running Drill + Physical Drill.	
		9-12pm	Instruction in Time, Elevating, Traversing Dial + Barrage Fire Instruction	(Phl)
		2-4pm	Company Drill with arms	

WAR DIARY or INTELLIGENCE SUMMARY.

Army Form C. 2118.

50 M.G. Coy.
July 1917.

Place	Date	Hour	Summary of Events and Information	Remarks and references to Appendices
St Nicolas	31-		Company Parade for Packing Limbers prior to Relief in Afternoon.	
			Relief by Daylight of 52 M.G. Coy. Left 13th Sector.	
			Map references of Portions.	
			N° 16. Gun. I.A.50.45. N° 12. Gun. I.7.6.05.35. } Cuba Trench.	
			- 15 " I.1.a.60.26. Cork Trench - 13 " I.7.6.00.45. } under	
			- 14 " I.I.C.80.90. } under Lt F.W.Davis. - 6 " I.7.6.40.30. Lt H.E.Smith	
			- 8 " I.I.C.75.75. - 6a " I.7.6.40.70. } Charlie Trench.	
			- 7 " I.I.d.60.00.	
			N° 24 Gun. H.6.d.50.10 } under - 23 " I.126.70.65 } Lt D. Irwin } Caniz Trench. 4 Guns in Reserve in Hudson under 2nd Lt E.Field.	
			- 30 " H.6.c.50.55. } Hawthorne. T.	
			Company H.Q. in Gavrelle Line (Hussar) Hill 6.75.96. Lt C.S.Merritt. Lt H.B.Morier-Williams	
			Rinding Post Coy Sgt Major + Signallers in Orgart Hussar.	
			Ration Dump. Cookhouse Dump. H.5.D.70.80	
			Relief Complete 6 p.m. 31.7.17.	H.B.M-W.

Cewrett Coy
O.C. 50 M.G. Coy

Army Form C. 2118.

WAR DIARY
or
INTELLIGENCE SUMMARY.
(Erase heading not required.)

50. M.G. Coy.
1st August. 1917.

Vol 18

Place	Date	Hour	Summary of Events and Information	Remarks and references to Appendices
XVII Corps Left Div Sector	1st		Company in the line. Reports from Officers as follows. Company Relieve 52. M.G. Coy by day. GREEN HOPKINS Sector. Relief complete 6.pm. Guns in Action. All Guns in Battle Position Casualties. nil. "A" Section. Lt. E.W. Davis Work done. nil General maneuvre. Change in Position. nil Material Required. nil General. Fairly quiet. "B" Section Lt. D. Irwin Guns in Action. nil Casualties. nil Change in Position. nil Work Done. nil. New emplacement to be constructed in Conrad. Positions improved Material Required. nil General. Fairly Quiet. Map Reference of the Guns as follows No.16. Gun. I.1.a. 50.45 ⎫ No.15. Gun. I.1.a. 60.25 ⎪ No.14. Gun. I.1.c. 80.90 ⎬ CORK TRENCH No.8. Gun. I.1.c. 75.75 ⎪ No.12. Gun. I.7.d. 05.35 ⎭ No.13. Gun. I.7.b. 00.45 ⎫ CUBA TRENCH. No.6. Gun. I.7.b. 40.30 ⎪ No.6A. Gun. I.7.b. 40.70 ⎬ CHARLIE TRENCH. No.7. Gun. I.1.d. 60.00 ⎭ "C" Section Lt. H.E. Smith. Guns in Action. nil Casualties. nil Work done. Improvement of Funk Holes and Saps. [Rain Slows progress.] Work to be done. Continuation of above. Change in Position. nil Material Required. 4" × 2" General. Situation Quiet. "D" Section 1/Lt. E.S. Fold. Guns in Action. nil Casualties. nil Work done. nil Work to be done. Deepening and repairing Trench. Change in Position. nil Material Required. 500 Sand Bags, and "Duck Boards". Situation Quiet. No.24. gun. map Ref. H.6.d. 50.10. ⎫ CADIZ No.23. gun. map Ref. H.12.b. 70.65. ⎬ TRENCH. No.30. gun. map Ref. H.6.c. 50.55. ⎭ 4 Guns in Reserve. HUDSON TRENCH Coy. H.Q. at:— H.11.b. 75.95.	

WAR DIARY or INTELLIGENCE SUMMARY

Army Form C. 2118.

50 M.G. Coy

August 1917.

(Erase heading not required.)

Instructions regarding War Diaries and Intelligence Summaries are contained in F. S. Regs., Part II. and the Staff Manual respectively. Title pages will be prepared in manuscript.

Place	Date	Hour	Summary of Events and Information	Remarks and references to Appendices
XVII Corps Left Div Sector	2nd		Guns in Action. 2	
			Rounds Expended. 2,500.	
			Casualties. Nil	
			Work done. Fire step made for No.30 Gun. Sap to New Emplacement at No.14 gun ordered. Receptacle made for Gun gear. Work done on Saps at Nos. 6A, and 7 Guns, and on Emplacement at Nos. 23 and 23 A. General maintenance and repair of Trenches and Emplacements.	
			Work to be done. Emplacements for Nos. 24 and 24A to be completed. Shelters for Nos. 23, 23A, 24, and 24A, to be constructed by R.E.S. HAWTHORN Trench to be improved, and Emplacements at Nos. 14, 15, and 8 to be revetted.	
"			General. Nos. 29, and 30 guns fired indirect at irregular intervals, from 10. PM – 12:30. AM. Target suspected Ration Dump at 19 a.1.8. Rounds expended. 2,500.	
			Situation. Enemy Shells CORK Trench at irregular intervals with 5.9.s in the Vicinity of No.16 Gun otherwise situation normal.	
"	3rd		Guns in Action. 5	
			Rounds Expended. 1,000	
			Casualties. Nil	
			Work done. At No. 23 position Trench deepened Duck Boards Laid. At No. 23A work done on building new dugout. At No. 8. alternative emplacement wired and Revetted. At No. 14 Gun Sap widened to new Emplacement. At No. 11. Gun alternative Emplacement revetted in CHARLIE & CUBA General Maintenance of repair to Trenches and Front Helen work Continued by R.E.S and Saps in vicinity of Nos. 6A, and 7. Duck Boards laid up to HAWTHORN, and work done on Trench 30,000 Rounds S.A.A. Carried up to Barrage Guns. Emplacements at Nos. 23A, 24, and 24A to be completed, and Shelters for same positions, Safety Frames to be adjusted and Checked. General up Keep of Trenches and Emplacements.	
			Work to be done.	

WAR DIARY or INTELLIGENCE SUMMARY

Army Form C. 2118.

50. M.G. Coy.
August 1917.

Place	Date	Hour	Summary of Events and Information	Remarks and references to Appendices
XVII Corps Left Div Sector.	3rd	cont.	**Change in Position.** nil. **General.** One Gun fired indirect from H.6.c.45.45 from 9.30 – 11.30 P.M. at irregular intervals. Target WEED Trench from I.2.d.30.05 – I.8.b.95.95. Rounds Expended 750. S.O.S. Tests 2 Golden Rockets were observed at 2.3.am fired from about 17b.90.10. Barrage Guns opened fire within fine seconds.	
"	4th		**Guns in Action.** Ammunition Expended 9,000 rounds. Casualties nil. **Work done.** Trench in Vicinity of 70S.29 & 30 Gun Duckboarded. Dugout frame made & erected at 70.23.A Position. Gun Emplacement revetted at 70.8. Work done on widening Sap to new Emplacement at 70.14. Alternative Emplacement revetted at 70.15. R.E.'s continue work on Saps at Nos. 6A. & 7. Dew Pit on at Coy. H.Q. General maintenance & repair of Trenches. **Work to be done.** Rifle Racks to be erected when to Rand & 70.23.A position to be completed. Emplacement for 70.24.A to be started. Dugouts for 70S.24 & 24.A & to be constructed. Fire step at 70.14 to be improved. Belts filled.	
"			**General.** In conjunction with the Artillery. 2 minutes bursts were fired on Tracks in Vicinity of I.18.b.30.50. I.8.b.40.40. I.8.6.80.20. I.8.a.80.00 and I.19.a.10.63. Indirect fire was maintained on these Tracks during the night until 10.am. One gun also fired indirect on WASH Trench at I.3.d.15.70. from 10.P.M – 1.a.m. Rounds Expended 9,000. **Situation.** Normal Some Shelling of CORK by S.9.s during the afternoon.	
"	5th		**Guns in Action.** 7 Rounds Expended 4,000. Casualties nil. **Work done.** Shelter at 70.23.A completed. Covered emplacement at 70.23.A carried on with. Latrine built at 70.23 and position improved. Emplacement at no.15 Gun being revetted. HAWTHORN Trench cleared and Duckboarded. **Work to be done.** Emplacement at 70.23.A to be completed. Emplacement at 70.24 & 24.A also shelters to be constructed. General maintenance of Dugouts & Trenches. Safety Frames to be erected & checked.	

WAR DIARY
INTELLIGENCE SUMMARY.
(Erase heading not required.)

Army Form C. 2118.

50. M. G. Coy.
August. 1917.

Place	Date	Hour	Summary of Events and Information	Remarks and references to Appendices
XVII Corps Left Div Sector.	5th cont.		General. In conjunction with Artillery. 7 Guns fired a short burst on Barrage lines at 11.30 P.M. in addition 3 Guns fired indirect from 10 PM - 1.30 AM. on Enemy Trenches + Tracks at irregular intervals. Rounds expended 4000	
			Situation. CORK shelled with 5.9.s. 5.9.s also fell in the Vicinity of HAWTHORN and CADIZ at various times during the night. CHARLIE Trench shelled in the morning also.	JW
"	6th		Guns in Action 6. Ammunition Expended 13,000 Rounds Casualties Nil. Work done. Emplacement at No 23A Completed. Work done on Shelter for No 24. Continuation of improvement of advanced emplacement at No. G.14. Revetting done at No. 15. Reconstruction of alternative emplacement to No. 16. which was destroyed by a direct hit. HAWTHORN Trench + indirect fire positions duckboarded + improved. S.A.A. carried up to 1/F guns also R.E. Material. Trenches round Coy. H.Q improved.	
"			Work to be done. Shelters at No 24A to be completed. Alternative emplacement at No 0.24 & No 24A + Shelter at No 24A to be constructed. General maintenance of Trenches + No 16 to be completed. Rifle Racks to the front when available.	
			General. At 10.30 PM in conjunction with the 51st Brigade Barrage fire was opened by 6 Guns on Targets as follows:- I 8 d 30.45, V 8 L 40.40, V 18 a 50.00, I 9 a 10.65, I 8 L 75.25 and I 9 a 00.90. Indirect fire was maintained on these Targets from 10.30 PM - 3 AM at irregular intervals. Ammunition Expended 13,000 Rounds. Enemy Aeroplanes fired on at 7 PM.	
			Situation. Enemy observed working in considerable numbers this morning on Western Slopes of GREENLAND HILL. Enemy had a direct hit on a T.M. emplacement which is in very close attendance to No 6 A Gun. in CHARLIE Trench. CORK Spasmodically shelled with 5.9.s + T.M.s. 3. Ammunition Expended 2,000 Casualties Nil.	JK
"	7th		Guns in Action 3. Ammunition Expended 2,000 Casualties Nil. Work done. Trench in Vicinity of No 23 position revetted Emplacement at No 23A Completed. Work continued on Shelter for No 24. R.E. Material + S.A.A. carried up to these positions. Work done on improving HAWTHORN Trench.	

WAR DIARY or INTELLIGENCE SUMMARY

Army Form C. 2118.

50. M. G. Coy.

August. 1917.

Place	Date	Hour	Summary of Events and Information	Remarks and references to Appendices
XVIII Corps Left Div Sector.	7TH Cont'd.		**Work done.** Revetting at Nos. 15, 14, + 8 continued. Grass cut in front of No. 16 Gun. Work done on improving CUBBY HOLES & Emplacements in CHARLIE + CUBA. **Work to be done.** Shelter for No. 24 to be completed. Emplacement at No. 24 to be constructed. General maintenance of Trenches and Emplacements. **General.** Guns in CHARLIE fired at Enemy Aeroplane. Rounds expended 200. 2 guns fired indirect on following targets. Enemy Tracks in I.8.b and C at irregular intervals. Time 9.30-11.30 am. 1000 Rounds Expended.	
"	8TH		**Situation.** CHARLIE and CORK shelled with 5.9.s and T.M.s during the night. **Guns in Action.** 7. **Casualties** nil. **Work done.** Ammunition Expended 5000 Rounds. Work done on Emplacement and Shelter at No. 24 position. General maintenance of repair to Trenches + Emplacements. Officers small dugout built in HAWTHORN. R.E. Material + S.A.A. carried up to Gun positions. **Work to be done.** Alternative Emplacement for Dos. 13. 12. and 6A to be completed. No. 16 Alternative Emplacement to be improved. Emplacement + Shelter at No. 24 to be completed. Emplacement and Shelter at No. 24 A to be constructed. **Change in Positions.** Gun Team of No. 24 moved back from present position to new position now almost completed. Complete in CADIZ. Reserve Gun Team to be moved into No. 23A position today. **General.** One Gun in CHARLIE, + one Gun in HAWTHORN fired on Enemy Aeroplane in conjunction with Anti-Aircraft guns. 6 guns fired Barrage fire on the following targets:- I.8.b.30.45. I.8.a.80.00. I.8.b.76.75. I.8.b.45.40. I.9.a.10.65 and I.9.c.00.90. Indirect fire was also maintained on these targets at irregular intervals during the night. Total Rounds Expended. 5,000.	
"	9TH		**Guns in Action.** 3. **Ammunition Expended** 4,000 Rounds. **Casualties.** 236 M.G. Coy. one O/R wounded accidentally. (500.) 50. M. G. Coy. Casualties nil. **Work done.** Work done on Emplacement at Nos. 24 + 23A. S.A.A. + R.E. material carried up to positions. Sap constructed for No. 27 Gun. Officers dug-out in HAWTHORN worked on. New Emplacement made for Nos. 25 Gun. **Work to be done.** Emplacements at Nos. 24A, 24, + 23/A. Shelters for Nos. 24, + 24 A to be revetted and completed.	

WAR DIARY
or
INTELLIGENCE SUMMARY.
(Erase heading not required.)

Army Form C. 2118.

50. M. G. Coy.
August. 1917.

Place	Date	Hour	Summary of Events and Information	Remarks and references to Appendices
XVII Corps Left DIV Sector	9TH	Cont'd	Work to be done. A.A. Emplacement to be made in CORK and CUBA. Alternative Emplacement to be made for ALL Guns in CHARLIE. General. 3 Guns fired indirect as follows No.23 Gun Target i 9 c 00.90 Time of firing 9.30 - 11.30 P.M. No 28 Gun Target WHIP X ROADS. Time of firing 11.15.P.M. - 1.45.A.M. No.25 Gun Target WHIP X ROADS. Time of firing 1.30.am - 3.0.am Total Ammunition expended 4,500 rounds	Cont'd
"	10TH		Guns in Action. 9 Ammunition Expended 6,500 Rounds Casualties NIL Work done. Resetting of Nos. 24A, IM, 23A, and 23 positions, work done on emplacement and Shelters at their positions. Work done on enemy Trenches in CORK, + CHARLIE, Emplacements, + Trenches repaired after the heavy rain. Shelters constructed for No.25 Gun. Emplacements at Nos 28, + 26 improved + Sap improved for gun position at No.27. Work to be done No. 23. Emplacement to be completed, also No.24. Nos.24A, + 24 Shelters to be completed + Emplacement improved safety Frames at ALL Positions to be checked. Trench at No.25 to be deepened Continuation of work at Nos. 28, 27, and 26 Positions. A.A. Positions to be made in CUBA and CORK. Alternative Emplacements to be made in CUBA and CHARLIE. General Maintenance.	
"			General. 6 Guns fired indirect from 12 midnight - 2 A.M. Targets: - 18 d 20.70 I 2 d 35.50, I 8 d 70.25, I 9 c.15, 35.95, @ I 9 c 00.90, + WHIP X ROADS Total Ammunition Expended. 6,500 Rounds. Enemy Aeroplanes were also engaged during the Day. In response to S.O.S. Calls our Guns fired at the following Times. 2 minute bursts:- 11.2 P.M, 11.14 P.M, 11.30 P.M, 2.19.A.M, and 2.21 A.M. Action was taken at once the first three S.O.S. Signals were put up from the Right Sector + the last two from the Left Sector Casualties 1 Rounds Expended 750. Casualties 1 O.R KILLED 236 M.G. Coy. Nil	
"	11TH		Guns in Action. Work done. AA Emplacement commenced in CORK. 2 Alternative Emplacements made in CHARLIE A.A. Emplacement started in CUBA. Trenches drained + repaired on nearly all Support Guns. R.E. Material and S. A.A. carried up to Gun Positions. Shelter for Pos. 26, + 25 Teams commenced.	

Army Form C. 2118.

WAR DIARY
or
INTELLIGENCE SUMMARY.
(Erase heading not required.)

50. M. G. Coy
August, 1917.

Place	Date	Hour	Summary of Events and Information	Remarks and references to Appendices
XVII Corps Left Div Sector.	11TH	Cont.d	Work continued on Officers dugout in HAWTHORN. Work commenced on Sap for Nos. 27. Gun. Work continued on Emplacements and Shelters at Nos. 23, 23A, 24, and 24 A. Work to be done:- Continuation of work above. General. One gun fired indirect between 3. and 5. P.M. Target I.8 to 30.45. Rounds Expended 750.	Cas'
"	12TH		Guns in Action. 3. Ammunition Expended 4,000 Rounds Casualties Nil. Work done. Work commenced on 3 Emplacements in TRENT Trench. Alternative emplacements carried on with CORK. A.A. position carried on with CORK. Work done on Shelters and emplacements in CADIZ. also work done on Shelters for Nos. 25, + 26. Gun Teams. Sap about completed for No. 27. Team. Work to be done. Alternative emplacement in CUBA to be completed. A.A. emplacement in CUBA and CORK to be completion. Three emplacements and Shelters in TRENT Trench to be finished. Shelters and emplacements in CADIZ Line to be completed. General maintenance and Repair. One Reserve Gun manned up to No. 24 A. Position. 3 guns fired indirect from 12 M.N. - 2.50. A.M. Targets :- I 13 a 30. b 25 and I 18 a 170.00. Rounds Expended 4,080.	
"	13TH		Guns in Action. H. Ammunition expended 6,000. Casualties Nil. Work done. Work done on emplacements + Shelters in TRENT Trench and at Nos. 23, 23A, 24, and 24 A positions. Alternative emplacement for No. 7. Gun completed. Work continued on A.A. position in CORK. Work also done on Emplacements + Shelters at Nos. 25, 26, 27, + 28. General maintenance + repair of Trenches. Work to be done. Continuation of above. General. Four Guns fired indirect between the hours of 9.30. P.M + 1.0 A.M. Targets :- V I2d 35.05 to I9a 15.90. I 8d. 05.55 to I 8b 15.38, and I 8b 00.60 to I 8b 20.50. Ammunition Expended 6,000. Rounds.	Cas'

Army Form C. 2118.

WAR DIARY
or
INTELLIGENCE SUMMARY.
(Erase heading not required.)

50. M.G. Coy
August. 1917.

Place	Date	Hour	Summary of Events and Information	Remarks and references to Appendices
XVII Corps Left Div Sector.	13TH		**Con'd Situation**— Twelve H.E. 2.5 fell in close vicinity of No. 25 Gun between 9.45 P.M + 10.0. P.M. accounted for undoubtedly by the fact that CHICKEN RESERVE is frequently being crossed by day.	CW
	14TH		**Guns in Action** 18. Ammunition Expended 6,000 Rounds Casualties nil. **Work done.** All positions in CORK and CUBA worked on. New Emplacements Commenced for Nos 14, + 13 Guns. Improvement made to Shelters + Emplacements at Nos 23, 23A, 24, and 24A Emplacements in TRENT Trench Completed. Shelters in TRENT Trench worked on. Shelters at Nos. 25, + 26 Guns Completed. Work continued on Saps for Nos. 27. + 28 Gun Teams. **Work to be done.** Continuation of above. **General.** In conjunction with the Artillery 8 Guns fired on Enemy Tracks in 18t., two vicinity of WHIP x ROADS. Rounds Expended. 6,000. **Situation** Enemy M.G's very active along CHICKEN RESERVE & CALF RESERVE & This due undoubtedly to unnecessary movement along this line by day.	CW
"	15TH		**Guns in Action** 14 Ammunition Expended 6,500 Casualties Nil. **Work done.** Work continued on improving positions at Nos. 23, 23A, 24, and 24A. New Emplacement for No. 13 Gun in CUBA Completed. A.A positions in CORK and CUBA Completed. Work continued on new emplacement for No. 14 Gun. Alternative emplacements, for Guns in CHARLIE Completed. Fire step at No. 15 Gun improved. Work done in vicinity of Nos. 25. + 26. Guns deepened. Trench done on Nos. 27. + 28. Gun positions. **Work to be done.** A.A Emplacement in CORK and CUBA new Emplacement for No. 14. Gun to be completed. Shelters for Team at No. 13. Gun position to be erected. No. 27. Gun Sap to be completed. **Change in position** 3 Reserve Guns moved into the Intermediate Line in General. Open Sketch Map forwarded. Targets WIBBLE Trench, WHIP x ROADS + Four Guns fired indirect. Dugouts at G12d 60.35. Rounds Expended 6,500.	CW

Army Form C. 2118.

WAR DIARY
or
INTELLIGENCE SUMMARY.
(Erase heading not required.)

50. M.G. Coy.

August. 1917.

Instructions regarding War Diaries and Intelligence Summaries are contained in F.S. Regs., Part II and the Staff Manual respectively. Title pages will be prepared in manuscript.

Place	Date	Hour	Summary of Events and Information	Remarks and references to Appendices
XVIII Corps Left Div. Sector.	16TH		Guns in Action 4. Ammunition Expended 5,000 Rounds. Casualties Nil. Work done. All alternative emplacements in CHARLIE and CUBA, + A.A. position completed. New Position in CORK for No. 14 gun completed. Also new emplacement for No. 13 gun in CUBA completed. 4 guns moved into them. Work done on improving positions at Nos 23, 13a, 24, + 24A. Emplacements + Trenches in vicinity of indirect + intermediate line improved. Work done on Nos. 25, 26, 27, + 28, + Emplacements improved.	cw
"			Work to be done Continuation of above.	
"			General. Four Guns fired indirect on Targets as follows:- (i) Tracks N.E. of WHIP X ROADS, 9-65. (ii) I.13.a.30.25. (iii) Dugouts at I.12.d.65. 57 and (iv) New work at I.12.d. 60. 35 from 9.30 PM - 12 Midnight. Rounds Expended 5,000. Company Relieved by 51. M.G. Coy. by day. Relief complete by 6. PM. Gun Teams on being relieved proceed in small Parties, independently to GRIMSBY CAMP St NICHOLAS.	cw
ST. NICHOLAS	17TH	7.0AM	Reveille 7. AM Company Parade at 12 noon, in New fighting order.	cw
"	18TH	5:30AM	Reveille Inspection and Roll Call. 2. P.M. Company turned out: for	cw
		8.0AM	5.30. AM. Interior Economy + Musketry Clean Parade. Full Pack Parade and Inspection	
		9.0AM	Cleaning Guns and Gun Gear.	
		2.0PM	Coy Parade for Close Order Drill with Arms.	
		3.0PM	Kit Inspection.	
"	19TH	5:30AM	Reveille 6:30. am. Interior Economy + Musketry Clean Parade.	cw
		8.15AM	Physical and Running Drill.	
		11.0AM	Church Parade Service	
"	20TH	5:30AM	Reveille followed by the usual Musketry Clean Parade + Interior Economy	cw
		8.15AM	Physical and Running Drill.	
		9.0AM	Rest of morning spent in Mechanism, Spare Parts, + Immediate Action. Company Parade for Baths.	
		1:45PM		
"	21ST	5:30AM	Reveille 6.30. Musketry Clean Parade + Interior Economy.	cw
		8.15AM	Physical and Running Drill.	
		9.0AM	Lecture on Trench Discipline. Gun Drill etc.	cw
		2.0PM	Close order Drill with Arms.	

Army Form C. 2118.

WAR DIARY
or
INTELLIGENCE SUMMARY.

(Erase heading not required.)

50. M. G. Coy.
August. 1917.

Instructions regarding War Diaries and Intelligence Summaries are contained in F. S. Regs., Part II. and the Staff Manual respectively. Title pages will be prepared in manuscript.

Place	Date	Hour	Summary of Events and Information	Remarks and references to Appendices
ST. NICHOLAS	22ND	5.30 AM	Reveille.	
		6.30 AM	Interior Economy and Muster Clean Parade.	
		8.15 AM	Physical and Running Drill.	
"		9.0 AM	Lecture on Range Cards.	
		10.0 AM	Box Respirator and P.H. Helmet, Inspection, and Drill.	
		11.0 AM	Company Parade for Baths.	w
ST. NICHOLAS	23RD	5.30 AM	Reveille.	
		6.30 AM	Interior Economy and Muster Clean Parade.	
		8.0 AM	Running and Physical Training.	
		9.0 AM	Company Parade for Gun Drill, Indirect Fire, Barrage Work, Bottle Lines, and Lecture on New Enemy Gas.	
"		2.30 PM	Close Order Drill and Saluting Drill.	
		2.45 PM	16 no. N.C.O.'s leave Camp for the Trenches, Chemical Works Sub Section.	w
ST. NICHOLAS	24TH	5.30 AM	Reveille.	
		6.30 AM	Interior Economy and Muster Clean Parade.	
		9.0 AM	Company Parade for Cleaning Guns, gun gear etc. & limbers etc. packed for the Lines. Later Section move off independently to the Trenches & relieve 52. M.G. Coy. [Chemical Wks Right Sub Sector] Relief complete by 6.0 PM. Casualties nil.	
FAMPOUX	25TH		Map References of the Guns as follows	

"A" Section
No. of Gun	Map Reference	
No. 21.	H.12 d. 72.32.	S.E.
No. 22.	H.12 d. 70.50.	N.E.
No. 31.	H.18 a. 75.45.	S.E.
No. 32.	H.18 a. 70.75.	N.E.

"C" Section
No. of Gun	Map Reference	
No. 2.	H.17 b. 25.15.	E.N.E.
No. 3.	H.17 d. 20.40.	S.E.
No. 6.	H.11 d. 95.25.	S.E.
No. 7.	H.11 d. 90.80.	N.E.

"B" Section
No. of Gun	Map Reference	
No. 1.	I.14 c. 65.35.	N.E.
No. 2.	I.14 c. 05.55.	S.E.
No. 9.	I.13 b. 50.17.	N.E.
No. 10.	I.13 b. 35.90.	S.E.

"D" Section
No. of Gun	Map Reference	
No. 3.	I.14 a. 20.55.	N.E.
No. 4.	I.8 c. 00.10.	S.E.
No. 5.	I.7 d. 90.25.	N.E.
No. 11.	I.7 d. 10.45.	N.E.

WAR DIARY or INTELLIGENCE SUMMARY

Army Form C. 2118.

50. M.G. Coy.
August 1917.

Place	Date	Hour	Summary of Events and Information	Remarks and references to Appendices
FAMPOUX	25TH	Cont	Guns in Action. 6. Ammunition Expended. 7,500 Rounds. Casualties nil. Work done. At No.17 Gun Dug out and Ammunition Stores worked on. No.19 Gun Revetting and deepening Trench & improvement of Position. No.20 Gun. Trench deepened & Traverse improved. General maintenance at all other Positions. Work to be done. Dug out at No.17 position to be completed. Majority of positions to be Camouflaged. Intermediate line gun position to be improved. Officers Dug out to the gun position constructed there. Relief of RWTH complete by 6.0 pm Casualties nil. 6 Guns fired indirect, at irregular Intervals as follows. No of Gun — Target — Time. No.31, No.32 — Dugouts along Ry Embankment in I.14.b.55.79 — 10.0 PM – 12 M.N. No.17 — I.14.b 60-70, No.18 — I.14.b 65-90, No.19 — I.14.b 55-99, No.20 — I.14.b 50-90 — 10.0 PM - till DAWN. Total Rounds Expended :- 7,500.	
FAMPOUX	26TH		Situation. Quiet. Guns in Action 5 Casualties nil Rounds Expended. 6,000. Work done. Sap Read at No.21 Gun Completed. No.2, and 9, positions Camouflaged. A.A position at No.1 Sand bagged and heightened. Parapet at No.1 Gun position repaired. Trenches near Intermediate line guns deepened, and Dug out for Officers commenced there. No.3 position improved, work done on cleaning up No.18 position. Sap at No.21 Gun to be revetted. Officers dugout in ½ Line to be completed. Sap for No.11 Gun to be constructed. General maintenance and repair of Trenches. No.18 position to be reconstructed.	

Army Form C. 2118.

WAR DIARY
or
INTELLIGENCE SUMMARY.

(Erase heading not required.)

50. M. G. Coy
August 1917

Place	Date	Hour	Summary of Events and Information	Remarks and references to Appendices
FAMPOUX	26th Cont		**General.** No. 32 Gun fired at Enemy Aeroplane about 6.30.P.M. 200 Rounds Expended. The following Guns fired indirect as follows:-	
			No of Gun / Target / Time	
			21. / N. End of RY Arch a I 9.0 / 11. P.M. - 12. M.N.	
			22. / Searching Tracks to I 9.b 80.25. / 2.0.a.m. - 3.0.a.m.	
			17. / PLOUVAIN X ROADS. / 11. P.M. - 12. M.N.	
			18. / PLOUVAIN X ROADS. / 2. a.m - 3. a.m.	
			Total Rounds Expended. 6,000. Casualties. Nil. Ammunition Expended 6.000.	cw
FAMPOUX	27th		**Guns in Action** 4. Casualties. Nil. Ammunition Expended. 6.000.	
			Work done. No. 21. Position Revetted. A.A. position off CAMEL commenced. Recess for Stores, and S.A.A. built at No.14 Position. Sapping out for new position for No. 11. Gun worked on. Parapet at No. 10. Sandbagged and built up. Recess for Bombs made at No.11. Work done on all positions in intermediate Line. Officers dug-out.	
			Work to be done. A.A. position at No. 31 Gun to be completed. Officers Dug out in 1/1. to be completed. General maintenance + repair.	
			General. 400 Guns fired indirect as follows:- Between the hours of :-	
			9.30 P.M. and 11.45. P.M. Guns again at 2.30 a.m. and 3. 30. A.M. Targets :-	
			Nos 17. and 18. Guns PLOUVAIN X ROADS	
			Nos 21. and 22. Guns Trenches on I 9 d 90.10.	
			Ammunition Expended. 6,000. Rounds.	cw
FAMPOUX	28th		**Situation** Normal.	
			Guns in Action. 8. Casualties Nil. Ammunition Expended. 148,000 Rds.	
			Work done. New Shelter made for No. 17. Gun Trench at No. 18. Position. Duckboarded and revetted. Teams from Nos. 19. and 20. Guns assist R. E. in construction of Dug outs. A.A. position at No. 31. Gun carried on with. Work done on Sap at No. 111. position. General maintenance of emplacements + Trenches. R.E. Material and S.A.A. carried up to gun positions.	

A 5834 Wt W 4073 M657 750,000 8/16 D. D. & L. Ltd Form C. 2118/13

Army Form C. 2118.

WAR DIARY
or
INTELLIGENCE SUMMARY.

(Erase heading not required.)

50. M. G. Coy.

August, 1917.

Place	Date	Hour	Summary of Events and Information	Remarks and references to Appendices
FAMPOUX	28TH	Cont.	Work to be done. Officers dug out in '/. line to be completed. Sap at No. 11. Gun position to be completed. Sap at No. 21. Gun to be revetted. A.A. position for No. 31. Gun to be completed. Dug out to be finished at Nos. 19 and 20. Gun positions.	
"			General. In conjunction with 3" stokes 6 guns Barraged a line at I 8 c 90.50 - I 8 a 50.00. In addition 2 Guns fired Indirect from 10.0. P.M. - 12. 45 A.M. and again at 2.30. A.M - 3.30. A.M. Target 19 a I 95.10. Total Rounds Expended. 14,000.	
FAMPOUX	29TH		Guns in Action 3. Ammunition Expended 6,500 Rounds. Casualties Nil. Work done. Work done Parapet at No 9. position repaired. Sap at No. 11. continued. Work continued on Emplacement at No. 5. Gun Parapet at No. 3. Gun repaired, & Sap revetted at No. 21. Gun position. Continued work at A.A. position for No. 31. Gun. Improvements made at Nos. 17, 18, 19 and 20 positions. Emplacement for 2.5 Gun constructed. Trench at I.7. Revetted.	
"			Work to be done General maintenance and continuation of above. 3. Guns fired Indirect as follows :-	

Target
Time of Firing.
No of Guns		
21.	I 9 d 90. 10.	10.0. P.M.
19.	I 15 b 45. 60.	To At Irregular
20.	I 15 b 45. 60.	3.30. A.M. Intervals.

Total Rounds Expended. 6,500.

Situation - Normal.

Army Form C. 2118.

WAR DIARY
or
INTELLIGENCE SUMMARY.
(Erase heading not required.)

50. M.G. Coy
August. 1917.

Instructions regarding War Diaries and Intelligence Summaries are contained in F.S. Regs., Part II and the Staff Manual respectively. Title pages will be prepared in manuscript.

Place	Date	Hour	Summary of Events and Information	Remarks and references to Appendices
FAMPOUX	30TH		**Guns in Action.** 8. **Ammunition Expended.** 7,000 Rounds. **Casualties.** nil. **Work done.** Trench Revetted in vicinity of No. 3 Gun. Work continued on Sap for No. 11 Gun. Work done on all positions in the Intermediate Line. Officers Dug out almost completed. Improvements to Trenches and Emplacements made in vicinity of Nos. 17, 18, 19, and 20 Guns. A.A. position for No. 31 Gun, and Sap for No. 21 Gun both worked on. **Work to be done.** Continuation of above. **General.** In conjunction with the Artillery Programme as per: Your SG 223 Intense bursts of fire on Targets as ordered, & at times as stated was carried out. Total Ammunition Expended 7,000 Rounds. **Situation.** NORMAL.	
"				
FAMPOUX	31ST		**Guns in Action.** 8. **Casualties.** nil. **Ammunition Expended.** 10,000 Rounds. **Work done.** Revetting at No. 21 position completed. Work continued on A.A. position at No. 31, and Revetting done at No. 20 gun position. No. 19 Rebuilding front of Gun Emplacement. At No. 18 Gun Emplacement improved. No. 17 Gun "Cubby Holes" repaired and improved. Officers Shelter in /1 line completed. Trenches at all positions in /1 line deepened. Trench at 17 Revetted. Positions Nos. 1, 2, 9, and 10. Camouflaged. 2 new A.A. Emplacements made for Nos. 1 and 2 Guns. No. 19 Gun position Sandbagged & revetted. No. 4 "post" Platform revetted, also Fire Step. No. 11 Revetting sides of Sap, and continuation of Sap. General maintenance. A.A. position for No. 19 and 10 Gun to be constructed. Saps at Nos. 21, and 11 Guns to be completed. A.A. Position for No. 31 Gun to be Completed. **General.** Reference Your SG 225, 8 Guns fired on the following Targets. At same times as Artillery ;— (A) I.15. c - I.15 Central " 10.30 p.m. (B) CLOD Trench between CUB and CLIFF. (C) Road from I.14 to 40.67. to PLOUVAIN. (D) I.9.d.00.50. to WINDMILL COPSE. Total Ammunition Expended. 10,000 Rounds. **Situation - Normal**	
"				

50th M.G. Coy

One Copy 14th Division
F. I. Note No 7 herewith for
information.

W. N Moyho
Lieut
Staff Officer
50th Inf Bde

Army Form C. 2118.

WAR DIARY
INTELLIGENCE SUMMARY.
(Erase heading not required.)

September 1917.

Place	Date	Hour	Summary of Events and Information	Remarks and references to Appendices
FAMPOUX	1st		**Guns in Action** 2. **Ammunition Expended**: 3,500 Rounds. **Casualties** NIL. **Work done**. Revetting No 29 Gun position, Alternative Emplacement for No.19 Gun being constructed. Resetting & improving Gun position generally. Rebuilding No 7 Gun position destroyed by fire yesterday. No. 31 A.A. position completed. A.A. positions made for Pos. 9 & 10 Guns A.A. position at No.1 Gun revetted. Revetting Fire Step and entrance to Sap at No. 5. Work continued on Sap at No. 11 Gun.	
"			**Work to be done**. Continuation of improvement at Nos. 17, 18, 19, and 20. Guns and A.A. position for No. 17 Gun to be improved. Sap at No. 11 position to be completed. General improvement and maintenance. **General**. No. 32 Gun engaged Enemy Aeroplane flying low at 8.30 A.M yesterday. 500 Rounds fired at Enemy Aeroplane driven off. 2 Guns fired indirect as follows. No. 32. Gun Target: I.78.a.75.05. No. 31. Gun Target: I.78.a.75.05. Total Rounds Expended, 3,500.	
			Situation normal.	
FAMPOUX	2nd		**Guns in Action**. 3. **Casualties**. NIL. **Ammunition Expended**. 5,000 Rounds. **Work done**. Work continued at No. 9 & 10. A.A. positions. Trench Repaired near No. 1. Gun. Work continued on No.11. Sap. Sap to No 2 Gun position widened and deepened. Continuation of work at A.A. Emplacement at No. 12. All Guns Tested and cleaned. General maintenance of condition and repair. Indian Company relief.	
"			**Work to be done**. No.10 A.A. emplacement to be revetted. No. 31. A.A. position to be Sandbagged. Shelters made for Gun Teams at Nos 24, & 31 positions. Trench between Shelter and Gun at 17 position to be deepened. No. 1.b position to be completed. Work continued at No. 11. Gun position. General maintenance of repair and condition. **General**. 5 Guns fired as follows: - No. 18. Gun Target: I.9 Central. Nos 17, 19, 20, 31 and 32. Guns Target: - I.9 d.00.05. to WINDMILL COPSE. Times of firing, 9.30 P.M. to 10.30. P.M. and again at 2.30 am to 3.30. A.M. Total Rounds Expended, 5,000.	

WAR DIARY or INTELLIGENCE SUMMARY

Army Form C. 2118.

September 1917.

Place	Date	Hour	Summary of Events and Information	Remarks and references to Appendices
FAMPOUX	3rd		Guns in Action. 8. Rounds Expended. 10,600. Casualties. Nil. **Work done.** Continuation of improvement at No.9 and 10. A.A. positions, & on Sap at No.11. Gun. Dug out commenced at No.17. Gun. No. 18, 19, and 20. positions improved. Trenches improved in vicinity of No. 31. Gun. Dug out started at No. 32 position. Aiming Posts checked. No. 12. A.A. position Camouflaged. S.A.A. Stores (rebuilt) Rifle Racks fixed. Trenches widened and deepened in Intermediate Line. Dakwalks laid. Guns Tested and Cleaned. General upkeep + maintenance of Condition. **Work to be done.** Dug-out at No.1 and 2 positions, + Trenches to be cleaned. Alternative position for No. 2 Gun to be made. Completion of A.A. positions for No. 9 and 10. Guns. Continuation of work on Sap at No.11. Position. Complete and improve dug outs + positions at No.17, 18, 19, and 20. Guns. Continuation of No. 32. Dug out. No. 31, and 32 A.A. Gun positions to be Camouflaged + positions revetted. Salvaging of Stores. General upkeep and maintenance of condition. **General.** Indirect Fire Guns fired as follows :-	Sw? Sw? Sw?

Gun — Time — Target

- 17, 18 — 9.30 P.M. to 3.30 A.M. — X. ROADS and TRACKS at PLOUVAIN – I.15.d.4.5.6.0.
- 19, 20 — — Dump and TRACKS – Vicinity of I.9.Central.
- 21, 22 — — GAVRELLE – PLOUVAIN RD about I.8.d.10.55. Dump + TRACKS. I.9.Central.
- 31, 32 — 7.0. P.M to 7.30. P.M. — WINDMILL COPSE.

No. 31 and 32 Gun fired on WINDMILL COPSE as stated above on receiving news from the Inf.y. that an Enemy relief was in progress in that vicinity.

WAR DIARY
or
INTELLIGENCE SUMMARY.

Army Form C. 2118.

September 1917

Place	Date	Hour	Summary of Events and Information	Remarks and references to Appendices
FAMPOUX	4th		**Guns in Action** No. 9 and 10 A.A. positions improved. Continuation on Sap at No. 11 Gun steps to dug-out at No. 4 position repaired. Rounds Expended 14,000. Casualties NIL. **Work done** No. 31. A.A. emplacement camouflaged. Work on No. 32 Gun Dug out Fire step and emplacement at No. 31 position revetted. Sap at No. 21 Gun widened. Work continued on Dug out at No. 11 Gun. Guns Tested & Cleaned. General maintenance of repair & condition. **Work to be done** Continuation of work in progress. Material to be salvaged. **General** General upkeep and repair at positions. A.A. Guns Nos. 31 & 32 fired from 7.0 A.M - 9.30 A.M. Indirect guns fired as under :- Gun / Time / Target 19 } 9.30 P.M. } GREENLAND HILL from 20 } to } I 8 Central to I 8 b 0060 31 } 3.30 A.M. } Tracks in I 8 b - 32 } } GAVRELLE - PLOUVAIN RD. No. 32 Gun fired from 3.0 P.M - 5.0 P.M. Target in CORN Trench.	SWR? SWR?
FAMPOUX	5th		**Guns in Action** 9. Rounds Expended 17,200. Casualties NIL. **Work done** Continuation on Sap at No. 11 Gun. New dug-outs at Nos. 17, +18 Guns worked on. A.A. Emplacement commenced in CRETE. Trenches deepened near No. 19. & 20 Guns, alternative position. Sap improved at No. 21 Gun. Continuation on dug-out at No. 32 position. No. 31 A.A. position Camouflaged. A.A. position Intermediate line altered and Trenches improved. Guns tested and cleaned. **Work to be done** Continuation of work in hand. No. 9 & 10 A.A. positions to be finished. Work to be continued on No. 11 Sap + new A.A. emplacement at No. 32 Gun. Trenches in the Intermediate line to be widened and Duckboarded - also A.A. position to be altered. General maintenance of repair and condition. **General** A.A. Guns Nos. 1, 31 and 32 Fired at 7.0 A.M. and 1.0 P.M - 1.45 P.M. Target :- Enemy Aeroplane, which was driven off.	SWR? SWR?

WAR DIARY
INTELLIGENCE SUMMARY

September 1917.

Place	Date	Hour	Summary of Events and Information	Remarks and references to Appendices
FAMPOUX	5th Cont'd		**Indirect Guns fired as follows:—** Gun. Target. Gun. Target. 17 } Tracks in 21 } Tracks in 18 } I.14.d. 22 } I.8.d. 19 } Tracks in 31 } Tracks in 20 } I.8.d. 32 } I.14.d. **Guns in Action.** 9. Rounds Expended 26,250. These Guns co-operated with the Artillery and intense bursts were fired at 10.30 P.M. – 11.0 P.M. – 11.15 P.M. Firing at these same targets was continued throughout the night from 11.30 P.M – 3.30 A.M. Casualties NIL. **Work done.** Continuation of work in progress. No. 9 and 10 A.A. positions improved. Work on Sap at No. 11. Gun continued, and A.A. position in CRETE also worked on. New Dug-out being made for No. 18. Gun position. Trenches deepened and revetted at No. 19 and 20. Guns position. Completion of Shelter at No. 32 position. Box Mounting fixed at No. 32 position. Latrine made at No. 1 & 2 Gun position. Trenches at No. 12, 15, 16, and 17 deepened and duckboarded. Material Salvaged. Guns tested and cleaned. General maintenance of repair and condition.	SW?
"	6th		**Work to be done.** Continuation of work in progress. No. 11 Sap to be completed. Slabs at No. 4 Dug-out to be repaired. A.A. Emplacement at No. 32 Gun to be completed. Box Mounting to be fixed at No. 31 Gun position. Trench to be deepened at No. 12 position. Latrine at No. 13 position to be moved. Fire Steps at all positions in Intermediate line to be duckboarded. Salvaging all available Material. General maintenance of condition.	SW?
"			**General.** A.A. Guns:- Nos. 1, 2, and 32 fired from 10.0 A.M. to 12 noon. Target Enemy Aeroplane, which was driven off.	SW?

WAR DIARY
or
INTELLIGENCE SUMMARY.

Army Form C. 2118.

50 Sy/M.C

September 1917.

(Erase heading not required.)

Place	Date	Hour	Summary of Events and Information	Remarks and references to Appendices
FAMPOUX	6th Cont'd		All Indirect Guns:- Nos. 17, 18, 19, 20, 21, 22, 31 and 32. fired as under:-	RSR

Target.   Time.
I 9 Central   9.30 PM to 9.31. PM Intense Fire.
 Main Tracks and Paths.   9.32. PM to 10. 0. PM Irregular bursts of fire.
I9c 00.15. New work.   10.30. PM to 10.31. PM Intense Fire.
 Tracks and WINDMILL COPSE.   10.32. PM to 11. 0. PM Irregular bursts of fire.
I 9 Central.   11.30. PM to 11.31. PM Intense Fire.
 Main Tracks and Paths.   11.32. PM to 12. 0. MN Irregular Bursts.
I9c 70.34. New work.   12.30. AM to 12.31. AM Intense Fire.
 Tracks and Cross Roads.   12.32. AM to 1. 0. AM Irregular Bursts.
Firing was carried out by all Guns on I9c 70.34 at irregular intervals
               from :- 1.30. AM to 3.30. AM.

Guns in Action. 2. Rounds Expended 4,000. Casualties. NIL.

Work done. Continuation of work in progress. Steps prepared at No. 4. Gun position.
Work done on A.A. Emplacement at No. 9. and 10 positions.
No. 17. and 72. positions under construction and improvement.
Work on Sap at No. 11. Gun still in progress.
Work done on New dug-out at No. 18. Gun.
COLT RESERVE deepened and Sandbagged in vicinity of No. 19. & 20. Guns.
Dug-out at No. 32. Gun position completed.
New Latrine built at No. 72. position. Guns Tested and Cleaned.
Salvage collected. General maintenance of repair and condition.

| FAMPOUX | 7th | | | SWR |

Work to be done. Continuation of above. No. 9. and 10. A.A. Emplacements worked on.
Sap at No. 11. Gun position to be continued.
Work on No. 17. A.A. Emplacement.
New dug-out at No. 18. Gun position.
A.A. Emplacement to be constructed for No. 32. Gun.

WAR DIARY
INTELLIGENCE SUMMARY

September 1917.

50th M.G.C.

Army Form C. 2118.

Place	Date	Hour	Summary of Events and Information	Remarks and references to Appendices

Yampoux	Sept 17		**Work to be done.** Cont'd. Concrete platform to be made for No. 31 Gun. Trench round No. 12 Gun to be deepened. Cookhouse to be made in Intermediate line. Salvage to be collected. General maintenance of repair & condition.
			
			 General. Indirect Fire was carried out as follows:—
			
			 Gun. Target. Time.
			 22. { 19.c.70.34. X.ROADS. } From
			       { New work K- WINDMILL COPSE. } 9.30. P.M.
			       { Railway Embankment + TRACKS. } to
			 17. { I.15.b. PLOUVAIN X ROADS - TRACKS. } 3.30. A.M.
			       { GAVRELLE PLOUVAIN ROAD. }
			
			 Ammunition Expended. 4,000 Rounds.
				Sgt. 7.

Yampoux	18		**Guns in Action &** Rounds expended 4,500. Casualties Wounded 1 O.R. **Work done.** Continuation of work in Load. Further work in Sept at No.11 gun Alternative position commenced for No. 31 gun. Trenches widened & deepened at 31 and 3.5 positions. Salvage collected. Ltr. Cpy asking if Nos. 17. 18. 19. and 20 guns. General maintenance of condition & repairs. **Work to be done.** Continuation of above completion of Nos. 9 and 10 A.A. emplacements. Sap at No.11 gun to be completed. A.A. position in CRETE sandbagged and revetted. Work on new dugout at No. 18 gun. Completion of emplacements at Nos. 19 and 20 gun. Deepening and revetting C.O.L.T. RESERVE in vicinity of guns. Concrete platform made for Nos. 31 and 32 guns. Salvage collected. General maintenance of repair and condition. Enemy machine guns fired at No.'s 17, 18, 19 and 20 guns during the night. Indirect guns fire as follows:- Gun. Target. 19 19.c.70.34. 18 I.9 central. 31 19.c.00.15. 32 19.c.00.15. Time 9.30 p.m to 3.30 a.m. No. 21 and 22 guns were shelled during the night	Sgt. 7. REMARKS. { New work { Cone Round { Tracks

WAR DIARY
INTELLIGENCE SUMMARY

(Erase heading not required.)

Army Form C. 2118.

September 1917.

Place	Date	Hour	Summary of Events and Information	Remarks and references to Appendices
Fampoux	Sept 9		Guns in Action. 8 Rounds expended 201,500. Casualties nil. Work done:- Extermination of work in progress. Work in No.11 Sap continued. Trenches & dugouts improved at No. 19, 17 & 18 guns. No.19 and 20 alternative positions wetted. Construction of concrete platform for No 31 gun. No 32 position prepared for making concrete platform. Hurdles duplicated & improved in intermediate line. Cookhouse at 32 finished. No.19 gun position improved. General maintenance of repair & condition. Guns tested & cleaned. Salvage collected. Work to be done. Formation of work in hand. No.11 Sap to be completed. No 19 AA position to be completed. Complete No. 18 dug-out & resitting No.19 position. Concrete platform finished at No. 32 gun. Emplacement at 38 gun to be made. General maintenance of repair & condition. Salvage to be collected. General - In accordance with Instructions received gun fired in conjunction with the operations by the left Brigade as follows:-	See A.7.
			Gun Target 17 58 &80·15 } Barrage 18 58 &60·6 } Harrassing 31 gun WEED in 59.a.F. Junction with WEASEL in 59.d: 32 gun 58&62.Y's Emplacement Harrassed & sinched. Miscellaneous. During this firing guns fired well. 3 damaged barrels (one burst), no injured and 1 burned. A bad cross fire to an internal explosion were the only stoppages occurred. Company relieved by 51 M.G. Coy by day, team in relief proved back independently to Camp ST NICHOLAS. Relief completed & all men safely under cover at 5.45 p.m. During 16 days in the line only no. casualty:- Pte Chalker - wounded (Skull, Face) Gun Target 19 58 &60·15 }Amanda Gun 20 52 &60·3 }Harassing 22 23 a. 20. 50 Emplacement 57.d. Junction 21 WEAR - in 52.b, Harrassing 5' Left and switched	See A.7.
St. Nicholas Camp	Sept 10		Reveille 7am. Break fast & an. Roll of morning spent in cleaning equipment, clothing etc, prior to muster parade at 12 noon. Dress fighting shelter, 2-3 pm, all men fitted with clothing etc. closely followed by bay parade.	See A.7.
	11	5.30	Reveille 5.30 am followed by muster clean parade from 6.30 to 7 am. Company parade under Section arrangements from 8.30 am to 4 pm for cleaning guns, gun & accessories, ammunition + Kit inspection. Several Officers, S/M, and a few N.C.O's went to canadier the best way to spend several hundred francs in the interest of the men of this Company and Lt was decided to hold a Canteen when we go to our next & any Coffer 2/6 to count in the Trenches during Sept month.	See A.7.

50th Bn MGC

Army Form C. 2118.

WAR DIARY
or
INTELLIGENCE SUMMARY.
(Erase heading not required.)

September 1917.

Place	Date	Hour	Summary of Events and Information	Remarks and references to Appendices
St Nicholas Camp	Sept 12		Reveille 5.30 am. 6.30 am Interior economy & am physical training 9 am. Company parade & knive clean parade. 10.15 am Bir Rafinale & P.H. Salonta inspection & drill. 11.30 am to 12.30 pm. Lecture on Range Cards. 2 pm to 3 pm clean and drill with arms.	S.W.P.
	13		Reveille 6 am. 7 am musketry clean parade & Interior economy. 8 am Company drill. 9 am mechanism & spare parts. 10.15 am Snovadi action. 11.30 am Snap shot drill. 2 pm Running drill practice for Brigade Race.	
	14		Reveille 6 am. 7 am Interior economy & musketry clean parade. 8 am physical & running drill. Rest of morning spent in mechanism, spare parts, immediate action & instruction in German machine Gun. 2 - 3 pm. Close order drill with arms.	S.W.P.
	15		Reveille 6 am. 7 am musketry clean parade & Interior economy. 8 am Running drill. Rest of morning spent in "Barrage work" indirect fire, battle lines, etc. 2pm Saluting drill & guard orders.	
	16		Reveille 6.30 am. Church parade during the morning. Limbers packed prior to going into the line. Company relieve 52nd M.G. Coy. in the GREENLAND HILL Sub sector to day Casualties NIL	S.W.P.
GREENLAND HILL Sub Sector	17			
	18		Guns in action & Rounds expended 8,250. Casualties NIL. Wire door Brigadier commenced to intermediate position. Lunch sent away by no. 25 Gun to clean obstruction caused to field of fire parapet cut away when it obstructed 'field of fire' to 'South line' of No. 23 & 3 gun. Running shine necessary. General maintenance of repair & condition	S.W.P.

+ in reserve
+ W. Ravenill General

WAR DIARY
or
INTELLIGENCE SUMMARY.

Army Form C. 2118.

50 My I.W.C.   September 1917

Place	Date	Hour	Summary of Events and Information	Remarks and references to Appendices
GREENLAND HILL SUB SECTOR.	18th		Map Reference of the Guns as under:—	

No of Gun.   Map Reference.

"C" Section.
- 16.   I.1.a 50.40.
- 15.   I.1.a 65.10.
- 8.   I.1.b 80.70.
- 14.   I.1.c 80.40.

"A" Section.
- 7.   I.1.d 63.40.
- 6.A.   I.7.b 40.60.
- 6.   I.7.b 35.35.
- 12.   I.7.b 00.45.
- 13.   I.7.a 90.70.

"B" Section.
- 23.   H.12.b 80.32.
- 23.A.   H.12.b 68.68.
- 24.   H.6.d 52.05.
- 24.A.   H.6.d 55.70.

"D" Section.
- 9.   H.11.a 75.92.
- 10.   H.5.c 98.40.
- 11.   H.5.a 81.20.

Remarks: Smy. Smy. Smy. Smy.

Army Form C. 2118.

WAR DIARY
or
INTELLIGENCE SUMMARY.
(Erase heading not required.)

Place	Date	Hour	Summary of Events and Information	Remarks and references to Appendices
Gunland Hill Sub Sector	Sept 18		Continued:— Work to be done :- Finishing dug-out for individuals position. Construction of A.A. emplacement. Pit Prop sheathings to be put in at No. 24 & 23 A. positions. Position to be camouflaged. RE's Construction of work on No. 23 A & 24 Sap. General sharpening up & maintenance of repair & condition. Gun screens to be made. The following guns fired at targets at times as follows:—	SWS7.
			Gun No. Target Times Rounds expended	
			23 Trenches J8 & 65.70. Trucks & M.G. 13a 20.50 9.30pm to 3.30 am 2900	
			24 Shell holes & tracks 13a 30.30 to 29d 60.40 9.30 pm to 8.30 am 1850	SWS7.
			26 C 26 & 60.20 10pm to 4 am 1950	
			28 to 23a 10.30 10pm to 4 am 1950	SWS7.

WAR DIARY or INTELLIGENCE SUMMARY

Army Form C. 2118.

50th Coy M.G.C.
September 1917.

Place	Date	Hour	Summary of Events and Information	Remarks and references to Appendices
Greenland Hill Left Sub Sector	Sep 19		Guns in action 8. Rounds expended 4,810. Casualties Nil. Work done - shelters completed & officers dug-out constructed in intermediate positions. A.A. positions at No. 23 and 24a guns under construction. Latrine commenced at 24 and 24a positions. Continuation on Sap at 23 position by R.E.'s. Obstruction of 'field of fire' cleared at No. 23 position. Positions re-camouflaged. Fire screens made. Trench leading to No.14 gun position deepened. General maintenance of repair & condition. Work to be done - Continuation of such work specified above, as is uncompleted. A.A. emplacement to be made at 23a also A.A. posts at No. 24 gun. No.7 new position to be finished. General maintenance of repair & condition. Indirect fire guns fired accurate burst at 2.30 am. 2 & 5 am and 3.10 am as follows:-	Eng.
			Gun No. — Target — Rounds expended	
			24a — (Tracks in 38a) & (and 33c) — 600	
			23a — (Tracks in 32b, 32d & 33c) & (32d & 6) — 800	
			25, 26, 27, 28 — (Tracks in C2 & 6, C2 & C, 93a) — 1060. In addition No. 28 gun Target 38.6.45.45 & 59 central intermittently thought high. No. of rounds 1250	
			Total number of Rounds 4 & 10. Rounds expended 10100. Casualties Nil.	
	20		Guns in action 6. Rounds expended 10,100. Casualties Nil. Work done - Anti-aircraft emplacement completed. Latrine constructed. Continuation of work on Sap at 23a by R.E's. Deepening Trench at No.14 position & putting down duckboards. Work carried on at A.A. positions. Repairs and A.A. emplacement finished at intermediate position. Maintenance of repair & condition.	Eng.

50 L.H.A.C. Army Form C. 2118.

WAR DIARY
or
INTELLIGENCE SUMMARY

September 1917

Place	Date	Hour	Summary of Events and Information	Remarks and references to Appendices
Gunland Hill Sub Section	Sept 20		General. Guns fired last night as follows:- Gun No. 25 and 27 rounds expended 1500 + 2000. Gun No. Target 24a) Long hunts) Gun No. Target 27a) throughout) 23a 20.40 23a) night from) 9 & 8 45.45 23b) 10 pm to 2 am) Rounds expended Targets 24a 320 & 66.55 27a 9 & 45.45 23a 9 & 20.40 23b 9 central Total 5750 At 6.5 am No 23 gun fired at junction of WEED + WART at approximately 9040.90 on information from Infantry that an enemy working party was there. Total 9250.	Sept 27
	21		Guns in action. 6 Rounds expended 10.325 Barwallia Nil work done Inch. dispersed at intermediate position and at No 14 gun position. 23 AP position completed. 24 A.A position completed. Cutination in Sap at 23a by RE3. General maintenance finished. Cutination in Sap and upkeep. Work to be done. - Bachination of such work specified above as not completed. Sap at No 24 gun impeded. General - Anti-aircraft guns fired as follows :- 23 at 10.45 am and 6.45 pm. 23a at 6.45 pm 24a at 10.45 + 6.45. Rounds expended 800. 27 + 28 also fired at aircraft. Rounds expended 125. Indirect fire guns fired as follows :- Gun No. Time Target Rds expdt 27 from dusk till dawn 23a 2000 28 8 pm to Midnight - 1000 27 Midnight to 4 am - 93a 1000 28 by dawn - 500 Total 4500 Squad fired 23 10 pm to 2 am 9 & 65.55 24a - 9 central 27a - 93a 20.40 23b - 9 & 45.45 Total 900.	Sept 27

A5334 Wt. W5973/M687 750,000 8/16 D.D. & L. Ltd. Forms/C.2118/13

Army Form C. 2118.

WAR DIARY
or
INTELLIGENCE SUMMARY.
(Erase heading not required.)

September 1917.

Place	Date	Hour	Summary of Events and Information	Remarks and references to Appendices
GREENLAND HILL SUB SECTOR	22nd		**Guns in Action.** 8. **Rounds Expended** 11,700. **Casualties.** 2. O/R wounded. **Work done.** Widening and deepening trench to No. 14 Gun position. Two A.A. emplacements completed at No. 23A. and 24 positions. Continuation of work on other A.A. Emplacements. No. 7. Box Mounting completed. Trench deepened at A.A. positions in intermediate line. Work on Sap at No. 24 position done. Continuation of work on Sap at No. 23A Gun by R. Es. General maintenance of repair and condition. **Work to be done.** Continuation of such work specified above, as is not completed. General maintenance of repair and condition. **General.** Anti-Aircraft Guns fired yesterday as follows:—	(sgd?)
"	"		Times of Firing. Gun No. 10.0. A.M. 23. 23 A. 6.0 AM and 1.0 PM to 6.30 PM. 24. 24 A. 6.0. AM and 6.35 PM. 10.0 AM + 1.0 PM to 6.30 PM. Rounds Expended 350. Indirect Guns fired as follows:— From 9.0. PM to 2.30. AM. at irregular intervals on following Targets. No. 28. Gun. 19 Central. No. 23. Gun. 13a. 20.40. also No. 23A. Gun. Rounds Expended:— 2,250.	(sgd?)
"	"		The following Guns fired one minute bursts at 2.30 AM. 2.45 AM. + 3.10 AM. Guns. Target. Rounds Expended. 23 and 23 A. I.3 a. 20.40. 2250. 24 and 24 A. I.2 d. 65.55. 1500. 25 and 26. I.9 Central. 2250. 27 and 28. I.8 d. 45.45. 1100. Total Rounds Expended, 9,100.	(sgd?)

WAR DIARY or INTELLIGENCE SUMMARY

Army Form C. 2118.

5th M Coy MMC September 1914.

Place	Date Sept.	Hour	Summary of Events and Information	Remarks and references to Appendices
Greenland Hill Sub Sect'n	23.		Gun in Action. Rounds expended 6900. Casualties Nil. Work done. All A.A. position completed. Trench to No. 8 position deepened. No. 6 alternative emplacement rebuilt. Maintenance of General repair condition. Work to be done. Pit Prop frames to be put in at Nos. 25 & 26 position. Construction of such went specified above as is uncompleted. Maintenance of general repair condition. General. A.A. gun fired 600 rounds at hostile aircraft during the day. Indirect fire guns fired between 9 pm & 2.30 am as follows :- Rounds expended. Gun No. Target 24 J3a 2.40 2500 24a J2d 65.55 2600 29 J9 central 1000 Total 6100	Sw.?
ARRAS. MANIN.	24		Company relieved by 183 M.G. Coy. & proceed to billets in ARRAS in completion of relief. Canadian N.L. Reveille 6 am. Breakfast 7. Dinner 11. Company paraded at 12.15 pm & march via Danville, Wailly, Boiseville, Amens - Le - Compte to Manin. Bien Full marching order. Distance about 14 miles. Company arrive in billets at 9 pm.	Sw.?
MANIN.	25		Reveille 7 am, gas & rifles were inspected by 10.30 am. A pay parade finished the day.	
BERLENCOURT	26		Reveille 6 breakfast 7. Billets cleaned & inspected & all gear packed by 9 am. Company paraded at 9.15 am & march via Evinchy - St Nole [...] marching order. [...] & billets by 12 noon.	Sw.?

Army Form C. 2118.

WAR DIARY
or
INTELLIGENCE SUMMARY.
(Erase heading not required.)

5MG140

September 1917.

Place	Date	Hour	Summary of Events and Information	Remarks and references to Appendices
BERLENCOURT	27.	6.0 AM.	Reveille. 8:30 am to 9.15 am Physical + Running Drill. Rest of morning spent in Cleaning and Checking Gun gear, Kit, Iron Rations, Box Respirators and P.H. Helmets. Swine were also inspected.	EW7
		1.30 PM to 4.0 PM.	Bathing Parade.	
"	28.	6.0 AM.	Reveille, followed by Physical Training from 8.30 - 9.15 am.	
		9.30 am to 12 noon.	Company Parade for Pack Saddle work, Stoppages. Attached Men receive Instruction on the Gun.	
		1.15 PM.	Company Parade and march to AMBRINES + go through a Gas Chamber to test Gas Helmets.	
"	29.	6.0 AM.	Reveille. 7.15 AM. Interior Economy + Muster Clean Parade.	EW7
		8.30 AM.	Physical Training. 9.30 am. Instruction in Belt Filling.	
		10.30 AM.	Lecture on Indication + Recognition of Targets.	
		11.15 AM.	Indication and Recognition of Targets on the Ground. Introducing Afternoon spent in firing Slippages on the Range. Fixing Blindfolded, and firing wearing Box Respirators. Attached Men receive Instruction on the Gun.	
"	30.	7.0 AM.	Reveille. 7.45 AM. Interior Economy + Muster Clean Parade.	EW7
		10.30 AM.	Parade Service for Nonconformists of ALL Denominations on Football Field at DENIER. (Corner of AMBRINES - BERLENCOURT - LIGNEREUIL Roads.) Parade Service for R.C.s BERLENCOURT Church. Rest of Morning Spent in Cleaning up Village.	

WAR DIARY
INTELLIGENCE SUMMARY.

(Erase heading not required.)

Army Form C. 2118.

50 M.G. Coy
October, 1917.
Vol 20

Place	Date	Hour	Summary of Events and Information	Remarks and references to Appendices
BERLENCOURT	1ST	6.0 AM	50th M.G. Coy. Reveille	
		7.15 AM	Interior Economy and Muster, Clean Parade.	
		8.30 AM	Physical and Running Drill.	
		9.30 AM to 11.0 AM	Two Sections "A" and "B" (i) Action from limbers (ii) Use of Pack Mules (iii) Supply of Ammunition Overhead Fire	a.H.S.
		11.0 AM to 12.30 PM	Two Sections "C" and "D"	
		2.0 PM	Sections Change Over. Company Parade for Brigade Tactical Scheme.	
"	2ND	6.0 AM	Reveille	
		7.15 AM	Interior Economy and Muster, Clean Parade.	
		8.30 AM	Close Order drill with Arms. [Special reference to March discipline.]	a.H.S.
		9.30 AM	Belt filling	
		10.30 AM	Testing and Cleaning Guns. Attached men instruction on the Gun.	
		11.30 AM	Pack & Saddlery drill Attached men further instruction on the Gun.	
		2.0 PM	Company parade for Brigade Tactical Scheme. Later in the day for Coy fixed out.	
"	3RD	5.45 AM	Reveille	
		8.30 AM	Brigade Tactical Scheme.	a.H.S.
		2.15 PM	Afternoon spent in cleaning Guns, Gun gear, and Packing Limbers prior to entraining for PEZELHOEK.	
"	4TH	7.0 AM	Reveille	
		8.30 AM	Physical and Running Drill.	
		9.30 AM	Company Drill with Arms. Rest of morning at disposal of Section Officers. Attached men instruction on the Gun.	a.H.S.
		2.0 PM	Packing Limbers	
		4.45 PM	Transport proceed by Road to SAULTY.	
		5.30 PM	Company march to SAULTY and entrain for PEZELHOEK.	
		9.30 PM	Company and Transport safely entrained.	

Army Form C. 2118.

WAR DIARY
or
INTELLIGENCE SUMMARY.
(Erase heading not required.)

October, 1917.

Place	Date	Hour	Summary of Events and Information	Remarks and references to Appendices
PROVEN AREA.	5TH	10.30 AM.	Company detrained and marched to PILCH CAMP [F.15.6.8.8.] PROVEN AREA.	att 8
		1.0 PM	Transport followed half an hour later.	
	6TH	6.0 AM	Rest of day spent in cleaning up Camp, Clothing and Equipment.	
		7.15 AM.	Reveille	att 8
		8.30 AM.	Interior Economy and Muster Clean Parade.	
		9.30 AM.	Physical and Running drill [Vicinity of Camp.]	
		10.45 AM.	Cleaning and Testing Guns	
		12.30 PM to 2.0 PM	Packing Mules, and Instruction in MAKESHIFT pack Saddlery.	
		2.0 PM	Attached men receive instruction on the gun. Immediate Action	
		3.0 PM	Attached men Mechanism and Spare Parts.	
		3.0 PM to 4.0 PM	Lecture and discussion on "Allotation of Duties". Lance Corporals receive special instruction.	
	7TH	7.0 AM.	Reveille	att 8
		7.45 AM.	Interior Economy and Muster Clean Parade.	
		9.30 AM.	Parade Service for C of E. Church Army Hut	
		10.0 AM.	Parade Service for Nonconformists of all Denominations [PITCHCOTT] Camp.	
	8TH	7.0 AM.	Reveille	att 8
		7.45 AM.	Interior Economy and Muster Clean Parade.	
		9.0 AM.	Muster Parade Dress New Battle Order.	
		9.30 AM.	Cleaning Guns, gun gear, etc and Packing Limbers.	
		10.30 AM.	Attached men instruction on the Gun.	
		2.0 PM.	All Iron Rations inspected and deficiencies made good.	
		3.0 PM.	Box Respirators and P.H Helmets inspected + donned.	
	9TH	7.0 AM.	Reveille 7.45 AM. Interior Economy + Muster Clean Parade	att 8
		9.0 AM.	Foot truction drill under Section Officers	
		9.30 AM	Rifle Inspection	
		10.0 AM	Sections parade under Sec Officers for lecture and discussion:—	
		To (a)	Employment of Machine Guns in captured positions (ii) Communication	
		12.Noon (iii)	Supply of Ammunition IV M Gs on Barrage work, and its importance	

A 5834 Wt.W4973/N687 750,000 8/16 D. D. & L. Ltd. Forms/C.2118/13

Army Form C. 2118.

WAR DIARY
or
INTELLIGENCE SUMMARY.   October 1917.
(Erase heading not required.)

Place	Date	Hour	Summary of Events and Information	Remarks and references to Appendices
COPPERNOLE CAMP.	9th	2.15 PM	Company march to PROVEN railhead and entrain	AHS
		7.0 PM	Company arrive at COPPERNOLE CAMP. Transport started by Road and arrive two hours later.	AHS
	10th	7.0 AM	Reveille	
		7.45 AM	Interior Economy and Muster Clean Parade.	
		10.0 AM	Rifle inspection	
		10.30 AM	Tube Sand bags for man issued to all Ranks as per Brigade Orders.	AHS
	11th	6.30 AM	Received standing to ready to move into the line at one hours notice.	
		2.0 PM	Morning spent in Testing and cleaning Guns etc. Packing limbers	
		3.0 PM	Company minus 6 Gun Teams paraded for Physical Training.	
		2.0 PM	Box Respirator and P.H. Helmet inspection and drill.	
			6 Gun Teams under Lieut. J.W. Telfer, leave Camp and arrive at Barrage positions at 8.0 PM and are in position along a line in 18 D Central,	
	12th		by 10.0 PM. Casualties 4 o/Ranks [Drivers] wounded.	AHS
		5.0 AM	Attack by 51 & Brigade. 6 Guns fired in accordance with orders issued by D.M.G.O. 15 Belt Boxes per Gun fired. Attack successful. Rest of Coy. still under one hours notice to move, carry on work.	
		9.0 AM	Arms drill, Immediate action, Mechanism, and spare parts	
		10.0 AM	Attacked men instructions on the gun.	
		12 Noon	Coy leave 6 Guns receive instructions to relieve 51. M.G. Coy in the line, and leave Camp at 2. PM and arrive at COY. H.Q. MARTINS MILL at 10.0 PM.	
MARTINS MILL.	13th	2.0 PM	2 Guns remain in reserve at COY M.Q. Four Guns relieve four Guns in vicinity of V.I.D TURENNES crossing. 2 Guns relieve 2 Guns 50 yards in front of GRAVEL FARM V8 a 10 & 10. 2 Guns relieve 2 Guns in vicinity of TRANQUILLE HOUSE V7 c 30 50 Relief complete by 5.0 AM the 14/10/17. Casualties nil	AHS
	14th		6 Barrage Guns withdrawn to PILKEM II Camp. 2 Guns in Reserve moved up to vicinity of CONDE HOUSE V13 a 30 90 in Position by 10.0 PM. Officers report enemy shelling severe. All Guns have excellent Fields of fire. Casualties wounded o/Ranks one	AHS

Army Form C. 2118.

WAR DIARY
or
INTELLIGENCE SUMMARY.   October 1917.

(Erase heading not required.)

Instructions regarding War Diaries and Intelligence Summaries are contained in F. S. Regs., Part II. and the Staff Manual respectively. Title pages will be prepared in manuscript.

Place	Date	Hour	Summary of Events and Information	Remarks and references to Appendices
MARTINS MILL.	15th		No Machine Gun Targets offered. Gun Teams do useful sniping with rifles. Shelling still heavy especially in vicinity of TRANQUILLE HOUSE. Casualties:- Wounded o/Ranks. 2.	AH8
"	16th		Hostile Aircraft very active during the night vicinity of Bde Transport Lines and tons of Bombs dropped. [Casualties Killed o/Ranks. one. Wounded o/Ranks. four. [Drivers.] Orders for relief by 102 M.G. Coy received. Relieving Teams leave Bde. H.Q. at BON GITE at 4.0 PM. Relief complete by 9 P.M. Casualties:- Died of wounds o/Ranks. one. Teams on relief proceed to BOESINGHE Station and bivouac for the night. Total Casualties :- Killed o/Ranks. one. Wounded o/Ranks. 1. Died of Wounds o/Ranks. 1. Wounded in Action o/Ranks. 11. Company less Transport entrain at BOESINGHE	AH8
BOESINGHE PROVEN.	17th	7.0 AM. 10.0 AM. 10.0 AM.	Station at 7.0 AM and occupy PARANA CAMP [e 17 d 12.] Company arrive at PROVEN at 7.0 AM. Transport leave the forward area by road, and arrive at PARANA CAMP at 1.30 P.M. Rest of day spent in cleaning up Camp, and arranging Transport Lines. Clothing and equipment cleaned, ready Muster Parade the following day	AH8

Army Form C. 2118.

WAR DIARY
INTELLIGENCE SUMMARY.
(Erase heading not required.)

October 1917

Place	Date	Hour	Summary of Events and Information	Remarks and references to Appendices
PARANA CAMP PROVEN. [C17d12]	18TH	6.30.AM	Reveille	
		7.30.AM	Interior Economy and Muster. Clean Parade.	
		9.0.AM to 12.30.PM	Company parade for Cleaning and Checking. Guns, Gun gear, Ammunition, etc.	a.q.s.
		2.0.PM	Kit and clothing inspection.	
		3.0.PM	Deficiencies in Kit made up, and Clothing issued out. [including Winter underwear.]	
"	19TH	6.30 AM	Reveille	
		7.30 AM	Interior Economy and Muster. Clean Parade.	a.q.s.
		9.0.AM	Muster Parade [Dress FULL Marching order.]	
		9.30 AM to 11.0.AM	Cleaning Wagons, Belts, Boxes Ammunition etc.	
		11.15 AM	Box Respirator and P.H. Helmet, inspection and drill.	
		2.0 PM	Arms drill	
"	20TH	3.0 AM	Reveille	a.q.s.
		4.45.PM	Company parade FULL Marching order and march to Billets in LE RIECLE. no one fell out on line of march.	
		11.15.AM	Company arrive safely in Billets.	
		1.30.PM	Foot Inspection. Rest of day spent in cleaning up Billets.	
LE RIECLE.	21ST	3.0 AM	Reveille	a.q.s.
		4.30 AM	Company parade, FULL Marching order and march to ARNEKE and entrain for AUDRUICQ.	
		11.0.AM	Company detrain and march to Billets in BERTEHEM.	
		6.0 AM	Transport move by Road, arriving 4.P.M.	
BERTEHEM.	22ND	7.0.AM	Reveille	a.q.s.
		9.0.AM	Squad drill with Arms. Rest of morning spent in Cleaning, + Checking, Guns, gun gear, etc.	
		2.0.PM	Guard Parade.	

WAR DIARY
INTELLIGENCE SUMMARY.

Army Form C. 2118.

October 1917

Place	Date	Hour	Summary of Events and Information	Remarks and references to Appendices
PERNES	23rd	6.30 AM	Reveille.	
		7.30 AM	Interior Economy and Muster Clean Parade.	
		9.0 AM	Physical and Training drill.	
		10.15 AM	Mechanism and Spare Parts.	
		11.15 AM	Stoppages.	
		2.0 PM	Lecture by Section Officers:- Range Cards and practical use of same.	aHS
		2.0 PM	Guard Parade.	
		2.0 PM	Sgts and Cpls Squad drill with Arms.	
		3.0 PM	Company pack out.	
	24th	6.15 AM	Reveille.	
		7.45 AM	Company parade and march to RECQUES for Baths.	
		11.0 PM	"D" Section and 2 Gun Teams of "B" Sec. proceed to GRASSE-RAVELLE to "Barrage Fire" in conjunction with 236 M.G. Coy.	aHS
		2.0 PM	Rest of Company Squad drill with Arms.	
		3.0 PM	Village Roads and Transport lines cleaned up. Limbers washed and Billets generally improved.	
	25th	6.15 AM	Reveille.	
		7.15 AM	Interior Economy and Muster Clean Parade.	
		9.0 AM	Physical Training.	
		10.15 AM to 11.15 AM	"A" & "C" Section and one Gun team of "B" Section Firing on the Range. Introducing (1) Stoppages (11) Firing with Box Respirators on. (111) Gun team of "B" Section parade for "C" Section and one gun team of "B" Section.	aHS
		11.30 AM	(1) Gun drill. (11) Use of Yukon Pack and Pack Mules. Demonstration as to the quickest method of moving forward with Gun, gun, etc.	
		2.0 PM	Sections Change round. Squad drill with Arms. Officers:- Map Reading Re Section.	

Army Form C. 2118.

WAR DIARY
INTELLIGENCE SUMMARY.
(Erase heading not required.)

Instructions regarding War Diaries and Intelligence Summaries are contained in F.S. Regs., Part II. and the Staff Manual respectively. Title pages will be prepared in manuscript.

October 1917.

Place	Date	Hour	Summary of Events and Information	Remarks and references to Appendices
BERTENEM.	26th	6.30 AM	Reveille	
		7.30 AM	Interior Economy and Muster Clean Parade.	
		9.0 AM	Physical and Running drill	
		10.15 AM	"A" Section and Two Guns Team of "B" Section firing on the Range. Attached Mens firing Stoppages. "C" Section Situation — Points before, during and after firing. Repairs and adjustments.	AHS
		11.30 AM	Section Change round.	
		2.0 PM	Arms Drill. [Sword Parade]	
		2.0 PM	Tactical ride for Officers. Surrounding country surveyed, re Bde Scheme.	
	27th	6.30 AM	Reveille	
		7.30 AM	Interior Economy and Muster Clean Parade	
		9.0 AM	Physical Training.	
		10.15 AM	"C" Section and one Gun Team of "B" Sec. arrange for Brigade Tactical Scheme.	AHS
		10.15 AM to 12.30 PM	"A" Section and one Gun Team of "B" Sec. parade "Battle Order" Route March.	
		11.45 AM	"C" Section and one Gun Team of "B" Sec. parade for Bde Tactical Scheme on the RECQUES. West Training Area.	
	28th		Brigade orders. A day of Rest.	
		7.0 AM	Reveille.	AHS
		10.0 AM	All Church Services as follows.	
			Church of England Service Voluntary	
		9.10 AM	Service for R.C's at NEILLES. Bn H.Q.	
		10.45 AM	Service for Nonconformists at NEILLES.	
		6.15 PM	Voluntary Service at ZUTKERKE followed by Holy Communion	

WAR DIARY
INTELLIGENCE SUMMARY.

Army Form C. 2118.

October. 1917

(Erase heading not required.)

Instructions regarding War Diaries and Intelligence Summaries are contained in F. S. Regs., Part II. and the Staff Manual respectively. Title pages will be prepared in manuscript.

Place	Date	Hour	Summary of Events and Information	Remarks and references to Appendices
ERTEHEM.	29th	5:0 AM	Reveille	AHS
		6:25 AM	Company parade [less 6 Gun Teams attached to 236. M.G. Coy.] for Brigade Tactical Scheme. Dress. Battle order. Haversacks empty and all Belt Cartridges left behind. All Yukon packs in limbers and Gun Tripod slings, and Ammunition Carriers carried on the animals.	
			Guard parade for instruction in Guard duties	
—"—	30th	2:0 PM		AHS
		6:30 AM	Reveille	
		7:30 AM	Interior Economy and Muster Clean parade.	
		9:0 AM	Lecture on Machine Gun Barrage.	
			Rest of morning spent in :-	
			Cleaning and Testing Guns	
			Instruction in Belt Filling Machine	
			Stripping the lock	
			Mechanism and Spare Parts.	
			Stoppages	
		2:0 PM	"A" Section will use the Range first followed by "C" and "B".	
			Squad drill with Arms.	
		2:0 PM	Lecture by C.O. to Sgts on New Barrage work and its importance.	
—"—	31st	6:30 AM	Reveille	AHS
		7:30 AM	Interior Economy and Muster Clean parade	
		9:0 AM	Company parade for "Route March" in Battle order	
		9:0 AM	Squad's parade for instruction in "Bugler Reading", flag drill etc.	
		2:0 PM	Guard parade for Instruction in Guard duties.	
		2:0 PM	Coy. parade for cleaning limbers + improving Transport lines	
		3:0 PM	All Belts Cleaned and refilled.	

31/10/17

Clements Capt
OC 50 MG Coy

No. 50. M.G. Coy.

WAR DIARY
INTELLIGENCE SUMMARY

NOVEMBER 1917.

Vol 2.

Army Form C. 2118.

(Erase heading not required.)

Instructions regarding War Diaries and Intelligence Summaries are contained in F.S. Regs., Part II. and the Staff Manual respectively. Title pages will be prepared in manuscript.

Place	Date	Hour	Summary of Events and Information	Remarks and references to Appendices
BERTEHEM.	1st	6.30 AM	Reveille.	J.H.S.
		7.30 AM	Interior Economy and Muster Clean Parade.	
		9.0 AM to 12 noon	Company parade for Cleaning Harness, Limbers, and Filling Belts.	
		2.0 PM	Guard paraded for instruction in Guard duties.	
		9.0 AM	All Officers attend a lecture on "Machine Gun Barrage".	
BERTEHEM.	2nd	6.30 AM	Reveille.	J.H.S.
		7.30 AM	Interior Economy and Muster Clean Parade.	
		9.0 AM	Physical and Running drill.	
		10.15 AM	Company parade for Semaphore drill, Communication drill and Instruction in Guard Duties.	
		11.30 AM	Officers, Sergeants and Corporals attend lecture on :- Machine Gun Barrage. Signallers parade for instruction :- Buzzer and Flag. All Steel Helmets covered with sacking, per Brigade Orders. and darkened.	
BERTEHEM.	3rd	5.15 AM	Reveille.	J.H.S.
		6.45 AM	Company parade for Brigade Tactical Scheme. Dress "Battle Order".	
BERTEHEM.	4th	7.0 AM	Reveille.	J.H.S.
		9.0 AM	Company parade under Section arrangements for :- Cleaning Guns, Gun gear, etc. All Belts cleaned and refilled, and Belt Boxes made up to establishment. All Church Services : Voluntary.	

Army Form C. 2118.

WAR DIARY

~~INTELLIGENCE SUMMARY~~

(Erase heading not required.)

NOVEMBER 1917.

Instructions regarding War Diaries and Intelligence Summaries are contained in F.S. Regs., Part II. and the Staff Manual respectively. Title pages will be prepared in manuscript.

Place	Date	Hour	Summary of Events and Information	Remarks and references to Appendices
BERTEHEM	5TH	6.30 AM	Reveille.	
		7.30 AM	Interior Economy and Muster Clean Parade.	
		9.0 AM	Squad drill with Arms	
		10.15 AM TO 12.30 PM	Sections parade under Section arrangements, special attention being paid to :- (i) Checking of Gun gear. (ii) Cleaning of Wagons (iii) Box Respirators & Gas Helmet. Inspection and drill. (iv) Kit inspection.	AHS
		2.0 PM	Company parade for Packing Limbers, prior to departure for the Line	AHS
BERTEHEM	6TH	6.30 AM	Reveille.	
		9.0 AM	Physical Training	
		10.15 AM	Guns cleaned and tested. Limbers packed. Warning order received. Company will be entraining on the 7 inst.	AHS
BERTEHEM	7TH	2.0 AM	Reveille.	
		3.45 AM	Company parade Full marching order and march to AUDRUICQ railhead.	
		7.0 AM	Company entrain with rest of Bde.	
		12.0 noon	Company detrain at ELVERDING HE and march to SOLFERNIO CAMP.	
		1.0 PM	All Ranks arrive safety in camp.	
		9.45 AM	Transport entrain at AUDRUICQ and arrive at new lines, situated near WHITE MILL at 2.0 AM 8/11/17. Enemy aircraft very active during the night, and Tons of Bombs dropped in vicinity of Brigade area. Casualties [this Coy. N, L.]	AHS
SOLFERNIO CAMP	8TH	7.0 AM	Reveille	
		9.0 AM	Foot fraction drill in Tents. Rest of day spent in "Revetting Tents, and cleaning up new Camp	AHS

Army Form C. 2118.

WAR DIARY
INTELLIGENCE SUMMARY.
(Erase heading not required.)

NOVEMBER 1917.

Place	Date	Hour	Summary of Events and Information	Remarks and references to Appendices
SOLFERINO CAMP	9TH	7.0 AM	Reveille.	
		9.0 AM	Foot Friction drill.	
		9.30 AM to 12 noon	Work continued on Resetting Tents, and a Trench dug round the Camp. Anti-Aircraft emplacement constructed.	
		2.0 PM	Company parade for gathering wood, for the purpose of laying a Track through the Camp.	JHS
SOLFERINO CAMP	10TH	7.0 AM	Reveille.	
		9.0 AM	Foot Friction drill.	
		9.30 AM	Company parade for Cleaning and Testing Guns, under Sec. arrangements.	
		11.0 AM	Box Respirator and P.H. Helmet inspection and drill.	
		2.0 PM	Work continued on cleaning up Camp, and resetting of Tents completed. During the night, small Bombing raid by the enemy over our lines and vicinity of Camp shelled with H.E. Shells.	JHS
SOLFERINO CAMP	11TH	7.0 AM	Reveille.	
		9.0 AM	Foot Friction drill. Rest of day spent in digging Trenches round Tents to draw away water after recent heavy rain. Transport lines moved to :- B.20 & 5.3.	JHS
SOLFERINO CAMP	12TH	7.0 AM	Reveille.	
		9.0 AM	Foot Friction drill.	
		9.30 AM	Physical Training.	
		10.30 AM	Company parade under Sec. arrangements :- New Transport lines visited and Tents erected for "Details". Floor Boards inserted in 6 Tents at SOLFERINO CAMP.	JHS
SOLFERINO CAMP	13TH	7.0 AM	Reveille.	
		9.0 AM	Foot Friction drill. Rest of morning spent in Cleaning Guns, and packing Limbers for the line. Lieut. J.W. Felton, and 3 Gun Teams of "A" Section Leave for the Line, followed by Lt. H.E. Smith 3 Gun Teams of "B" Sec., & archeon Team of "A" Sec. Coy. H.Q. DROP HOUSES.	JHS

Army Form C. 2118.

WAR DIARY
or
INTELLIGENCE SUMMARY.

NOVEMBER 1917

(Erase heading not required.)

Place	Date	Hour	Summary of Events and Information	Remarks and references to Appendices
DROP HOUSES	14th		7 Gun Teams on the line. 51 M.G. Coy being relieved. Casualties. Wounded O/R. One. Map Reference of the Guns as follows :-	

No. of Gun   Map Reference.
1.   V 7 a 25.50.
2.   V 7 c 62.95.
3.   V 7 b 07.17
4.   V 7 a 93.20.
5.   U 7 d 20.20
6.   U 13 b 50.50
7.   STRING HOUSES
    DROP HOUSES
    COY. H.Q

No. 5 and 6. Guns are also employed on A.A work. The Div on our left have 2 guns approximately at U 12 d 30.70 firing down the Railway, and one gun at EGYPT HOUSE firing across listed Railway. The Div on our right have 1 Gun at HELLES HOUSE firing across our front and /2 Guns in vicinity of POLE CAPELLE BRY firing in a N.E direction.

Transport lines are at B 20 b 5.3.

Army Form C. 2118.

WAR DIARY
INTELLIGENCE SUMMARY.   NOVEMBER 1917

(Erase heading not required.)

Instructions regarding War Diaries and Intelligence Summaries are contained in F. S. Regs., Part II. and the Staff Manual respectively. Title pages will be prepared in manuscript.

Place	Date	Hour	Summary of Events and Information	Remarks and references to Appendices
DROP HOUSES.	15th		1. Observations. (a) Own — Nil (b) Enemy's — Nil 2. Artillery Observations. (a) Own. Active throughout the day, except during intense periods. (b) Enemy. Slight retaliation on light field guns. 5.9s and 4.2s noticed TAUBE and GENERAL Farms, from 3.0 PM – 3.30 PM. Also around the area J.11.a. 6.5.8 from 4.15 PM – 5.0 PM. Then round my SP 5.6 and 7. Guns shelled about 3.30 PM. DROP HOUSES shelled with 5.9s from 3.15 PM – 4.0 PM. Shells apparently coming from direction of HOUTHULST FOREST. Enemy appear to have one or two light field guns close up on the night of STADEN RAILWAY. 3. Enemy's Defences. (a) New work — None observed (b) Wire — None observed (c) M. G's — One Gun was reported checkered tracks throughout the night. (d) T. M's — None observed (e) Dumps — None observed (f) State of Ground — Bad. Water logged generally. Enemy's Communications — None observed. Nothing to report. Enemy's A Dispositions — None observed. Movement —	H.J.S. F/S/9

Army Form C. 2118.

WAR DIARY
INTELLIGENCE SUMMARY.
NOVEMBER 1917

(Erase heading not required.)

Place	Date	Hour	Summary of Events and Information	Remarks and references to Appendices
DROP HOUSES	15th	7	Aeroplane Activity - Nil	
		8	Miscellaneous	
			(i) Belt line ammunition in more top gear a slate but gradually being replaced by fresh Belt boxes.	
			(ii) A Straggler presumably a Frenchman reported at one of our Officers H.Q at 12 d 5.8 yesterday afternoon 4.0pm and Guide was sent on to Brigade H.Qs. by 2nd Infantry.	AHS
DROP HOUSES	16th	1	Operations	
			(a) Ours - Nil	
			(b) Enemy - Hostile Bombardment opened up at left at 5.30 PM S.O.S sent up to which Artillery and M.Gs replied.	
		2	Artillery Activity	
			(a) Ours - Replied to S.O.S signal at 5.30 PM HOUTHOULST FOREST received a good deal of attention.	
			(b) Enemy - Active throughout the day. G.B. 12. noon 15/11/17 — 2.0. P.M. at 6.30 P.M 8. 5.9's shelled with 5.9's and 2.0 P.M OLGA HOUSES. Registration of duckboards and 5.9's fell in close proximity to defended locality cannot tell whether the day about 40 light field Gun shells were dropped in quick succession at 10.0 P.M. in vicinity of LE 1.2.5.7.8 The STADEN RAILWAY received attention on and off during the day and night.	AHS

Army Form C. 2118.

WAR DIARY
INTELLIGENCE SUMMARY. NOVEMBER 1917

(Erase heading not required.)

Instructions regarding War Diaries and Intelligence Summaries are contained in F. S. Regs., Part II. and the Staff Manual respectively. Title pages will be prepared in manuscript.

Place	Date	Hour	Summary of Events and Information	Remarks and references to Appendices
DROP HOUSES	16th	Cont'd.		
		3	**Enemy's Defences.**	
			(a) None observed.	
			(b) None observed.	
			(c) 1 One M.G. firing from the direction of GRAVEL FARM at irregular intervals.	
			" 1 One M.G. firing from the direction of the cross roads and Railway at H.12.d.1 at irregular intervals during the night	
			(d) One suspected to be firing from direction of ASEN HOUSE at 5.30 p.m.	
			(e) Nil	
			(f) Dyer still very wet.	
		4	**Enemy Communications.** — None observed.	
		5	**Enemy Dispositions.** — None observed.	
		6	**Movement behind Enemy's lines.** None observed. Visibility too low	
		7	**Aeroplane Activity.** Enemy planes very active during the day. Bombs dropped 20 yards to the left of HQ 70 1 Queens. Enemy planes also dropped unlighted along our front lines at dawn 15/11/17.	
			Bombs were dropped on Railway Infantry	
			Two Enemy observation Balloons, one in one another - one mid Lamis	
			Signalling to one another.	
			A long slow trail of heavy white smoke was seen during an E.N.E. direction in vicinity of ADEN HOUSES at 7.0. AM 15/11/17. Phosmine/Pist Box? fired HS	
		8	Miscellaneous. Movement of men also suspected	

Army Form C. 2118.

WAR DIARY
or
INTELLIGENCE SUMMARY.
(Erase heading not required.)

NOVEMBER 1917.

Place	Date	Hour	Summary of Events and Information	Remarks and references to Appendices
DROP HOUSES	17th		1. Operations. (a) Ours. } Nil (b) Enemy's. } 2. Artillery Activity. (a) Ours. Active throughout day and night. (b) Enemy's. Active throughout day and night. Concentrated bombardment on DROP HOUSES. Any 5.9s and Shells of higher calibre from 3.15 PM – 4.30 PM and intermittently throughout the night. 3. Enemy's Defences. (a) New Works (b) Wire (c) Machine Guns } No information (d) Trench Mortars (e) Dumps (f) State of ground. Improving. 4. Enemy's Communications } None observed 5. Enemy's Dispositions 6. Movement behind Enemy's lines. 7. Aeroplane Activity. 5 Gothas flying low flew over DROP HOUSES and dropped Bombs in vicinity of AU BON GITE, at 3.15 PM. My relieving Teams sniped at with Machine Guns from Aeroplanes. 8. Miscellaneous. Indian Company Relief successfully carried out yesterday. Casualties = Wounded O.R. One.	JHS

Army Form C. 2118.

WAR DIARY
INTELLIGENCE SUMMARY.
NOVEMBER 1917.

(Erase heading not required.)

Instructions regarding War Diaries and Intelligence Summaries are contained in F. S. Regs., Part II and the Staff Manual respectively. Title pages will be prepared in manuscript.

Place	Date	Hour	Summary of Events and Information	Remarks and references to Appendices
DROP HOUSES	18th		1. Guns in Action. Nil. Ammunition Expended. Nil. Work done. Improvement of positions. Work to be done. S.A.A. carried up to each Gun position and general maintenance and improvement of positions. 2. Observations (a) Ours } Nil (b) Enemy's } Artillery Activity (a) Ours. Not observed. (b) Enemy's Active during the whole day. DROP HOUSES and vicinity bombarded from 10.15 am - 11.15 am and 3.15 pm - 4.30 pm and at intervals during the night with 5.9's. Gas Shells used at intervals. OLGA HOUSES shelled at intervals, and received special attention at 2.30 pm 3. Enemy's Defences. (a) New work. None observed. (b) Wire. None observed. (c) Machine Guns. M.G. fires from vicinity of GRAVEL FARM. (d) Trench Mortars. None observed. (e) Dumps. None observed. (f) State of Ground. Bad. 4. Enemy's Communications. } going away from the Duckboards. 5. Enemy's Dispositions. } None observed 6. Movement behind Enemy's lines. 7. Aeroplane Activity. One of our observation planes flying low at 3.0 pm was fired on by our own Infantry. 8. Miscellaneous. Nil.	

Army Form C. 2118.

WAR DIARY
INTELLIGENCE SUMMARY. NOVEMBER 1917

(Erase heading not required)

Instructions regarding War Diaries and Intelligence Summaries are contained in F. S. Regs., Part II. and the Staff Manual respectively. Title pages will be prepared in manuscript.

Place	Date	Hour	Summary of Events and Information	Remarks and references to Appendices
DROP HOUSES	19th		Guns in Action 1. Ammunition Expended 500 Rounds. Targets :- GRAVEL FARM and vicinity. Times of Firing. 6.pm - 9.pm - Direct Fire -	
			1. Operations (a) Ours. } Nil (b) Enemy. }	
			2. Artillery Activity (a) Ours Barrage put down on Divisional Front at 7.AM 18-11-17. (b) Enemy's. Enemy retaliated in less than one minute to our Barrage. LANGEMARK is evidently in his Barrage lines as we were heavily shelled and around OLGA HOUSES, DROP HOUSES, and VULCAN LANE were heavily shelled during the night at intervals. Gas Shells again fell around Coy. H.Q. at night at intervals.	
			3. Enemy's Defences. (a) Bad work. } None observed. (b) Wire. } (c) Machine Guns. Enemy M.G. fired from direction of GRAVEL FARM on to BERTHIER and TAUBE FARMS. (d) Trench Mortars. Enemy T.M fired from direction of MEMLING FARM at 12 midnight. Enemy T.M also ballooned to be firing from VAN DYKE FARM. None observed.	
			(e) Dumps. (f) State of Ground. No improvement. Enemy's Communications. } Nothing to report. Enemy's Dispositions. } Movement behind Enemy's lines. None observed.	
	4/5/6			

Army Form C. 2118.

WAR DIARY

INTELLIGENCE SUMMARY.

NOVEMBER 1917.

(Erase heading not required.)

Instructions regarding War Diaries and Intelligence Summaries are contained in F. S. Regs., Part II and the Staff Manual respectively. Title pages will be prepared in manuscript.

Place	Date	Hour	Summary of Events and Information	Remarks and references to Appendices
DROP HOUSES.	19th		7. Aeroplane Activity. (a) Ours. Our Planes flew low at dawn from our Enemy Posts and appeared to patrol all day along the front. (b) Enemy. Enemy Planes were about soon after dawn. One of our Planes was seen to crash 8. Miscellaneous. Lights were observed in RUBENS and VAN DYCK FARMS from 6.0 PM onwards	AHS
DROP HOUSES.	19th	5.0 PM 9.0 PM 11.0 PM to 12. M.N.	Relief. Company relieved by 51 M.G. Coy. Teams on relief proceed independently to Transport Lines at B20 b 5.3. All Ranks safely under Canvas. Casualties NIL. Camp and Transport Lines Shelled at regular intervals. Trenches round the Camp occupied during shelling. Casualties Wounded "Ranks" Two. Vicinity of B20 b 5.3 again shelled during early hours of the morning 20.11.17 at irregular intervals. G.S. Limber conveying Guns etc. from DROP HOUSES encountered heavy shelling. One L.D. Horse being killed and half the Limber damaged.	AHS
CARDOEN CAMP.	20th	7.0 AM 9.0 AM 10.30 AM	Reveille. Fighting Limbers packed prior to the Sections moving back to CARDOEN CAMP [A18 a 9.6] Sections paraded and march to new Camp and occupy 1½ Huts in conjunction with 50 T.M. Battery, B20 b 5.3. Transport remain in present location B20 b 5.3. Cleaning up Huts. Rest of day spent in Cleaning Clothing & Equipment and Improving Latrines	AHS

Army Form C. 2118.

WAR DIARY
INTELLIGENCE SUMMARY.

NOVEMBER 1917

(Erase heading not required.)

Instructions regarding War Diaries and Intelligence Summaries are contained in F.S. Regs., Part II. and the Staff Manual respectively. Title pages will be prepared in manuscript.

Place	Date	Hour	Summary of Events and Information	Remarks and references to Appendices
DROP HOUSES	20TH		Detachment. Casualties :- Killed O/Ranks One. Wounded O/Ranks Two. Total Casualties :- Killed P/Ranks One. Wounded P/Ranks Six.	JHS
CARDOEN CAMP.	21ST	7.0 AM	Reveille	
		7.45 AM	Interior Economy and Muster Clean Parade.	
		9.0 AM	Foot friction drill	
		9.30 AM	MUSTER PARADE "Brass Battle Order"	
		10.0 AM	Box Respirator and P.H. Helmet Inspection. Rest of morning spent in Cleaning Guns, gun gear, and wagons.	
		2.0 PM	Kit and Iron Ration inspection.	
		3.0 PM	Company paid out	JHS
CARDOEN CAMP.	22nd	7.0 AM	Reveille	
		7.45 AM	Interior Economy and Muster Clean Parade.	
		9.0 AM	Foot friction drill	
		9.30 AM	"MUSTER PARADE" dress Battle Order.	
		10 AM to 12.30 PM	Rest of morning spent in Cleaning and Checking Guns, gun gear, Ammunition Boxes Belts etc.	
		2.0 PM	Company parade for revetting Huts and improving Camp.	JHS
CARDOEN CAMP.	23rd	7.0 AM	Reveille	
		7.45 AM	Muster Clean Parade and Interior Economy.	
		9.0 AM	Foot friction Drill	
		9.30 AM	Physical Training.	
		10.30 AM to 12.30 PM	Instruction in Mechanism and Immediate Action. Attached men special Instruction in Mechanism.	
		2.0 PM	Arms drill	JHS

WAR DIARY

INTELLIGENCE SUMMARY

NOVEMBER 1917

Army Form C. 2118.

Place	Date	Hour	Summary of Events and Information	Remarks and references to Appendices
CARDOEN CAMP.	24th	7.0.AM.	Reveille.	
		7.45AM	Interior Economy and Muster Clean Parade.	
		9.0.AM.	Foot Friction drill.	
		9.30.AM	Officers Lecture on :- (I) Reports. (II) Communication. (III) Map Reading.	
		10.30.AM.	Arms Drill.	
		11.30.AM	Gun Drill. Attached Men instruction in Mechanism and Stoppages.	
		2.0.PM	Instruction in Guard Duties.	
			Signallers instructed in Buzzer and Flag throughout the day.	JHS
CARDOEN CAMP.	25th	6.0.AM.	Reveille.	
		7.15AM	Interior Economy and Muster Clean Parade.	
			Church Parade Services as follows :-	
		9.0.AM	Nonconformists of all Denominations parade Service in CINEMA THEATRE	
		9.45.AM	Service for R.C's. in CARDOEN FARM Chapel.	
			Holy Communion Services as follows :-	
		8.0.AM.	Church Army Hut. ROUSSEL FARM.	
		8.30.AM.	Y.M.C.A. Tent at DAWSONS CORNER.	
			Evening Services all Voluntary.	
			Fighting limbers packed prior to moving to New Area.	JHS
MORTAR CAMP.	25th	10.30AM	Company parade and march to MORTAR CAMP.	
		12.Noon	All safely arrive at New Camp. 5. Nissen Huts, and S. Tents being occupied.	
		1.30AM	Rest of day spent in cleaning up Camp, and resetting of Huts and Tents commenced.	
MORTAR CAMP.	26th	7.0AM	Reveille.	
		7.45AM	Interior Economy and Muster Clean Parade.	
		9.0.AM	Foot Friction drill.	
		9.15AM	All Socks inspected, and deficiencies made up. Every Man to be in possession of 3 pairs of Socks.	
		9.30AM to 12.30PM	Company parade for resetting Huts, Digging Trenches round the Camp and Sand bagging Transport Lines.	JHS

Army Form C. 2118.

WAR DIARY
INTELLIGENCE SUMMARY.

(Erase heading not required.)

NOVEMBER 1917.

Instructions regarding War Diaries and Intelligence Summaries are contained in F. S. Regs., Part II and the Staff Manual respectively. Title pages will be prepared in manuscript.

Place	Date	Hour	Summary of Events and Information	Remarks and references to Appendices
MORTAR CAMP	26th	2.30 PM	"H.Q." and "A" Sections parade for Baths. "Div¹ BATHS"	AHS
		3.0 PM	and "C" Sections "Baths"	
"	27th	7.0 AM	Reveille	
		7.45 AM	Interior Economy and Muster Clean parade.	
		9.0 AM	Foot Friction Drill in Huts	
		9.30 AM	Instruction in Mechanism and Stoppages.	
		10.30 AM to	Company parade for improving Camp – Huts and Tents revisited	
		12.30 PM	and trenches dug round the Camp Safeguard against Hostile Aircraft. Duckwalk track also laid, all round the Camp	AHS
		2.0 PM to	Barbed wire removed from vicinity of Billets and Shell holes	
		4.0 PM	filled in. Work continued at Transport lines. B 20 & S 3	
MORTAR CAMP	28th	7.0 AM	Reveille	
		7.45 AM	Interior Economy and Muster Clean parade	
		9.0 AM	Foot Friction drill in Huts	
		9.30 AM to 10.30 AM	Physical Training Vicinity of Camp	
			Box Respirator and P.H. Helmets Inspection and Drill	
		11.30 AM to	Gun Drill Introducing Stoppages wearing Box Respirators	
			Special instruction for Attached Men in Mechanism and Stoppages	AHS
		11.30 PM	Signallers Buzzer and Flag Reading	
		2.0 PM	All Guns cleaned and Tested	
MORTAR CAMP	29th	6.30 AM	Reveille	
		7.45 AM	Interior Economy and Muster Clean Parade	
		9.0 AM	Foot Friction Drill in Huts	
		9.30 AM	Arms Drill	
		10.30 AM	Pack Mule Drill	AHS

Army Form C. 2118.

WAR DIARY
or
INTELLIGENCE SUMMARY.

(Erase heading not required.)

NOVEMBER 1917.

Place	Date	Hour	Summary of Events and Information	Remarks and references to Appendices
MORTAR CAMP	29th	Can.Ed. 11.30 AM	"Indirect Fire" (1) Lecture. (1) Practical. Throughout the day "B" Section continue work at Transport lines:- Re-sitting new lines and Tents. Vicinity of MORTAR CAMP shelled throughout the night at intervals.	AHS
MORTAR CAMP	30th	6.30 AM 7.45 AM 9.0 AM 9.30 AM 10.30 AM 11.45 AM 1.30 PM	Reveille Interior Economy and Muster Clean Parade Foot Friction drill in Huts Physical Training, vicinity of Camp. Instruction in (1) Map Reading (11) Compass. Stripping the Lock, Spare Parts, etc., in Huts. "A" and "B" Section's parade for Foot Baths. Resetting of New Transport lines at B20b 5.3 completed.	AHS

30/11/17

Cummon Capt
OC 501 F.C.

WAR DIARY
or
INTELLIGENCE SUMMARY

50. Machine Gun Coy.

Army Form C. 2118.

December 1917.

Place	Date	Hour	Summary of Events and Information	Remarks and references to Appendices
LANGEMARCK SECTOR "Drop Houses"	Dec 1/17		Company relieved 52 M.G. Coy. in the line by day. Company H.Q. DROP HOUSES. Relief completed by 5 pm. Casualties NIL. Tactical Report: Guns in action NIL. Reports received: Ropes firing direct on to GRAVEL FARM from BERTHIER FARM supposed by him. A.A. engagements being made for No.6 gun near ETOILE HOUSE. New position being made for No.1 gun on the railway, old position having been rocked out. Night defence carried out. General harassing of enemy positions.	Ann
	-2		(1) Artillery (A) Ours: unknown on night apparently making an attack at 2.0 am 2nd morning. (B) Enemy's: NIL Military Activity (A) Machine Gun: carried out bombardment at 6 pm yesterday & again at 2 am on LANGEMARCK country morning. (B) Trench Mortars: Replies to our bombardment at 2 am. Shelled enemy firing points around enemy defences. (A) W.T.s: None observed. (B) T.M's: None observed. (C) M.G's: Machine guns again firing from GRAVEL FARM. (D) New Trench: None observed. (E) Dumps: None observed. (F) Ground: Ground apparently frozen in morning. Tanks: None observed. (4) Enemy's Communications: None observed. (5) - Inspirations: None observed. (6) Movement behind enemy's lines: None observed. (7) Aeroplane activity: None observed. (8) Situation on the whole seems quieter than the last time when the Brigade were in the line.	Obs

WAR DIARY
or
INTELLIGENCE SUMMARY.

50. Machine Gun Coy.

Army Form C. 2118.

December 1917.

Place	Date	Hour	Summary of Events and Information	Remarks and references to Appendices
LANGEMARCK SECTOR. Coy. H.Q. DROP HOUSES.	3		Enemy action: Nil. Proposed operations: direct fire from BERTHIER FARM on 5 GRAVEL FARM from 6 pm. to 8 pm. tonight. (Battalion concurred) wounded J. General maintenance and repair of positions. New position completed from No.1 gun. Coy. H.Q. (DROP HOUSES) sandbagged. Operations (A) Guns: Nil. (B) Subunits: Nil. Shelling activity (A) Enemy: "Creeping" barrage put down at 8.30 pm. in accordance with programme. (B) Enemy's apparently no reply to barrage at 6.30 pm. DROP HOUSES vicinity shelled from 3.30 pm. to 5 pm. 1 direct hit on Coy. H.Q. Shelling otherwise normal. Enemy's outposts New break) None observed. Wire (C) M.G's, GRAVEL FARM M.G's again active (D) T.M's Rifled F fire at GRAVEL FARM from 2 shots at 5.30 pm. (E) Dumps. Enemy dump seen to go up at about 4.45 at 8.45 pm. (F) State of ground. but still very bad. improving	(i)
	4		Operations (A) Enemy infantry patrols reported having been at GRAVEL FARM about 2 am. M.G's at BERTHIER FARM fired on Germans at GRAVEL FARM at intervals from 6 pm. to 8 pm. (B) Enemy's held.	(ii)

Army Form C. 2118.

50 Machine Gun Co/
WAR DIARY
or
INTELLIGENCE SUMMARY. December 1917.
(Erase heading not required.)

Instructions regarding War Diaries and Intelligence Summaries are contained in F. S. Regs., Part II. and the Staff Manual respectively. Title pages will be prepared in manuscript.

Place	Date	Hour	Summary of Events and Information	Remarks and references to Appendices
LANGEMARCK SECTOR	Dec 4 (Continued)		Artillery activity (a) Ours. Normal. GRAVEL FARM fired on by killed guns. Enemy opposed to the shoot of the target. (b) Enemy's. During the day many shells on CONDÉ HOUSE. EGYPT HOUSE. LANGEMARCK STATION with 5.9's and at 4.25 (a) Forest shelled with 5.9's and shrapnel during the morning Enemy defences. (2) New work) have observed (3) Wire) (C) M.G.'s M.G. fired about knots from a position SSW of my (d) T.M's No 2 gun Heavy T.M's heard firing from a position night of the Railway during the night (E) Dumps) have observed (f) State of ground. must frozen Enemy's communications. Enemy's dispositions. Movement behind enemy's lines] None observed Our air activity (a) Ours. Several NEWPORT SCOUTS up own and Hun during 9 p.m. day (b) Enemy's. Enemy planes heard at night specially morning Miscellaneous. Snipers busy on TAUBE FARM during the day. At 6 p.m. two lights sent up field of enemy's lines, both white, a shower of yellow. No apparent news forward	aw

A 5834 Wt. W4973/M687 750,000 8/16 D. D. & L. Ltd. Forms/C.2118/13

50. Machine Gun Coy.

Army Form C. 2118.

WAR DIARY
INTELLIGENCE SUMMARY.
December 1917

(Erase heading not required.)

Instructions regarding War Diaries and Intelligence Summaries are contained in F. S. Regs., Part II. and the Staff Manual respectively. Title pages will be prepared in manuscript.

Place	Date	Hour	Summary of Events and Information	Remarks and references to Appendices
LANGEMARCK SECTOR	Dec 5	5½	Operations. (a) Ours. Infantry sent out patrol at 6 pm 4/2/17 who reached V17.55.65 when they were fired on by an enemy working party from just in front of them who apparently retired to the sixth side of BROMBECK. Enemy estimated 15 to 20 men. (b) Enemy's Nil. Artillery activity. (a) Ours. Fairly active during the day. Shells appeared to be dropping short of GRAVEL FARM nothing definite known. No rounds prematire. Unit offence unknown. (b) Enemy's. Very normal. Enemy Defences. (a) M.G. Concentration on N. Bank of BROMBECK about V7.8.77 (b) M.G's. Nil (c) T.M's. None reported on seen to-day. (d) Dumps. Nil (e) State of ground. Unknown. Unknown in places. Enemy's Dispositions. Not Known. Movement behind enemy's lines. None seen. Aircraft activity. Very little. One enemy plane flying at about 1200 ft. over Tank Farm this morning was engaged by one with M.G. Fire but made away over enemy's lines. Miscellaneous. Between 7 and 9 am 4/12/17 a dense white low cloud of smoke a steam about 1 mile in length moving from TURENNE CROSSING 5 ft. of EGYPT HOUSE in a N.W. direction. Another similar cloud was seen to issue in direction about 5 pm 4/11/17. Company relieved in night. Cigarettes extra. Post duties Nil. Rest of morning checking stores loading guns 10/R have been at night on a search of a landing near.	
MORTAR CAMP	Dec 6	8.30.		

Army Form C. 2118.

50 Machine Gun Coy

WAR DIARY

INTELLIGENCE SUMMARY. December 1917.

(Erase heading not required.)

Instructions regarding War Diaries and Intelligence Summaries are contained in F.S. Regs., Part II. and the Staff Manual respectively. Title pages will be prepared in manuscript.

Place	Date	Hour	Summary of Events and Information	Remarks and references to Appendices
MIXTAR CAMP	7		Company prepare to move to rest area. All surplus kit to B.Sc H.Q. by 6 a.m. Company parade at 12.15 pm & march off to ELVERDINGHE STATION. Entrain to AUDRUICK arriving there at about 11 pm. Coy then march to BERTENEM and arrive at 2 a.m.	ans
BERTENEM	8	9 am	Reveille.	ans
		9-9.30	Foot friction drill & inspection	
		10.30	hourly. Clean parade.	
		afternoon	Rest of morning was spent in the Transport lines. Sectional football match.	
	9	7 am	Reveille. Company Parade at 8.30 - 9.15 Foot drill with arms	ans
		9.30-10	full marching order. Remainder of morning spent on Lectures, gas helmets, inspection, etc.	
		afternoon	Kit, Box respirators, gas helmets & iron rations were inspected during the morning. Football match.	
	10	10.30 am	Company leave BERTENEM & march via WOLPHUS, LA RECOUSSE, NORDAUSQUES, EPERLEQUES to OUEST MONT & arrive in billets at 1 pm.	ans
OUEST MONT	11	7 am	Reveille	ans
		6.30-9.15	Signal drill with arms	
		9.30-10.30	Taking & cleaning guns	
		afternoon	Rest of morning spent in fitting of clothing boots etc. 2 p.m. Games.	
	12	7 am	Reveille. 8.30 to 9 foot friction rule. 9.15 to 10.15 Physical training. Remainder of morning spent on Mechanism & Immediate action. Afternoon. Intersectional football match.	ans
	13	7 am	Reveille. Foot friction drill & Physical training as usual	ans
		10.30-11.30	Gun drill. 11.30 - 12.30 pm Pack saddling. afternoon. Intersectional football match.	

2/Lt. F. Paret joins company.

WAR DIARY

INTELLIGENCE SUMMARY

50 Machine Gun Coy.
December 1917.

Army Form C. 2118.

Place	Date	Hour	Summary of Events and Information	Remarks and references to Appendices
BERTENCH	1917 14	8.30 am 4— 8— 7 am	Reveille. Breakfast. All kitts cleaned + gear packed for moving. Company Parade + march to ST OMER via HOULLE, MOULLE etc + entrain to ACHIET LE PETIT. Company detrain + march through BAPAUME & halt near LE TRANSLOY arriving at about 11 pm.	July
LE TRANSLOY	15	4.45a 9.15-9.30 10.30-11 11-12.30 Afternoon	Reveille. Foot friction rub + inspection. Company Parade — Inst. handing over for inspection. Leaning + cleaning guns, gun gear etc. Sports.	Aug
	16	9.30 am Afternoon	Reveille. Company parade for Church services during the morning. Lecture for NCOs at noon by the C.O. Semi-Final Hinder Sectional football match.	Aug
	17	7 am 7.45 8.30-9 9.15-10.15 Afternoon	Reveille. much clean parade + interior economy. Foot friction rub. Clean rifle hill. Rest of morning, firing Stoppages on the range. Sports.	Aug
	18	9.30-10.15 10.30 to noon Afternoon	Reveille - much clean parade + foot friction rub as before. Physical training. Firing Stoppages on the range. Instruction regarding Discipline were read out. Afternoon — Football match.	Aug

WAR DIARY or INTELLIGENCE SUMMARY

50 Machine Gun Coy
Army Form C. 2118
December 1917

Place	Date	Hour	Summary of Events and Information	Remarks and references to Appendices
LE TRANSLOY	Dec 19	7 am.	Reveille	
		7.45-	Muster clean parade & interior economy	
		8.30-9	Foot drill drill	
		9.15-10	Physical training	(iv)
			Rest of morning was spent in "Stoppages" lecture on antics in the line	
		2-3	Lecture for Open & 'ple	
		3-6	Clean for backsand run	
			Afternoon. Football match.	
	20	7am	Reveille	
			Muster clean parade, foot drill – rifle & physical training as previously	(iv)
		10.15-11.30	Firing Stoppages	
		11.30-12.30	Use of dialling, changing dials & the Clinometer	
		11.30-12.30	Lecture for Sergeants & Corporals on "Indirect fire".	
			Afternoon. Sports.	
	21	7am	Reveille	
		7.45-	Muster clean parade + interior economy	
		8.30-9.	Foot drill rifle drill	(iv)
		9.15-10.	Arms drill.	
		10-12.30.	Gun drill & immediate action & a lecture by section officers	
			Afternoon. Final of Inter- Section football match.	
	22	7	Reveille	
		7.45	Muster clean parade + interior economy	
		8.30-9.	Foot drill rifle drill + 9.15 5.10 am. Physical training	(iv)
			All gear packed on limbers by noon. Company paraded at 2.45 & march via HAPLINCOURT & BERTENCOURT arriving at about 6 p.m. This village was hardly big enough to cover all in one N.L.	

50 Machine Gun Coy

Army Form C. 2118.

WAR DIARY

INTELLIGENCE=SUMMARY. December 1917.

(Erase heading not required.)

Instructions regarding War Diaries and Intelligence Summaries are contained in F. S. Regs., Part II. and the Staff Manual respectively. Title pages will be prepared in manuscript.

Place	Date	Hour	Summary of Events and Information	Remarks and references to Appendices
BERTENCOURT.	23.	7.30 a.m.	Reveille	App 1
		11.50	Company parade full marching order & march to OLD BRITISH FRONT LINE via RUYALCOURT & HAVRINCOURT WOOD arriving about dusk. Transport are up near RUYALCOURT.	
OLD BRITISH FRONT LINE. HAVRINCOURT	24.	7.15	Reveille	App 2
		8.30–8.45	Foot friction drill	
		9.9.15	Rifle inspection	
			Remainder of day cleaning up kit & improving shelters. Company all now in shelters. Cavalier N.L.	
	25		Christmas day in the hut again. The Company made the best of it in the OLD BRITISH FRONT LINE & one wanted with Xmas pudding. One 1 gun team was cleaned.	App 3
	26		Foot friction drill, rifle inspection & cleaning up in general carried on the morning. Company Parade full marching order march to TRESCAULT arriving 5.30 p.m. at 4 p.m.	App 4
TRESCAULT.	27	7.15 a.m.	Reveille	App 5
		8.30–9	Foot friction drill.	
			Guns & gear were checked and cleaned prior to going into the line.	
	28	3 p.m.	Foot friction drill & cleaning up & hill recommend the morning Company parade in Battle order & relieve 52 M.G. Coy in the line. Packs & surplus stores are taken to the transport lines. Company head quarters are at GRAND RAVINE and relief in complete by 7 p.m.	App 6
FRESQUIERES				

50 Machine Gun Coy

Army Form C. 2118.

WAR DIARY
INTELLIGENCE SUMMARY.
December 1917

(Erase heading not required.)

Instructions regarding War Diaries and Intelligence Summaries are contained in F. S. Regs., Part II. and the Staff Manual respectively. Title pages will be prepared in manuscript.

Place	Date	Hour	Summary of Events and Information	Remarks and references to Appendices
FRESQUIRES	29		**Operations:** Relief of Gunners carried out as reported yesterday. **Enemy:** Nil. Artillery activity. **Ours:** No great activity. Shrapnel action in vicinity of HAVRINCOURT and HAVRINCOURT - FLESQUIERS RD from 2.45 p.m. to 3.30 p.m. **Enemy defences:** Nothing new to report. Ground hard & slippery - difficult for transport. No enemy communications in disposition available. No movement observed behind enemy lines. **Aeroplane Activity:** Slight activity on our front. Enemy planes fairly active between 10 - 12 noon. **Miscellaneous:** Guns in action - Nil. Work to the Gunners Construction of AA emplacement & general maintenance of repair & condition.	OW
	30		**Operations:** OURS — NIL ENEMYS — NIL Artillery activity. Nothing particular to report. ORIVAL WOOD shelled at intervals.	OW

50. Machine Gun Coy.
Army Form C. 2118.

WAR DIARY
INTELLIGENCE SUMMARY. December 1917

Place	Date	Hour	Summary of Events and Information	Remarks and references to Appendices
FLESQUIERES SECTOR	30		Artillery activity Enemy's. FLESQUIERES and HAVRINCOURT shelled at intervals. Gas shells at K24 & 70.20. Shelled with 5.9's between 5.30 pm & 7.45 pm. Heavy bombardment commenced at 6.25 am. Enemy's Defences New work — none observed Wire " M.Gs. " T.M.s " Dumps " State of ground. Still very hard. Slippery. Movement behind enemy's lines Movement observed throughout the day in GRAINCOURT & ORIVAL WOOD transport been seen at intervals on road South of BOURLON WOOD (F20 a and b) Aeroplane activity. Quiet throughout the day. Miscellaneous. Nil. Guns in action 3 Rounds expended 5000 Casualties Nil Targets engaged on following:- No. 9 gun. New work in L9a " 10 " ORIVAL WOOD & vicinity " 11 " new work in L9a and L9d Indirect bursts of fire throughout the night from 8 pm to 3 am	AN/

50 Machine Gun Coy.
Army Form C. 2118.

WAR DIARY
INTELLIGENCE SUMMARY. December 1917.

Place	Date	Hour	Summary of Events and Information	Remarks and references to Appendices
FRESQUIRES SECTOR.	31		Operations. Guns. Nil Enemys. Nil Artillery. Ours. No great activity. ORIVAL WOOD and GRAINCOURT shelled at intervals. Enemys. FRESQUIRES - HAVRINCOURT ROAD shelled at intervals throughout the period. HAVRINCOURT shelled during the morning with gas shells. Enemy defences. New trench } have have been observed. Wire } M.G.s Very active in right flank at 5.30 pm. T.M's. None observed. Dumps. A dump was observed to go up on the right flank at 5.30 pm. State of ground. Very hard & slippery. Movement behind enemy lines. Was not noticeable owing to poor visibility. Aeroplane activity. Very slight. Guns in action 3 Rounds expended 6000 Casualties Nil Gun positions last night as follows. No. 9 gun. Trench work & tracks in L9a " 10 " GRAINCOURT " 11 " New work in L9a and L8d.	Apps

Instructions regarding War Diaries and Intelligence Summaries are contained in F. S. Regs., Part II. and the Staff Manual respectively. Title pages will be prepared in manuscript.

WAR DIARY
or
INTELLIGENCE SUMMARY.
(Erase heading not required.)

50. Machine Gun Coy.   Army Form C. 2118.

January 1917.

Vol 23

Place	Date	Hour	Summary of Events and Information	Remarks and references to Appendices
GRAINCOURT SECTOR.	JAN. 1		Operations Artillery (Ours)... nil (Ours) Quiet except from 7.15 am 8.30 am on Right Flank (Enemy's).. nil (Enemy's) Active on right from 7.15 am - 8.30 am otherwise quiet. Enemy defences. New Work } hone observed. Wire } M.G's.... Normal — a M.G. firing from ORIVAL WOOD sweeps the road running through K.13a and K.13c at intervals. T.M's } None observed. DUMPS } State of ground. Hard + slippery. The snowfall last night obliterated all tracks. Movement. Transport + men observed at intervals at road K.19 and 20. South of BOULON WOOD. Aeroplane activity. a patrol of ours flew towards enemy lines about 9.30 am. otherwise no aeroplanes seen. Miscellaneous nil. Guns in action ... 3 Rounds expended 2,500 Casualties nil Change in position nil Work done. Continuation of yesterday. Guns tested + cleaned + belts filled. General maintenance of repair + condition Work to be done. Construction of A.A. emplacement. Construction of alternative position. General maintenance of repair + condition. Flash screens made.	AW

WAR DIARY

50 Machine Gun Coy Army Form C. 2118.

INTELLIGENCE SUMMARY

January 1918.

Place	Date	Hour	Summary of Events and Information	Remarks and references to Appendices
GRAINCOURT SECTOR Coy HQ	Jan 1		**Work to be done**: Positions in mchguns, trackdown of mchguns Targets engaged last night as follows:- No. 9 gun. New work & tracks in L9c No. 10 " GRAINCOURT No. 11 " New work in L8a and L8d } Time of firing 5.0 p.m – 5.30 a.m	
	2		**Observations** Ours } Nil Enemy's } **Artillery** Ours ... Quiet Enemy's ... Steady from 3.45 pm to 5 pm shared K.16d & S.6.2 M.G. positions at K.16d & S.9's and 4.2's and 5.9's at 3 pm with 4.2's and 5.9's at 2 pm **Enemy defences** New work } None observed Wire } M G's × roads in K24 & received attention at intervals throughout the night. T.M's A trench mortar was believed to be firing at 2 pm from about L.13 ~ 80.50 **Dumps** None observed. Stationary ground	Out

Army Form C. 2118.

WAR DIARY
INTELLIGENCE SUMMARY
(Erase heading not required.)

50 Machine Gun Coy
January 1918

Instructions regarding War Diaries and Intelligence Summaries are contained in F. S. Regs., Part II. and the Staff Manual respectively. Title pages will be prepared in manuscript.

Place	Date	Hour	Summary of Events and Information	Remarks and references to Appendices
GRAINCOURT SECTOR	2nd	Cont'd	Enemy Communications 7/d. Continual movement observed on road Movement Behind Enemy Lines south of BOURLON WOOD. Aeroplane Activity: Slight activity on both sides from 9.30 AM - 3.30 PM. Miscellaneous 7/d. Guns in Action 3 Rounds Expended 3,000. Casualties 7/d. Change of Position Left Section HQ moved to K23B 65.60. Work done Improvement of 7 & 5 Gun position. Coy HQ at K15d 90.15 strengthened. All positions and dugouts cleaned. Guns tested and cleaned. Belts filled. General maintenance of prepare and condition. Work to be done Continuation of above. A.A and alternative emplacements constructed where conditions of ground become suitable. Salvage collected and sent down. Miscellaneous Targets engaged last night as follows :- Target Gun LA JUSTICE X ROADS 9 GRAINCOURT 10 new work in 48.D. 11 3.0 PM Irregular bursts of fire from 8.0 PM - 3.0 AM	S/H/S J.H.S S/H/S

Army Form C. 2118.

WAR DIARY
INTELLIGENCE SUMMARY
(Erase heading not required.)

50 Machine Gun Coy
January, 1918.

Instructions regarding War Diaries and Intelligence Summaries are contained in F. S. Regs., Part II and the Staff Manual respectively. Title pages will be prepared in manuscript.

Place	Date	Hour	Summary of Events and Information	Remarks and references to Appendices
GRAINCOURT SECTOR	3rd		Guns in Action. 3. Rounds expended. 1500. Casualties. Nil. Change in position Nil. Guns listed and cleaned. Work done. Trench at No. 5 position deepened. Bells fitted. Salvage collected and sent down. General repair and condition of emplacements and dugouts maintained. Work to be done. Continuation of work in progress. AA. and alternative emplacements to be constructed when snow disappears. Salvage collected. General upkeep maintained. Miscellaneous Targets engaged last night as follows :-	AHS
			Gun Target	
		9	New work and Tracks in L 8 D.	
		10	GRAINCOURT	
		11	New work and Tracks in L 8 D. New work and Tracks in 8.0. PM - 3.0. AM.	
			Irregular bursts of fire from 8.0. PM - 3.0. AM.	
"	3rd		Operations Nil. Artillery Activity. (a) Ours. Active between 10.0. AM - 12 noon, and again at 3.30 PM - 4.15 PM (b) Enemy. Active between 3.0. PM - 4.30. PM. Special attention being paid to FLESQUIERES and RIBECOURT ROAD. Enemy Defences. (a) New work. None observed. (b) Wire. " " (c) MGs. Active between 10.0. AM - 11.0. AM. (d) TMs. None located (e) Dumps. Unable to make any observation owing to mist (f) State of Ground. Much softer after the recent thaw. Better for Traffic on roads and Tracks.	AHS

Army Form C. 2118.

WAR DIARY
INTELLIGENCE SUMMARY

(Erase heading not required.)

50. Machine Gun Coy.
January 1918.

Place	Date	Hour	Summary of Events and Information	Remarks and references to Appendices
GRAINCOURT SECTOR.	3rd Cont		Enemy Communications. Unable to get information concerning same. Aeroplane Activity Nil. Unable to get observation. Visibility too low. General Situation Calm. Miscellaneous Nil. Guns in Action. 3. Rounds expended. 3,000. Casualties Nil. Change in position. Nil. Work done. New emplacement constructed for No. 12 Gun. French deepened and cleaned at No. 5 Gun. Material salvaged. Guns tested and cleaned. Belts filled. General maintenance of repair and condition. Work to be done A.A. positions and alternative emplacements to be constructed when weather conditions are suitable. Position to be reconnoitred and constructed to cover sunken road in L.13 Material Salvaged General maintenance of repair and condition. Miscellaneous Targets engaged last night as follows:-	
			Gun Target 9 LA JUSTICE X ROADS 10 GRAINCOURT 11 New work in L.8.D. Irregular bursts of fire from 6.0 P.M - 1.0 A.M. Traversed 1° right and 1° left.	
"	4th		Operations Nil. Artillery Activity (a) Ours Active Between 10.30 P.M - 3.30 P.M. Otherwise normal. (b) Enemy. Extremely active throughout the day, especially between 10.0. A.M - 12 noon, when back areas and own batteries received special attention with gas shells. Tracks and Roads shelled with 5.9.S.	

Army Form C. 2118.

WAR DIARY
INTELLIGENCE SUMMARY.
(Erase heading not required.)

50 Machine Gun Coy
January 1918

Place	Date	Hour	Summary of Events and Information	Remarks and references to Appendices
GRAINCOURT SECTOR	7th	Cont'd	**Enemy Defences.** (a) New work. Enemy appear to be trench digging in L.1.8 and 9. (b) Wire. None observed. (c) MGs. " " (d) TMs. Enemy TM appears to fire from the right of ORIVAL WOOD about 7.0. pm 3.1.18. Gas shells being used. (e) Dumps. None located. (f) Slate & ground. Hard and slippery especially at night. Frost continues. **Aeroplane Activity.** (a) Ours. Active throughout the day. (b) Enemy. Extremely active all day. **Miscellaneous.** S.O.S. went up last night on left about 5.30 PM. Our Artillery opened out. No attack developed. 10 Enemy Observation Balloons up all day. Cloud of steam seen in vicinity of BOURLON WOOD probably Train on light Railway bringing up supplies. 1 Round expended 1500. Casualties Dil.	J.H.S.
	8th		**Guns in Action.** Continuation of above. Guns cleaned and tested. **Work done.** Belts filled. Salvage returned. General maintenance of repair and condition. New emplacement constructed for No. 12. Gun. AA and alternate emplacements to be built in BILHEM CHAPEL SWITCH. Salvage collected and returned. General maintenance of repair and condition. **Miscellaneous.** Targets engaged last night from 6.0 pm – 1.8. AM. GRAINCOURT.	J.H.S.

Army Form C. 2118.

WAR DIARY
INTELLIGENCE SUMMARY.
(Erase heading not required.)

50. Machine Gun Coy.
January, 1918.

Instructions regarding War Diaries and Intelligence Summaries are contained in F. S. Regs., Part II. and the Staff Manual respectively. Title pages will be prepared in manuscript.

Place	Date	Hour	Summary of Events and Information	Remarks and references to Appendices
GRAINCOURT SECTOR	5th		Operations Nil	
			Artillery	
			(a) Ours Very active throughout the day with intense fire on Enemy line also succeeded in silencing Hostile batteries during the night. Field batteries active all day, & throughout the night with harassing fire on Enemy lines.	
			(b) Enemy. Active between 2.0 PM - 3.30 PM	
			Enemy Defences	
			(a) New work } None observed.	
			(b) Wire }	
			(c) M.G.s Enemy M.G. very active during the night firing from direction of ORIVAL WOOD	
			(d) T.Ms. Hostile T.M fired on one from sunken road right of ORIVAL WOOD.	
			(e) Dumps Nil	
			(f) State of ground Hard and slippery.	
			Enemy Communications Nil	
			Enemy Dispositions Nil	
			Movement behind Enemy lines Men are seen walking about in large numbers in front of TRIANGULAR WOOD and in sunken road R/o the right front	
			Aeroplane Activity	
			(a) Ours Our planes very active throughout the day over Enemy lines	
			(b) Enemy. Hostile aircraft active during the early morning and fire down the road leading from RIBECOURT to FLESQUIÈRES.	
			Miscellaneous Nil	

Army Form C. 2118.

WAR DIARY

INTELLIGENCE SUMMARY.

(Erase heading not required.)

50 Machine Gun Coy
January 1918.

Instructions regarding War Diaries and Intelligence Summaries are contained in F.S. Regs., Part II. and the Staff Manual respectively. Title pages will be prepared in manuscript.

Place	Date	Hour	Summary of Events and Information	Remarks and references to Appendices
GRAINCOURT SECTOR	6th		Guns in Action 1. Rounds Expended 1200. Casualties Nil	
			Change in Position — No 7 and 8 Guns moved to BILHEM CHAPEL SWITCH in K29 d 60 90.	
			Work done Positions completed in BILHEM CHAPEL SWITCH for No. 7 and 8 Guns, accomodation made for teams. Guns tested and cleaned. Belts filled. Salvage collected. General upkeep maintained.	
			Work to be done Continuation of above. Positions for No. 7 and 8 Guns to be completed. AA and alternative positions to be made when weather conditions are suitable. AA and alternative positions to be constructed by BILHEM CHAPEL SWITCH Section HQ at K19 a 2060 to be cleaned and reconstructed where necessary. Salvage to be collected and sent down. General maintenance of gas mask. Kept up. No. 10 Gun fired on GRAINCOURT at intervals throughout the night. Traversing 1° Right and 1° Left.	AHS
			Miscellaneous. Nil	
	6th		Operations Nil	
			Enemy Defences Nil	
			State of Ground. Still hard + slippery bad for traffic.	
			Artillery Ours very active own left front Enemys Quiet.	
			Aeroplane Activity Both sides active all day.	
			Miscellaneous. Nil	AHS

WAR DIARY

INTELLIGENCE SUMMARY

50. Machine Gun Coy.
January 1918.

Army Form C. 2118.

Place	Date	Hour	Summary of Events and Information	Remarks and references to Appendices
	6TH		Night of Jan. 6, 1918. Company relieved in the line by 141. M.G. Coy. Relief complete by 9.0 A.M. Casualties :- NIL. Guns Teams on relief march to BILLETS near HAPLINCOURT and occupy Huts at SANDERS CAMP [Q.4.B.4.D] Ground still very hard and slippery. Bad for marching and Horse traffic. Company arrive safely in Camp 1.0 A.M. 7/1/18. No one fell out on line of march. Total Casualties :- NIL.	SMS
SANDERS CAMP	7TH	7.0 A.M.	Reveille. 12 noon. Muster clean parade. Afternoon spent in :- Building Cook Houses digging Latrines improving Beds in Huts, and improving and cleaning up Camp	SMS
"	8TH	6.30 A.M.	Reveille 7.30 A.M. Company parade for BATHS at HAPLINCOURT. Foot friction drill in Huts under Section Officers. Rest of morning spent in cleaning and checking Guns and Gun gear under Section arrangements. Kit and clothing inspection. 3.0 P.M. Iron Ration and Box Respirators inspection. 4.0 P.M. Sections parade for refitting clothing and all deficiencies in Kit made up.	SMS
		2.0 P.M.		
"	9TH	5.0 A.M.	Hostile Aircraft busy over our lines, and Bombs dropped in vicinity of HAPLINCOURT. Casualties :- NIL.	SMS
		7.15 A.M.	Reveille. 7.45 A.M. Interior economy and Muster Clean Parade.	
		8.30 A.M.	Foot friction drill. Rest of morning spent in completion of checking Gun gear, etc., followed by Cleaning and Testing Guns and cleaning Limbers.	
		2.0 P.M.	Pos. of each Gun Team parade under Section Sergeants and drawn Gun Limbers etc. New A.A. precautions constructed. Rain fell during the night, and Thaw replacement brought into force.	
"	10TH	7.0 A.M.	Reveille. 8.30 A.M. Company parade for a march. 9.15 A.M. Foot friction drill. Rifle and equipment inspection 11.0 A.M. Company paid out Warning order to stand to ready for the Line received. Fighting Limbers packed and full preparations carried out. Coy M.Q. established at J.35.d.2.6	SMS
		10.0 A.M.		
		12 noon		
		3.0 P.M.	Company proceed to take up positions in reserve. Coy M.Q. established at J.35.d.2.6 Casualties :- NIL.	
"	11TH		After standing to for one night. Company march back to Huts at SANDERS CAMP, vacated the day previous. Situation Normal. One man reported missing at Roll Call but reports himself later in the day. Casualties NIL. Heavy rain fell Rest of day spent in cleaning of Clothing and Equipment during the night	SMS

WAR DIARY
INTELLIGENCE SUMMARY.
(Erase heading not required.)

Army Form C. 2118.

50 Machine Gun Coy
January 1918

Place	Date	Hour	Summary of Events and Information	Remarks and references to Appendices
SANDERS CAMP.	12TH	7.45 AM	Reveille. 9.0 AM. Foot traction drill. 9.45 AM. Coy parade for cleaning Guns, Gun gear, Ammunition Belts, and Limbers. 11.30 AM. Lecture by Section Officers. Duties in the line. 12 noon. All Nos 2 of each Gun Team proceed to the line — to receive necessary information regarding positions Field's of fire, etc, prior to 52 M.G. Coy being relieved the day following, on the GRAINCOURT SECTOR.	S.H.S.
"	13TH	7.15 AM	Reveille. 9.0 AM. Packing Limbers for the line under Section arrangements. Rest of morning spent in cleaning Billets under supervision of Section Officers. 12 noon. Coy parade for the line. I proceed by ROYAULCOURT and PLANK TRACK to HAVRINCOURT SQUARE where guides conduct Company to COY. H.Q. [K.15.d.90.15.] and Gun Teams are taken to their respective positions in the line. Details move by Transport to VELU WOOD. Relief complete 9.50 PM. 13/1/18. Casualties NIL. Trenches very bad in places.	S.H.S.
COY IN LINE. GRAINCOURT SECTOR.			Map Reference of Guns as follows:—	S.H.S.

COY. H.Q. - K.15.d.90.15.

"A" Section	"B" Section	"C" Section	"D" Section
Sec. H.Q. K.16.b.35.60	Sec. H.Q. K.10.d.85.70	Sec. H.Q. K.22.b.60.60	Sec. H.Q. K.16.a.95.70.
No. 1. Gun. K.17.b.55.55	No. 3. Gun. K.10.d.80.67	No. 9. Gun. K.16.d.90.50	No. 11. Gun. K.16.b.65.75
No. 2. Gun. K.17.b.40.60	No. 4. Gun. K.10.d.80.70	No.10. Gun. K.16.b.50.60	No. 12. Gun. K.16.b.10.90.
No. 5. Gun. K.16.b.35.65	No. 7. Gun. K.10.d.20.50	No.13. Gun. K.22.b.49.80	No. 15. Gun. K.16.a.52.90.
No. 6. Gun. K.17.b.35.70	No. 8. Gun. K.10.d.15.65	No.14. Gun. K.22.b.50.75	No. 16. Gun. K.16.a.55.95.

WAR DIARY

INTELLIGENCE SUMMARY.

(Erase heading not required.)

Army Form C. 2118.

50 Machine Gun Coy.

January 1918.

Instructions regarding War Diaries and Intelligence Summaries are contained in F.S. Regs., Part II. and the Staff Manual respectively. Title pages will be prepared in manuscript.

Place	Date	Hour	Summary of Events and Information	Remarks and references to Appendices
GRAINCOURT SECTOR.	14th		Guns in Action :- NIL. Casualties :- NIL. Rounds Expended :- NIL. Change in Position :- Company moved from SANDERS CAMP to right Sector of Divisional front. Work done :- Guns Tested and cleaned. Belts filled. A.A. emplacements constructed. Trenches in vicinity of Gun positions cleaned, and improved. Salvage Collected. Work to be done :- General maintenance of repair and condition. Operations. (a) Own Relief of HUMOUR yesterday 13/1/18. (b) Enemy NIL. Artillery Activity (a) Own Below normal. (b) Enemy Quiet. A Barrage was placed on the left Divisional Sector at 5.0 P.M. lasting for 15 minutes. Enemy Defences. (a) Dug work (b) Wire (c) M.Gs (d) T.Ms (e) Dumps — None observed. State of Ground. Occasional bursts sweeping our Parapets. Movement behind Enemy Line. Nothing to report. None observed owing to mist. Very bad for the patrol till nightfall, when Raid Front set in, made at fumes. None observed. Aeroplane Activity (a) Own Active all day. (b) Enemy Fairly Active. Four observation Balloons were up for the greater part of the day being drawn down about 4.0 P.M. An Enemy plane brought down one of our observation Balloons in flames. Forcing both occupants to descend by Parachute.	S/H/S

Army Form C. 2118.

WAR DIARY
INTELLIGENCE SUMMARY
(Erase heading not required.)

50. Machine Gun Coy
January 1918

Place	Date	Hour	Summary of Events and Information	Remarks and references to Appendices
GRAINCOURT SECTOR	15th		Guns in Action :- 2. Rounds Expended :- 1500. Casualties :- NIL.	
			Change in Position :- NIL.	
			Work done :- Dug outs, Trenches and Gun positions cleaned and improved. Zero lines checked. Guns tested and cleaned. Belts filled. Salvage Collected. General maintenance of repair and condition. A.A. emplacements constructed. Gun positions revetted and improved generally. Trench No.15 Gun position deepened. dug Trench at No.15. Gun position deepened. Salvage collected and sent down.	
			Work to be done :- General maintenance of repair and condition. Targets engaged last night as follows :- No.9. Gun Deswork and area in K.5.D. No.10. Gun. Enfilading Trenches in K.4.D. Irregular bursts from 10.0.P.M. - 12 midnight.	
			Miscellaneous :- NIL.	
			Operations. (a.) Ours. (b.) Enemys. } Quiet throughout the day. Fairly Quiet. CANAL at K.20.B. shelled during the afternoon, and HAVRINCOURT shelled during the night. Active on night at 10.15.P.M.	
			Artillery Activity. (a.) Ours. (b.) Enemys. }	
			Enemy Defences. (a.) New work. (b.) Wire. (c.) M.Gs. } None observed. Enemy M.G fires along our Parapet at K.16.D. every night.	
			(d.) T.Ms. Enemy T.M. fired at 4.0.P.M. from approximately a position in K.4.D.	
			(e.) Dumps. Nothing to report. Are same.	

WAR DIARY

INTELLIGENCE SUMMARY.

50. Machine Gun Coy.
January 1918.

Army Form C. 2118.

Place	Date	Hour	Summary of Events and Information	Remarks and references to Appendices
GRAINCOURT SECTOR.	15TH	Cont'd	State of Ground. Very soft, and water logged. Enemy Communications } Nothing to report. Enemy Dispositions } Movement behind Enemy Line. None observed owing to mist. Aeroplane Activity. None observed. Weather conditions not favourable. Miscellaneous. NIL. Guns in Action:- 2. Rounds Expended:- 1,500. Casualties:- NIL Change in Positions. NIL Work done.	JHS
"	16TH		Continuation of work in progress. Water and mud removed from Gun positions. Trenches and Dug outs generally cleaned. [This has hindered further work] Guns cleaned. Belts filled. Maintenance Section. Repair and condition. Continuation of above. H.Q. dugout at No. 14. Gun repaired Sump Pits dug when ductwork are available. All Saps generally cleaned and repaired. Trenches and Gun positions cleaned and drained of water. A.A. positions to be completed. General repair maintained. Work to be done. Miscellaneous. Targets engaged last night as follows:- No. 13. Gun. :- Tracks and new work S.E of K 5.D. [B ZONE] No. 14. Gun. :- Tracks and new work in K 6.D. [C ZONE] No. 13. Gun. fired from 7.0. PM - 10.0. PM. No. 14. Gun. fired from 1.0. AM - 4.0. AM. Total Rounds expended :- 1,500. Enemy Defences. (a) New work } (b) Wire } NIL. (c) Dumps. } (d) M.G's } QUIET (e) T.M.s. } Enemy Communications } } No information. Enemy Dispositions } Aeroplane Activity. Enemy M.G very active on Railway in vicinity of K.16 & 35.65. Low visibility rendered observation impossible. NIL.	JHS
"	16TH		Operations. (a) Own. } NIL. (b) Enemy. } Artillery Activity. (a) Ours. } QUIET (b) Enemy's } State of Ground. Very bad. Movement behind Enemy Line. None observed. Aeroplane Activity. NIL	JHS

Army Form C. 2118.

WAR DIARY
INTELLIGENCE SUMMARY.

50 Machine Gun Coy
January 1918

(Erase heading not required.)

Instructions regarding War Diaries and Intelligence Summaries are contained in F. S. Regs., Part II. and the Staff Manual respectively. Title pages will be prepared in manuscript.

Place	Date	Hour	Summary of Events and Information	Remarks and references to Appendices
GRAINCOURT SECTOR	17th		Guns in Action 3. Rounds Expended. 3000. Casualties:- NIL. Change in Position. NIL. Work done. Continuation of work in progress. Entrance to Nos 3 and 4 Guns dugouts revetted. All other dugouts cleaned out. Trenches and Gun positions improved. Trench commenced to No. 16 Gun position. Guns tested and cleaned. Belts filled. Salvage Collected and sent down. General maintenance of Sap and condition. Work to be done. Continuation of above. Sap entrances to be revetted. Trench to Nos 16 Gun completed. Sump Pits dug and positions completed. Moving Nos 3 and 11 guns and Arrangements made for connecting Guns with O.Ps. Salvage to be collected. General repair and condition maintained. Miscellaneous. test night in co-operation with Artillery Nos 9, 10, and 13. Guns fired on the same targets at the same time.	JAHS
GRAINCOURT SECTOR	17th		Operations (a) Ours. } Nil (b) Enemy. } Artillery Activity (a) Ours. Half minute bursts on Enemy lines of communication from 6.0 PM. to 8.50 PM. (b) Enemy. GEORGE STREET AREA in K.15.D. shelled during the morning. Vicinity of K.17.b. 35 70 shelled intermittently during evening. Enemy Defences (a) New Work } None observed. (b) Mine. } (c) M.Gs. Enemy M.G. sweeps parapet in vicinity of K.16.d. 0675, K.16.d. to 90, K.16.a. 6290 and K.16.a. 5595. One also appears to be trained on K.16.b. 35 65 (d) T.Ms. 8. T.M. shells fell between K.16.b. 0675 and K.16.a. 5595 about 8.30. PM. (e) Dumps. None observed.	AAHS

Army Form C. 2118.

WAR DIARY

50 Machine Gun Coy.
January 1918.

INTELLIGENCE SUMMARY.

(Erase heading not required.)

Instructions regarding War Diaries and Intelligence Summaries are contained in F.S. Regs., Part II. and the Staff Manual respectively. Title pages will be prepared in manuscript.

Place	Date	Hour	Summary of Events and Information	Remarks and references to Appendices
GRAINCOURT SECTOR.	17TH	Cont.	State of Ground: Still very wet - with no improvement. Movement behind Enemy Line: None observed. Visibility bad. Enemy Dispositions: None available. Enemy Communications: Nil. Aeroplane Activity: Nil. Bad weather conditions prevents flying. Miscellaneous: Nil. Guns in Action: 2 Rounds Expended 3500. Casualties: Nil. Change in Position. No. 3 Gun moved to K16c 60.60. No. 11 Gun moved to K16c 60.55.	A.H.S.
"	18TH		Work done. Continuation of yesterday. No. 12 position reconstructed. Position of No. 3 and 11 Guns constructed. Trenches cleaned and improved in vicinity of all Gun positions. Continuation of cleaning and clearing out Dug outs. Trench to No. 15 and No. 16 Guns cleared and rebuilt where fallen in. Sump Pits dug. Salvage Collected. Guns tested and cleaned. General maintenance of repair and condition. Work to be done. Trenches and positions revetted. Continuation of work in progress. A.A. Emplacement constructed. Salvage to be Collected. General repair maintained. Miscellaneous. Guns fired last night as follows:- No. 5 Gun Target. 13 K 5 B. Tracks (G. Zone) 14 K 6 C. Tracks (C. Zone) Irregular bursts from 7 P.M. to 10 P.M., and 1 A.M. to 4 A.M.	

WAR DIARY
INTELLIGENCE SUMMARY.

50. Machine Gun Coy
January 1918.

Army Form C. 2118.

(Erase heading not required.)

Place	Date	Hour	Summary of Events and Information	Remarks and references to Appendices
GRAINCOURT SECTOR	18TH	Cont'd	Operations (a) Own } Nil (b) Enemy } Artillery Activity (a) Ours. Quiet. (b) Enemy. General shells EASTERN and of POST OFFICE TRENCH with 5.9s at 3.10 PM.? Odd shooting into HAVRINCOURT at intervals. Enemy Defences (a) Newwork } None observed (b) Wire } (c) M.P.Gs. Quiet (d) T.Ms. Nil (e) Dumps. None observed. Low visibility (f) State of Ground. Stiff. Very hard. Enemy Dispositions. Nil. Enemy Communications. Nothing to report on same. Aeroplane Activity. Bad weather conditions prevent flying. Miscellaneous. Nil. Guns in Action: 3. Rounds Expended 6000 rounds. Casualties Nil. Change in Position. Nil. Work done.	AHS
	19TH		Continuation of yesterday. New emplacement constructed for No. 10 Gun. All emplacements cleaned and improved. Duckboards constructed for Nos. 15 and 16 Gun positions. Trench from No. 15 and 16 gun positions cleared. Sump pits dug at Coy HQ Trenches and gun positions cleared and generally improved. General maintenance of condition. Guns tested and cleaned. Belts filled.	AHS

Army Form C. 2118.

WAR DIARY
INTELLIGENCE SUMMARY.
(Erase heading not required.)

50 Machine Gun Coy.
January 1918.

Place	Date	Hour	Summary of Events and Information	Remarks and references to Appendices
GRAINCOURT SECTOR	19th		Work to be done. Continuation of work in progress. Trench from Do 15 and 16 positions to be dug. Sap head at 17o.4. Gun position to be rebuilt. Unknown in General improvement to all positions. A.A. mountings put in position. Salvage to be collected and sent down. Miscellaneous Guns fired last night on enemy in { K 4. B } C. zone. No. 3 Gun. Target :- Tracks in K 4. B No. 11 Gun. Target :- Tracks in K 5 No. 14 Gun. Target :- New work and M.G. positions at K 11. B 10. 60. (A zone) Irregular bursts of fire at intervals, in accordance with shooting programme. Operations. (a) Ours. } Nil. (b) Enemy. } Artillery Activity (a) Ours. Quiet except for occasional 18 pdr shooting at intervals during day. Retaliation fire for enemy barrage on left Sector at 6.25 P.M. and on Left Battn Sector at 2.0 A.M. (b) Enemy. Very active. Left Battn Sector shelled from 2 A.M.- 3 A.M. Barrage placed on left Battn Sector at 6.25 P.M, and dieing at 7.10 P.M. Barrage placed on left Brigade Sector at 2.0 A.M. Enemy Defences (a) New work. } (b) Wire. } None observed (c) Dumps. } (d) M.G's. Fairly active (e) T.M's. A great number of T.M's fired during each hostile barrage.	

WAR DIARY / INTELLIGENCE SUMMARY

50. Machine Gun Coy.
January 1918

Place	Date	Hour	Summary of Events and Information	Remarks and references to Appendices
GRAINCOURT SECTOR	19th Cont'd.		State of Ground: Trenches bad. In many places impassable. Enemy Dispositions: Nil. Enemy Communications: Nil. Movement behind Enemy Line: Troops observed in GRAINCOURT at intervals. Aeroplane Activity: (a) Ours: Except for Artillery "Spotters" our planes were not very active. (b) Enemy: A flight of six Enemy planes were over our lines from 6.0 A.M to 11. 10 A.M. Guns in Action: 3. Rounds Expended: 3,250. Casualties: Wounded O/R One. [Rifle fire.] Work done: Continuation of yesterday's work continued on No. 10 emplacement. New position for No. 2 Gun constructed. Trenches and positions cleaned and cleared. A.A. Mountings fixed at No. 3 and 11. Positions. Guns listed and cleaned. Belts filled. Salvage collected and sent down. General maintenance of repair and condition.	@AHS
"	20th		Work to be done: Continuation of above. Completion of No. 10 position. Fixing tracks & A.A. mountings when available. Reconstruction of Trench at No. 3. position where blown in by Shell fire. Trenches and gun emplacements cleaned out. General maintenance of repair and condition. Guns in Action: No. 6 Gun fired against Hostile aircraft from 11. A.M. – 12. noon. Usual Night firing done by No. 13 and 14 Guns. Target engaged :– GRAINCOURT. [C. ZONE.] Bullets at irregular intervals from 7.0. P.M. to 10.0. P.M and 1.0 A.M. to 4.0. A.M.	@AHS

WAR DIARY
INTELLIGENCE SUMMARY
(Erase heading not required.)

Army Form C. 2118.

50. Machine Gun Coy.
January 1918

Place	Date	Hour	Summary of Events and Information	Remarks and references to Appendices
GRAINCOURT SECTOR	20th Con't		**Operations.** Nil. **Artillery Activity** (a) **Ours.** More active than for the last few days. The front opposite the Division on left being shelled with Heavies throughout the day. BOURLON WOOD and GRAINCOURT were fired on during the period. (b) **Enemy.** More active than usual along the whole front. — Though not systematic. HAVRINCOURT was shelled with 5.9s throughout the day, getting more lively towards dusk. Shells falling once every three minutes. During the afternoon Gas Shells and Whizz Bangs fell in K.18.D and K.21.B. Counter Battery work carried out during the day. **Enemy Defences** (a) Dug work.} No new work of mine observed. (b) Wire.} (c) M.Gs. The usual parapet sweeping, but not so much indirect fire. (d) T. Ms. Quieter yesterday than previously. (e) Dumps. None observed. (f) Stati & Ground. Still very wet. No improvement. **Movement behind Enemy line.** The usual individual movement observed in GRAINCOURT and vicinity throughout the day. **Enemy Communications.** Nil **Enemy Dispositions.** Nil	

Army Form C. 2118.

WAR DIARY
INTELLIGENCE SUMMARY

50 Machine Gun Coy.
January 1918.

(Erase heading not required.)

Place	Date	Hour	Summary of Events and Information	Remarks and references to Appendices
GRAINCOURT SECTOR	20th		**Aeroplane Activity**	
			(a) Ours. Active all day. A Patrol flew over the Enemy lines at 8.0 A.M. From 8.0 AM Two flights of Camels were over the Enemy lines evidently for protection for the numerous BE 2 c. in flight. These planes were heavily engaged by Hostile A.A. Guns. BE 2c were very active throughout the day and were engaged by A.A. Guns whenever they were in range.	
			(b) Enemy. A flight of Hostile planes crossed our lines at dawn. At 8. o'clock three small black Machines crossed our lines. They were engaged by A.A. and M.G. fire and caused to split up into no formation, eventually being driven back to their own lines. Individual Planes were active throughout the day and were very numerous, the majority being on Patrol.	
			Miscellaneous. Enemy Machine Guns were not so much in evidence firing against Our Planes in the Brigade Sector, as in the Sectors of Division on Flank.	

WAR DIARY

INTELLIGENCE SUMMARY

(Erase heading not required.)

Army Form C. 2118.

50. Machine Gun Coy.
January 1918.

Place	Date	Hour	Summary of Events and Information	Remarks and references to Appendices
GRAINCOURT SECTOR	21st		Guns in Action: 4. Rounds Expended. 8,000. Casualties. NIL. Change in Position: NIL Work done: Continuation of work in progress. A.A. mounting fixed at No. 6. Gun. Completion of emplacement at No. 10. position. Telephone fixed up to No. 9. Sniping Gun and Brigade O.P. No. 15 Gun position improved. Nos. 9 and 2. emplacements revetted. Ammunition cleaned. All emplacements in vicinity cleaned. Belts filled. Guns tested and cleaned. Salvage Collected. General maintenance of repair and condition. Work to be done: Continuation of above. A.A. mounting fixed at No.12. position. Fixing further A.A. mountings when available. Salvage to be collected and sent down. Guns fired last night as follows:— Miscellaneous. No. 3. Gun } No. 11. Gun } Tracks etc and road at K5a9060. No. 13. Gun } GRAINCOURT and TRACKS in K5D. [C. Zone] No. 14. Gun } No 3 and 11 Guns fired in accordance with notification that probable hostile relief was in progress. Fire applied at irregular intervals from 10 PM - 3. AM. Nos.13, and 14 Guns fired bursts throughout the night from 10. PM - 4. AM. Operations. NIL. Artillery: (a) Own. Normal. (b) Enemy. Quieter than previous day:- more attention being paid to back areas - Counter battery work also carried out.	A.F.S.
"	21st		Enemy Defences: (a) Dew work } None seen. (b) Wire } (c) M.Gs. One observed firing from left near corner of ORIVAL WOOD (d) T.Ms. NIL (e) Dumps } None observed. (f) State of ground. Very muddy still.	A.F.S.

WAR DIARY
INTELLIGENCE SUMMARY.

50. Machine Gun. Coy.
January. 1918.

Army Form C. 2118.

Place	Date	Hour	Summary of Events and Information	Remarks and references to Appendices
GRAINCOURT SECTOR	21st Cont.		**Movement behind Enemy lines.** Troops observed in GRAINCOURT at intervals throughout the day. Otherwise not noticeable as usual. **Aeroplane Activity** (a) Ours. Fairly Active. Artillery planes up all day, and were shelled when within range of enemy A.A Guns. (b) Enemy. Active though mostly Artillery planes. A flight of five fighting planes flew own lines and then turned track towards their own lines at 12.30 PM by A.A fire Enemy plane accounted for one of ours behind GRAINCOURT at 11.0 PM. 20/1/18. **Miscellaneous** An orange coloured Rocket was sent up by the Enemy. from the head of BOURLON WOOD at about 4.15 PM. No appeared action followed. One of own planes was firing Tracer bullets into GRAINCOURT at 4.30 PM. 20/1/18. **Guns in Action.** 4. Rounds Expended. 3,200. Casualties. NIL. **Change in Position.** No. 11 Gun to K16c 58 65. **Work done.** New emplacement constructed for No. 11 Gun. No. 15 position improved. Find slip remade at No. 12 position. Trenches and dugouts generally cleaned and improved. Material carried to positions. Guns tested and cleaned. Belts filled. Salvage collected and sent down. General maintenance of repair and condition. **Work to be done.** Continuation of work in progress. Pit prop mountings for AA proceed at No. 5 and 11 positions. Camouflaging No. 9 Sniping Gun position. Telephone fitted to Div. O.P. from Sniping Gun. Trenches cleaned and repaired. General maintenance of repair and condition.	JHS.
"	22nd			JHS.

WAR DIARY

INTELLIGENCE SUMMARY.

50. Machine Gun Coy
January, 1918

Army Form C. 2118.

Place	Date	Hour	Summary of Events and Information	Remarks and references to Appendices
GRAINCOURT SECTOR.	22nd	Cont'd	**Miscellaneous** Targets engaged last night as follows:- Gun Target 3 GRAINCOURT and TRACKS (C. zone) 10 E28 D 40.20 and Trenches etc. 11 GRAINCOURT (C. zone) 14 " Irregular bursts of fire applied from :- 1.0. A.M. to 7.0. A.M. No. 3 Gun fired 200 rounds at hostile plane at 7.0. A.M.	
"	23rd		**Operations** NIL. **Artillery** (a) Ours: Quiet during the day. Battery fire carried out frequently by 18 Pdrs during the night and ordinary gun fire frequently. Quieter than previous day. (b) Enemy: **Enemy Defences** (a) Bell work K } None seen (b) Wire (c) M.Gs. Usual fire at intervals. Indirect fire during night (d) T.Ms. None located (e) Dumps (f) State of Ground Muddy and still a great impediment to movement. Movement behind Enemy line: None observed except the usual individual movement in GRAINCOURT, which appears to be less. **Enemy Dispositions** None available. **Enemy Communications.** Nil. **Aeroplane Activity** Slight on both sides. **Miscellaneous** The same orange coloured light as reported yesterday was again sent up from the WEST near of BOURLON WOOD at 4.0. P.M.	

WAR DIARY
INTELLIGENCE SUMMARY.
(Erase heading not required.)

Army Form C. 2118.

50. Machine Gun Coy
January 1918.

Place	Date	Hour	Summary of Events and Information	Remarks and references to Appendices
GRAINCOURT SECTOR	23rd		Guns in Action 3 Rounds Expended 6,500 Casualties NIL.	
			Change in position NIL.	
			Work done Continuation of yesterday. Positions for No. 3 and 41 Guns dugout at No. 3 position cleaned out and repaired. No. 1 and 2 positions revetted. AA position completed at No. 12 Gun. Trench cleared to No. 15 and 16 Guns. No. 9 Sniping emplacement complete. Improvement to road to ration Dump near Coy H.Q. K15A 90.15. All positions and dugouts cleaned and repairs maintained. Guns tested and cleaned. Belts filled.	
			Work to be done Continuation of above. No. 3 and 11 positions completed. General maintenance of repair and condition.	
			Miscellaneous AA Guns fired 2,008 rounds at Hostile planes during the day. Targets engaged last night as follows:-	

			Gun Target.
			     3 K5A 80.66. Tracks + Roads.
			     11 X Roads. K5B 50+0.
			     14. K5A 80.60. Tracks + Roads.	

			Irregular bursts of fire from 1.0 A.M. — 4.0 A.M.	
			Operations NIL.	
"	23rd		**Artillery**: (a) Own: Quiet till dark when various Targets were engaged, and usual harassing fire carried out.	
			(b) Enemy. Quiet all day. AA Guns very active against our planes. Shelling of HAVRINCOURT COPSE at K22 A and CANAL at intervals throughout the day. HAVRINCOURT Gas shells sent into HAVRINCOURT during the night	

Army Form C. 2118.

WAR DIARY
INTELLIGENCE SUMMARY

(Erase heading not required.)

50. Machine Gun Coy
January 1918

Instructions regarding War Diaries and Intelligence Summaries are contained in F.S. Regs., Part II. and the Staff Manual respectively. Title pages will be prepared in manuscript.

Place	Date	Hour	Summary of Events and Information	Remarks and references to Appendices
GRAINCOURT SECTOR	23rd Contd		Enemy Defences	
			(a) Dew work. Done Observed	
			(b) Wire. " "	
			(c) M.G.s. Not so active as usual.	
			(d) T.Ms None located	
			(e) Dumps. Nil	
			(f) Stats of Ground. Still very bad.	
			Enemy Communications. NIL. Enemy Defences. None available	
			Movement behind Enemy Line. Not so noticeable as previously	
			Slight movement in GRAINCOURT during day.	
			Movement observed round FACTORY in JE2+C	
			Aeroplane Activity	
			(a) Own. Active throughout the day.	
			(b) Enemy. Very active during the morning from daybreak. Three flights of five planes each in the air at about 10.30 AM. apparently guarding slower flying machines.	
			One was driven off and formation broken up by AA. and M.G. fire.	
			Miscellaneous	
			From 3.30 P.M. – 3.45 P.M. Lamp Signalling was observed from K16c65 60 on a true bearing of 54° at about a distance of 2,000 yards.	
			Red light being used.	

Army Form C. 2118.

WAR DIARY
INTELLIGENCE SUMMARY.
(Erase heading not required.)

50 Machine Gun Coy
January. 1918.

Instructions regarding War Diaries and Intelligence Summaries are contained in F.S. Regs., Part II. and the Staff Manual respectively. Title pages will be prepared in manuscript.

Place	Date	Hour	Summary of Events and Information	Remarks and references to Appendices
GRAINCOURT SECTOR.	24th		**Guns in Action** 3. **Rounds Expended** 3,500. **Change of Position** NIL. **Casualties Wounded in Action** Officers. One LIEUT J.E. MILLS (T.F.) Ranks Three. [All Gassed.] **Work done.** Continuation of yesterday. Resetting sides and cleaning Travel Dugouts at No.1, + 2. AA guns. AA position at No.12 Gun completed. Belts filled positions all cleaned. Material cannot up. Gun tested and cleaned. General maintenance of repair and condition. Salvage collected and conditions maintained. **Work to be done.** Continuation of above. **Miscellaneous** Guns fired last night as follows:-	
			Target. Tracks etc in K5A K5A 8060 and vicinity. GRAINCOURT	
			Gun Bursts of fire from 10.0 p.m – 4.0 A.M	
			3	
			11	
			14 Irregular	
			Operations NIL.	
			Artillery. (a) Ours. Quiet - Usual harassing fire throughout the period. (b) Enemy. Very active during the morning with Gas shells. No. 13 and 14 GdNs in K22A were heavily shelled from 9.0 A.M – 10.0 A.M. HAVRINCOURT and FLESQUIERES were also shelled about 10 per minute during the morning with Gas shells.	ffHS
— " —	24th		**Enemy Defences.** Dew work Wire Done Observed. M.G.S Usual Indirect Fire. T.M.S Quiet. A. Zone located. **State of Ground.** Still Very bad.	ffHS

Army Form C. 2118.

WAR DIARY
INTELLIGENCE SUMMARY.
(Erase heading not required.)

50. Machine Gun Coy.
January 1918

Instructions regarding War Diaries and Intelligence Summaries are contained in F. S. Regs., Part II. and the Staff Manual respectively. Title pages will be prepared in manuscript.

Place	Date	Hour	Summary of Events and Information	Remarks and references to Appendices
GRAINCOURT SECTOR	24th	Cont'd	Movement behind Enemy Line — None Observed. Enemy Communications — Nil. Enemy Dispositions — Nil. Aeroplane Activity — Slight. Guns in Action — Ammunition Expended 2250 rounds in Action:- Casualties — Officers One 2/Lt E.S. FORD (T.S.) % Rank's Four. [ALL gassed.] Change in Position — Nil. Work done — Continuation of work in progress. Trenches cleaned. Position at No 12 Gun altered. Belts filled. Guns listed and cleaned. Salvage collected. General maintenance of repair and condition. Work to be done — Continuation of above. New S.O.S. line laid Trench to No. 15 and its position to be completed when Material is available. Trenches cleaned at No. 1 and 2 Gun positions. Miscellaneous — Targets engaged last night as follows.	Att's
"	25th		Gun — Target 13 — K5.a.2075 } and vicinity. 14 — K5.d.8075 } Bursts of one minute duration at the following times:- 7.15 p.m. 8.30 p.m. 8.45 p.m. 10.0 p.m. and 4.30 A.M. 500 rounds were fired at hostile aircraft during the day. No. 9 Sniping M.G in connection to Bde. O.P. fired at movement at 12.30 p.m 1.15 p.m and 2.0 p.m with good results one man seen to fall. Party scattered	

WAR DIARY
INTELLIGENCE SUMMARY.
(Erase heading not required).

Army Form C. 2118.

50 Machine Gun Coy.
January, 1918.

Place	Date	Hour	Summary of Events and Information	Remarks and references to Appendices
GRAINCOURT SECTOR	25th		Operations (a) Own. On receipt of message on the phone from Bde. O.P. To 9. Sniping Gun successfully dealt with party of the enemy at 12.30 pm 1.15 pm and 2.0 pm. (b) Enemy. Nil. Artillery (a) Own. Quiet. A.A. Guns active against Enemy planes (b) Enemy. Very active from 4.0 pm to 6.45 pm. HAVRINCOURT was heavily bombarded with Mustard Gas shells. Usual activity on CANAL during the day. A.A. Guns less active than usual. Enemy Defences (a) New work None seen (b) Wire. (c) M.G.s Usual Indirect fire (d) T.M.S. None located. (e) Dumps None available (f) State of Ground. Bad. Movement behind Enemy line. Slight. The usual movement in GRAINCOURT Enemy Dispositions. Nil Enemy Communications. None available Aeroplane Activity. Both sides very active throughout the period. The Enemy A.A. Guns were not so active against our planes as usual. Miscellaneous. Nil	

WAR DIARY
INTELLIGENCE SUMMARY

Army Form C. 2118.

50. Machine Gun Coy
January, 1918.

(Erase heading not required.)

Place	Date	Hour	Summary of Events and Information	Remarks and references to Appendices
GRAINCOURT SECTOR	26TH		Guns in Action 3 Rounds Expended 4,500 Casualties Wounded O/R One [Gas] Work done Continuation of yesterday Gas barrage lines laid out General maintenance of repair and condition Guns tested and cleaned All Belts filled Work to be done Miscellaneous Continuation of above and handing over to incoming Coy. [51 M G Coy]	Nil Change of Position Nil
"	26TH		A.A. Guns fired 1500 rounds throughout the day at Hostile aircraft. 70, 13 and 14 Guns fired into GRAINCOURT at intervals from 10.0 p.m. to 4.0 a.m. Six Hostile Balloons up during the morning and were taken down about 2.30 p.m. Operations (a) Own Brigade relief carried out during period (b) Enemy Nil. Artillery (a) Own (b) Enemy's Quiet except against hostile planes. Active Sector on right, shelled during morning HAVRINCOURT and area shelled throughout the day. AA. Guns active against our planes. Enemy Defences. (a) New work None seen (b) Wire (c) M Gs Usual activity (d) T Ms (e) Dumps None yet seen (f) State of Ground Ground much heavier, and worse for movement	

Army Form C. 2118.

WAR DIARY
INTELLIGENCE SUMMARY
(Erase heading not required.)

50. Machine Gun Coy.
January, 1918.

Instructions regarding War Diaries and Intelligence Summaries are contained in F.S. Regs., Part II. and the Staff Manual respectively. Title pages will be prepared in manuscript.

Place	Date	Hour	Summary of Events and Information	Remarks and references to Appendices
GRAINCOURT SECTOR.	26th	Cont'd	Enemy Communications Unknown. Enemy Dispositions Unknown. Movement behind Enemy Line None observed. Aeroplane Activity (a) Ours. Very active all day. Three BE2c returned from a long distance behind the enemy line, but were not attacked except by AA and M.G. fire. Many patrols crossed the enemy lines during the day. (b) Enemy. Very active throughout the day. A formation of four GOTHAS were broken up by fire of our scouts and driven back behind line at 2.0 p.m. Two machines came down apparently in difficulties. Enemy planes were very active during the night. Bombs were dropped on HAVRINCOURT, and back areas. Miscellaneous Total Casualties for the 13 days in the line, GRAINCOURT SECTOR Wounded. Officers Two Lt. J.E. MILLS (T.F.) 2/Lt. E.S. FOLD (T.F.) Wounded. O/Ranks Eight [All Gassed] Machine Gun Corps Wounded O/Ranks one Rifle Fire. (6th DORSETSHIRE REGT) attached	

WAR DIARY

INTELLIGENCE SUMMARY

Army Form C. 2118.

50. Machine Gun Coy.
January 1918.

Place	Date	Hour	Summary of Events and Information	Remarks and references to Appendices
GRAINCOURT SECTOR	26TH	Cont'd	Company relieved in the line by 51. M.G. Coy. Relief complete by 9.25 P.M. 26/1/18. Casualties Nil. Company on relief entrain at Q.2.A.51, (Light Railway) and detrain at Station 82 near PHIPPS CAMP, and march to Billets in SANDERS CAMP. All safely arrive in Billets. 10 a.m. 27/1/18.	JHS
SANDERS CAMP.	27TH	8.0 A.M.	Reveille. Rest of morning spent in cleaning clothing and equipment, renetting Huts, building A.A. emplacements, and improving Camp generally.	JHS
		2.0 P.M.	Kit Inspection.	
		3.0 P.M.	Clothing exchanged, and deficiencies in Kit made up. Telephone fixed up with HEART.	
"	28TH	6.45 A.M.	Reveille	JHS
		7.45 A.M.	Interior Economy and Muster Clean parade	
		8.30 A.M.	Physical and running drill vicinity of Camp. Rest of morning Coy Parade for cleaning and checking Gun gear, and cleaning Limbers.	
		12.30 P.M.	Company Parade for Baths at HARLINCOURT.	
		3.0 P.M.	Foot Baths at HERRICK CAMP. Hostile Aircraft very active during the night, and Bombs dropped in vicinity of HAPLINCOURT and BERTINCOURT.	
"	29TH	6.45 A.M.	Reveille.	JHS
		7.45 A.M.	Interior Economy and Muster Clean parade.	
		8.30 A.M.	Foot Friction Drill in Huts.	
		9.0 A.M.	Physical Training Vicinity of Camp.	
		10.45 A.M.	Muster parade Dress Full Marching order.	
		11.30 A.M.	Company parade under Section arrangements for Inspection of Iron Rations, Box Respirator, P.H. Helmet, and Ammunition.	
		2.0 P.M.	Guns tested and cleaned. Afternoon Games.	

Army Form C. 2118.

WAR DIARY
INTELLIGENCE SUMMARY.
(Erase heading not required.)

50 Machine Gun Coy
January 1918

Place	Date	Hour	Summary of Events and Information	Remarks and references to Appendices
SANDERS CAMP.	30TH	6.45 AM	Reveille	
		7.45 AM	Interior Economy and Muster Clean parade	
		8.30 AM	Foot Fraction drill in Huts	
		9.0 AM	Close order Drill vicinity of Camp	
		10.15 AM	At disposal of Section Officers	
		11.30 AM	Equipment fitting dres. Back order	
		a noon	Taking Guns cleaning and Laying tackle	AH&S
		2.0 PM	Company parade for Inspection of Equipment. Drop Backs order Huts. Afternoon spent in erecting Huts and improving Camp. Nothing except active during the night over our lines Bombs dropped	
	31ST	6.45 AM	Reveille	
		7.45 AM	Interior Economy and Muster Clean parade.	
		8.30 AM	Foot fraction drill in Huts	
		9.0 AM	Physical and Running drill vicinity of Huts	
		10.0 AM	Company fall out	
		11.0 AM	Gun drill by sections and in Mass formation	
		11.45 AM	Cleaning Guns and Gun gear	AH&S
		2.0 PM	Reverting Huts continuation of work in progress	

G.W. Downs Capt.
O.C. 50 M.G. Coy

HEADQUARTERS
AG/389/22
5th DIVISION

Dvl MGBee

Herewith War Diary
of 30th May 96y. Please acknowledge

J W Harris
Captain
A/DAAG 17th Div

4th M3.
M.G 22
1/3/18

HQ
17th Division.

Herewith I beg to return 50 M.G.
Coy. ~~Doc~~ War Diary completed to 23/2/18.
A War Diary will be sent you for
17th Battalion M.G.C. from 24/2/18 to
28/2/18 inclusive.

[signature]
Lt & Adjt
17th Battalion M.G.C.

Army Form C. 2118.

WAR DIARY
50th M.G. Coy
INTELLIGENCE SUMMARY

(Erase heading not required.)

Place	Date	Hour	Summary of Events and Information	Remarks and references to Appendices
SANDERS CAMP.	FEB 1	7 am	Reveille. 8 am Parade. 9 am Physical training	
		10-11 am	Cleaning guns, gun gear, packing limbers for the line + relief. 5.2 M.G. Coy on the Left Brigade Sector. Relief Completed by 9 pm. Casualties NIL.	
		1.15 pm	Coy. Parade	
LEFT BRIGADE SECTOR.	2.		Guns in Action 4. Rounds expended 3000. Casualties NIL. Change in position. Company moved from SANDERS CAMP to the relief of HUMOUR. Relieving HUMOUR as above. Guns tested + cleaned. Work done. Barrage lines checked. All positions improved in with AA + alternative positions constructed. Salvage collected. General improvement of dugouts + saps improved. Bellie filled. Work to be done. Repair + condition of miscellaneous. Guns fired last night as follows.	ANS
			Guns.
R. 5. —
R. 6. —
R. 7. 3
R. 8. 5	
			TARGET.
K4 & 50.40 . Road junction etc.
K3 & 65.75 Trench + Road junction.	
			Irregular bursts in BARRAGE LINE.	
			Time of firing:- Irregular bursts from 7 pm 1/2/18 to 7 am 2/2/18	
			Observations.
(a) Ours. Relief of HUMOUR completed by 8.30 pm 1/2/18.
(b) Enemy's. NIL.
(c) Artillery. Barrage fire from 6 pm to 9 pm. Otherwise quiet.
(d)	

50th M.G. Coy.

WAR DIARY / INTELLIGENCE SUMMARY

February 1918.

Army Form C. 2118.

Place	Date FEB	Hour	Summary of Events and Information	Remarks and references to Appendices
LEFT BRIGADE SECTOR.	2 Cont'd		Enemy defences. N.L. Movement. N.L. Miscellaneous. Owing to which not being completed till dark there is nothing to report. Map reference of guns as follows:- Coy. H.Q. — K.14.f.10.30 R - 2 K.15.b.60.40 S - 1 K.10.c.30.85 R - 3 K.15.a.95.50 S - 2 K.10.c.00.85 R - 4 K.9.c.45.82 S - 3 K.9.b.05.50 R - 5 K.15.d.20.68 S - 4 K.9.b.45.52 R - 6 K.14.d.29.85 S - 5 K.9.a.10.38 R - 7 K.14.b.12.25 S - 6 K.8.d.80.98 R - 8 K.8.c.80.85 S - 7 K.8.d.55.98 K.8.c.34.00 S - 8 K.9.b.00.35	Ans/
	3		Guns in Action 16 officers 80 o.r. Casualties N.L. Work done. Rounds expended 8000. Consolidated at Coy. H.Q. all positions cleaned & improved. Cook house constructed. Barrage lines checked. Cleaning S.4 and S.5 positions. Bell's field. Guns boiled & cleaned. General maintenance of condition & retention. Work to be done. A.A. position fixed (when available). Column alarm position sited & constructed. S.4 and S.5 positions revetted. All positions & trenches in readiness improved. Miscellaneous. Guns fired last night as under. Guns Target R.5 } Area E.29.c 10.35 R.8 Area E.29.d.40 Road + tracks. R.6 } Camps Bridge & R.7 } Road attacks. Huguelen barrels from 9.30 pm to 3 am.	

WAR DIARY

INTELLIGENCE SUMMARY. February 1918.

50. M.G. Coy.

Army Form C. 2118.

Place	Date FEB	Hour	Summary of Events and Information	Remarks and references to Appendices
LEFT BRIGADE SECTOR.	3	Contd.	Operations. (a) Ours. } NIL (b) Enemy's } Artillery. (a) Ours --- Quiet. (b) Enemy's --- LOCK 7 shelled at intervals. BULLEN TR. slightly shelled with H.E. at intervals. A.A. guns fairly active. Enemy defences. New work } None observed Wire } T. M's. Quiet M. G's. Active during hours of darkness on CAREY TR. and RYDER ST. State of ground. Fair Movement behind enemy's lines. None observed Enemy Communications ------ None observed Aeroplane activity. (a) Ours. Active all day, but with the exception of a few B.E.2.C all were at high altitude. (b) Enemy's Active during the forenoon all engaged with A.A. fire. An hostile aeroplane brought down in flames in the vicinity of HERMIES at midday. Miscellaneous. No targets were reported to sniping M.G. from DIV or BDE. O.P.	Ours

50th M.G. Coy.

WAR DIARY
INTELLIGENCE SUMMARY. February 1918.

(Army Form C. 2118.)

Place	Date FEB.	Hour	Summary of Events and Information	Remarks and references to Appendices
LEFT BRIGADE SECTOR.	4		Guns in Action 4. Rounds Expended 41,250. Casualties NIL. Change in positions NIL. Work done Dugout at S8 position improved. Alternative positions also and constructed for S1 and S2 Trench deepened and Sub Ranch improved at S2. All Gun positions camouflaged. Trenches in vicinity of positions cleaned. Baths Attack Guns tested and cleaned. Salvage collected. General maintenance of repair and condition done. Work to be done Continuation of work in progress. Flash screens to be constructed. AA positions to made. Alternative positions completed. Salvage Collected. General Maintenance work R.S. R.M. Gun engaged Enemy Party between 30pm-40pm. 250 Rounds fired. Targets engaged last night as under. Gun Target R.5 E.26.D.34.15 Irregular Bursts of fire R.6 Trenches and Tracks in [ ] from 10.45 PM – 1.0 AM R.7 [uncertain]	
"	"		Operations :- NIL. Artillery (a) Quiet during the day. Several observer rounds than during the 7 hours of darkness. (b) Quiet during the [?] — [?] night except for desultory shelling. which penetrated towards night S.3 and S.8 Gun positions area shelled. Shrapnel at 8.0 ¹PM CAREY TRENCH — H.E. and S.1 positions shelled during 9.45 PM — 10.15 ?PM. Usual attention paid to — 9.40RY 7. Enemy Defences Dug-work Wire Done Increased. M.Gs. Quieter than previous period. Usual night burst. T.Ms. Fairly active during the day — More active at Night. BROWN AVENUE and ALBAN TRENCH Subjected to Trench. [?] dry throughout the night. State of ground — firm — Improving	

Army Form C. 2118.

50 Machine Gun Company

WAR DIARY
or
INTELLIGENCE SUMMARY.
(Erase heading not required.)

Feb. 1918

Instructions regarding War Diaries and Intelligence Summaries are contained in F. S. Regs., Part II. and the Staff Manual respectively. Title pages will be prepared in manuscript.

Place	Date	Hour	Summary of Events and Information	Remarks and references to Appendices
LEFT BRIGADE SECTOR.	Feb 4 cont'd		Movement behind enemy line none observed. No targets were presented by sniping M.G.R.G. from O.P.s. Enemy communications. None available. Aeroplane Activity. Both active during the day. Always engaged by AA and M.G fire when within range. Guns in Action 5. Rounds Expended. 2760. Casualties NIL Change in Position NIL Work Done :- Entrance to Saphead at coy HQ constructed. Duck boards cleaned and relaid. Latrine improved. Trench deepened at S.1 position. Dugouts at S.1 and S.2 positions cleaned. S.5 position revetted and camouflaged. S.8 emplacement revetted. Gun position cleaned and improved. Ant Trenches in vicinity of Gun pested and cleaned. Salvage collected. General maintenance of repair Belts filled. and conditions. Work to be done. Continuation and completion of work in progress. Construction of another entrance to Saphead at Coy. H.Q. Steps improved and Sump Pits dug. Entrance to R.3 dugout improved. AA positions constructed when materials available. Miscellaneous Machine Guns carried out a shoot on the following Targets: Guns and times as stated :- Target	AH 3
	5 II		R2 R4 R5 R6 R7 } TRENCHES TRACKS and AREA E.26.D. 75.10 } Bursts of Thirty Seconds duration from 11.45 PM to 12.30 AM TOTAL Rounds Expended. 2,700.	

Army Form C. 2118.

50. Machine Gun Coy.

WAR DIARY
INTELLIGENCE SUMMARY.
(Erase heading not required.)

Feb 1918

Instructions regarding War Diaries and Intelligence Summaries are contained in F. S. Regs. Part II. and the Staff Manual respectively. Title pages will be prepared in manuscript.

Place	Date Feb	Hour	Summary of Events and Information	Remarks and references to Appendices
LEFT BRIGADE SECTOR	5th		**Operations** (a) Ours Inter Battalion relief carried out last night. (b) Enemy Nil. **Artillery** (a) Ours Active along Divl. front at 11.30 AM and 11.50 AM and again at 2.40 PM - 3.10 PM. Harms were very much in evidence. (b) Enemy Quiet during the day and no response to this. Two bombardments about Lock 7 and vicinity of K5 and K11. At 11.25 AM CANAL CUTTING and front line in vicinity of K5 a shelled. At 3.0 PM front line & Bat. H.Q. shelled for five minutes. 11.40 PM Several heavy shells fell over and seemed to fall at K26 central. At 5.45 PM a Barrage was placed on the LEFT leading up to 6.30 PM. During this bombardment the CANAL CUTTING and LOCK 7 were heavily shelled also G.9a. Movement behind Enemy lines. A party of the enemy were observed on the high ground at E28c.0 at 10.30 AM. **Enemy Defences** Dew'ork and wire. Done observed. MGs Quieter than usual. The Railway at K14.8 was intermittently fired on during the night. T. Ms Active during day & night. State of Ground - Fair - Improving. Enemy Communications A party of men were observed at intervals during the day with a Tape evidently marking trenches on the ARRAS - CAMBRAI road at approx. K.13. **Aeroplane Activity** (a) Ours Very few machines up during the day. Two of gun machines crossed enemy lines at 5.0 PM. Our planes crossed Enemy lines again at dusk. (b) Enemy NIL. **Miscellaneous** During operations yesterday morning enemy shells were observed to fall short & drop in Enemy's front line. On two nights lights being sent up the range was increased.	

50 Machine Gun Coy Feb. 1918

Army Form C. 2118.

WAR DIARY
INTELLIGENCE SUMMARY
(Erase heading not required.)

Place	Date	Hour	Summary of Events and Information	Remarks and references to Appendices

LEFT BRIGADE SECTOR	6th		**Enemy in Action** Rounds Expended, 8100. Casualties NIL.
			 Change in Position NIL
			 Work done Continuation of yesterday. Sapkeal entrance at Coy HQ completed. Sec S6 dug out commenced. Sump pit dug. Trench widened and improved generally at S2, and S2 boulders deepened. Trench at S2 widened. Commencement alterations positions for R2 and R5 gun. Entrance to M.G. R3 covered with camouflage. Dugouts for S7 and S8 team prepared. S8 emplacement revetted. R5 and R6 improved. Dugouts cleared. General improvement of positions. Trenches in enemy sump tested and cleaned. Salvage collected and sent down. Belts filled. Maintenance of repair and condition.
			 Work to be done Continuation and completion of work in progress. Sapkeal entrance at Coy HQ completed. S8 dugout completed. Sump pit dug. Salvage collected. R3 position revetted. Maintenance of condition and repair.
			 Miscellaneous Visual night firing as under:—
			    Gun Target
			 M.G. S.2 Party of Enemy in CANAL CUTTING 1.30 A.M.
			 M.G. R.25 XRbada E27D6080
			 M.G. R.5 Tracks and Bridge E27c1035
			 M.G. R.6 Area K4 a 20,10
			 M.G. R.7 Area K4 a 2050
			    Tracks and emplacement K4 B 0520
			 Irregular bursts from 9.0 pm — 3.0 A.M. During the day 1000 rounds were fired at hostile aircraft.	

50 Machine Gun Coy.   Feb 1918

Army Form C. 2118.

WAR DIARY
INTELLIGENCE SUMMARY.
(Erase heading not required.)

Place	Date	Hour	Summary of Events and Information	Remarks and references to Appendices
LEFT BRIGADE SECTOR	6th		Operations Nil	

Artillery (a) Enemy's shelling throughout the day unusual. Intermittent fire at night.
6.30 AM 8.0 AM forward trenches shelled
Unusual shelling at LOCK 7 during day.
11.0 PM few gas shells in barrage - PERNIES etc.
(b) A/A guns very active against our planes

Enemy Defences
(a) New work } None observed
(b) Wire }
(c) M.Gs } Usual indirect fire during the night
(d) T.Ms } Not active as usual.
(e) Dumps } None located
(f) Sites of Guns }

Movement behind Enemy lines. Throughout the day men in twos
and threes walked along the CANAL in E.27.c
At 6.30 PM a party of 20 hastily was scattered by M.G. S.A.
Continual movement during afternoon on ROAD running
NORTH and SOUTH through J.K.3

Enemy Communications None available. Enemy Communications NIL.

Aeroplane Activity
(a) Ours. Active all day. B.E.2c machines heavily engaged over left
Divl. front. Day enemy artillery AA Guns
Daneuvre often situations up throughout the day
A patrol of 3 CAMELS went right behind enemy lines at
2.15 PM. A patrol of NIEUPORT FIGHTERS evidently as
protection for numerous B.E.2c in flight, were up
most of the afternoon. Many gun bombing planes
crossed the Enemy lines at dusk.
(b) Enemy's Active all day,— only 3 succeeded in crossing our lines
were driven back by AA and M.G. fire. AT formation
of 9 enemy planes flying in V shape patrolled our
Lines at 3.0 PM

50 Machine Gun Coy

WAR DIARY

INTELLIGENCE SUMMARY.

(Erase heading not required.)

Army Form C. 2118.

Feb. 1918

Place	Date	Hour	Summary of Events and Information	Remarks and references to Appendices
LEFT BRIGADE SECTOR.	6th		Aeroplane Activity. (H) Enemy. When over GRAINCOURT this formation was broken up and Machine gun fire opened to their own lines. A few hostile planes were heard during the night. Enemy Anti-Aircraft Balloons were seen on the Miscellaneous. Balloons magneta (mauve) K 14 B 19 25 at 10.30 am 90 – 12 90 – 21 90 – 52 o – 65 0 – 76 80 70 Targets have not yet been received by M.G.R.6. Smoking Guns from any O.Ps.	HS
	7th		Guns in Action. 5. Rounds Expended. 7000. Casualties. NIL Change in Position NIL Work done. Continuation of work in progress. Saphead entrance at Coy H Q completed and further pump pits dug. Saphead entrance at R.5. improved. Alternative position in connection for M.G.R.2. M.G.S.1. Trenches widened and deepened in front of M.G.S.1. (Right) and M.G.S.2. positions, and latrines built for M.G.S7. these Gun Teams. Ammunition shelter for M.G.S7. improved. Dug-outs and positions generally cleaned and upkeep maintained. Ammunition, Belts and Guns cleaned, Belts filled — Guns cleaned and tested. Salvage collected and sent down. Work to be done. Continuation of above. R.E. Material required from dump to See H.Q. AA mountings fixed. Flash screens made. Salvage collected. General maintenance of repair and condition. Miscellaneous Guns fired last night as follows :- Guns Target M.G.R.1. E 27 D 9 20 Tracks and Trenches. M.G.R.2. E 28 a 20. X Roads and Tracks. M.G.R.5. E 4 a 52. Area and Tracks. M.G.R.6. E 26 D 31 5 Tracks and Trenches. M.G.R.7. LOCK 5. Irregular Bursts of 30 seconds duration from 7 PM – 3 AM	

Army Form C. 2118.

50 Machine Gun Coy.

WAR DIARY
INTELLIGENCE SUMMARY
(Erase heading not required.)

February 1918

Instructions regarding War Diaries and Intelligence Summaries are contained in F.S. Regs., Part II. and the Staff Manual respectively. Title pages will be prepared in manuscript.

Place	Date	Hour	Summary of Events and Information	Remarks and references to Appendices
Left Brigade Sector	7th		Operations Nil. Artillery (a) Fairly active throughout the front. Bowler Wood shelled with heavy howitzers throughout the afternoon. Normal fire on working parties and harassing fire at night. (b) Lost 7 shell firing heavily at 7.0am and intermittently throughout the day. Railway in K.14.b shelled with 77 mm at dusk. Area K.14.b shelled from 2.0pm – 2.30pm and from 7.0pm – 7.30pm. AA gun inactive. Movement behind enemy lines – Usual individual movement in canal bedding at intervals. Enemy communications – Nothing to report. Enemy dispositions – Nothing to report. Enemy defences – New work now observed. Wire. None observed. T.M's none located. M.G's – guns in chair sound. State of ground – Frozen. Aeroplane activity – (a) Artillery planes up during afternoon, and a fighting patrol flew at no great height over our lines from 3.0pm – 4.0pm. (b) Nil Miscellaneous – Hostile AA guns were very inactive during the period against our planes. M.Gs showed more activity. Guns in action. 5. Rounds expended 3,100	AHS
	8th		Miscellaneous – Guns laid yesterday on enemy support of G. R.6. Target – Park of trees. Fired E.27.c.89 at 9.15am. 9. Target – Lagging party E.22.c.34 at 10.15pm. Fired E.27.c.9.5 at 1.45pm. Third trough men engaged on wirage returned from O.P. A cask instance the enemy were manflicted. Gun field these night O/s wires. M.G.B.5. M.G.R.6, M.G.R.7. Each fired at Target – seen on ridge of Fork 6 – Bursts of 1 minute duration fired at 9.0pm, 1.30pm, sundry 7.30pm. Normal general fire throughout the night from 10.0pm – 3.0am on enemy M.G.R1 – Target Track and shrub. of Plough E.27.d.60.35. M.G.R.2 – Target Track in E.27.c. M.G.Q.5 – Target Track in K.4.a. M.G.R.6 – Target Enemy Punctions E.29.al. M.G.A.7 – Target Fork 6.	AHS

WAR DIARY or INTELLIGENCE SUMMARY

Army Form C. 2118.

50 Machine Gun Coy.

February 1918

Place	Date	Hour	Summary of Events and Information	Remarks and references to Appendices
Left	8th cont.		Cheveton Wd. Artillery – (c) Quiet during the day. Usual shelling for 15 minutes. (b) Double during day. Usual shelling of Railways. M.G. at night. Enemy Defences – New moved about 1am. Trench Mortars – T.M.s none to notice. On target not heard. Enemy Employment – None noticed. Harassed (Lewis) all through. None met with ammn. (quite quiet here all day) 9.15m Parts of system E.27.c.89. 12.15a.m. D.21.98. Also 9.20	
Brigade			E.27.c.3.4. 4.45m. Moderate Art. 9.15.m 29 m. M.G. fire. 10.30 R. as practised by shifting July 29. m. M.G. fire 10.30 R. Harassing Artillery – Quiet on both lines.	
Sector	9th		Wire Dumps – Wypet wet, attack too light to hop. at M.G. 96 – 57. Ammn. Stores for transp. remained out another day or so. Target reported M.G. 52.21 at rear of W. Menin Rd. Smashed out ammunition gun mounted and tried. Approaching clouds gnat are of tracks and expended all machine and dug-in Ground cold. Bois Hw Wotan. collected and sent again the line. Gun in Action – S. Round expended 6500 Casualties – Nil Changes in position. Observations – Lights (a) E. I. hill as under 9 am 9 am Target E.27.d.55.Lighten 1 scattered 8 to 9 working to entry. 1.0 pm target M.G.a.39 Working. entry M.G.a. Rt. Target x Rails + Roads E.27.c.80.85. Gun R. 2 – light fire in under Gun Rt. Target E.29.d.20 Target x Roads + Rails E.23.c.75 Gun R.1 – Target + Junction E.2.f.4. G.L. Rt. – Target + Road + Junction E.27. 19.35 Gun R.3 – Target roads. Gun lane bend through be night from 8.0pm – 6.0 am Target bn were to have seen at O.b.l. 20.90 # Bemellons unit	

Army Form C. 2118.

50 Mushin Gron Bay.

WAR DIARY

INTELLIGENCE SUMMARY

(Erase heading not required.)

February 1915

Place	Date	Hour	Summary of Events and Information	Remarks and references to Appendices
Left Brigade Sector	9th		Shelling - Nil. Artillery - (a) During night (b) Combat 11:15 a 4.5 at W of 10:30 and 11.0 a.m. from road in grenade throughout the trench. Enemy aeroplane brought down near Lille. 11.0 a.m. Bright French shelled 11:15. Bunch of 11:15 of 4.5 & Shell and H.E. & shrapnel. 1.0 p.m. Blan. Amen shell 11:15 77 m/m 11:40 h. Reinforcements W.L.n 4 11:5 m. S. Chr. d. 58 pt 77 m/m - a wood about H15 n 45.87. Enemy Dispositions - None available. Enemy Defences - None available. Enemy Communications - None observed. T.M.'s, Nigh velocity shells of enemy H.pm - Ammunition — None. Movement behind enemy lines — The unidentified angle was engaged by shipping at E. R 6 is to send recce of obsts. in trench used reported from S.R. 4 2.0 - another pat. E 77 d 55 1:6 p.m. Working party N 4 a 67. Aeroplane activity — 1 hostile plane brought down at 8:32 a.m. by M.G. and Infy fire as noted yesterday at situated O.B.'s of billets and W.L. Weak O.P.'s - Observation — confirmed of our F4 gunners taking to M.G. with Horace at by 7.6 wireless. Laterne 2/1 enemy observed and bombardier observed in view from M.G. 58 + M.G. 51 Touts at Nb 2.52 registered in different countries lab N.B.s contact a M.G. 22 cm line position a ammunition reported. Artillery brought together by the R7 companies General shelling & machine gun fire. action & not shelled + dropped & ... 2 fills. during 2 officers 1 other + most seen 2 ...	

(Appx.) Wt. W2859/M1893 750,000 1/17. D.D. & L., Ltd. Forms/C:2118 24.

50 Machine Gun Coy.   Feb. 1918.   Army Form C. 2118.

WAR DIARY
INTELLIGENCE SUMMARY
(Erase heading not required.)

Place	Date	Hour	Summary of Events and Information	Remarks and references to Appendices
LEFT BRIGADE SECTOR	10th		Guns in Action 5. Rounds Expended 3750. Casualties NIL. Change in position NIL. Miscellaneous 70 Targets were necessed by Sniping M.G.R.6. from O.P. Guns fired last night on usual Targets:- Gun Target M.G. R.1 x Roads and Tracks E.27.d 60 85. M.G. R.2 do E.28.a 20 00. M.G. R.5 Tracks, Trenches Etc. E.26.D M.G. R.6 Roads and Tracks M.G. R.7 LOCK 6. E.27.c.10 35. Irregular bursts from 8.0 PM to 3.0 AM. Operations NIL Artillery (a) Own Fairly quiet during day - Back area shelled at dusk. (b) Enemy BULLEN TRENCH shelled with H.E from 9.0 AM - 11.0 AM at 15 minute intervals. At 9.30 AM Dugout at K15 c 87 shelled with 5.9s. CANAL CUTTING shelled from 11.0 AM - 11.30 AM At intervals during day and front line system was shelled with 2 Guns of small calibre. 4.0 AM Three minutes bombardment of enclosed field on K15 B with Gas and H.E followed by salvoes two minutes later. Movement behind Enemy Line Not so noticable as usual. No targets were received by Sniping M.G.R.6. Enemy Defences New work, and wire. Done observed. M.Gs. More active during the day, scattering two of our working parties and arresting certain movement. Active against our planes. Visual indirect fire at night. T.Ms. Saw not in great evidence. About 20 shells fell near S6 + S8 Guns during morning. Fairly active all day. Front line shelled at intervals.	JHS

50 Machine Gun Coy

WAR DIARY / **INTELLIGENCE SUMMARY**

Army Form C. 2118.

Feb 1918

Place	Date	Hour	Summary of Events and Information	Remarks and references to Appendices
LEFT BRIGADE SECTOR	10th	Cont'd	**State of Ground** Fair. Trenches drying and improving. **Enemy Dispositions** None observed. **Enemy Communications** NIL. **Peacetime Activity** (a) Our Activities all the morning. (b) Enemy – G. Plane attempted to cross our lines at 4.0 pm but was driven back by A.A. and M.G. fire. **Miscellaneous** NIL. **Work done** Continued to fit up the pepper's MGs to prepare to withdraw and report at C.H.Q. S17, MGS to prepare at MGS17 and MGS18 for new dugout entrance. Construction of alternative position for MGR3. Sap head ammunition shelf finished and work on Sap head commenced. MGR6 ammunition store finished. MGR7 Shelters, ready. Dugouts taken from 2/L. MGR8 AA emplacement commenced. Salvage collected. Bombs dried and cleaned. Dugouts and Trenches in sector generally improved, maintenance of approx. and condition.	NIL
	11th		**Enemy Action** 5 Rounds expended 5000. Casualties NIL. **Change in position** NIL. **Miscellaneous** AA Some fired at Hostile Aircraft during afternoon. No Target where passed by support MGR6. Enemy fired during night as under. Enemy Target. MGR1 | Convoys and Transport MGR2 | AA. MGR3 | Strong point. MGR6 | Tracks MGR7 | Trenches + emplacements. Rate +25 MGS | Trenches + M.Gs. Irregular bursts from 7.0 pm – 1.0 am.	E4736085 E170 KHA2510 KHA2515 KH1129

50 Machine Gun Coy

WAR DIARY

Army Form C. 2118.

February 1918

(Erase heading not required.)

Place	Date	Hour	Summary of Events and Information	Remarks and references to Appendices
LEFT BRIGADE SECTOR	11th cont.		Observations — Nil. Artillery — (a) Fairly quiet. Enemy active at intervals towards Battery, which carried out during the day blind harassing fire at night. (b) 6.30 a.m - 6.30am - lock 7 shelled with 4.2's & 5.9 9 am - 11.30am Shelling of K14 & K15 by Battr. Tr. Road K9, K5030 high pierced N. K1B & George Street 2.30 to 3.30pm Whizzbangs running through K16 & K17 & d. shelled with H.E. (heat registry) Enemy Defence. — New work twice, none observed. M.G. unusual activity during Relief of M.G. in engaging our planes & my Tresly who worked with Royal T.M.B. firing. 2.30pm to 4.0pm Pullman Trench fire on continuously - state of trench - Inferred. Movement behind enemy line — 9.25 am one seen in front of K136. He was shot on by M.G. auxiliary & was seen to fall. He ran but taken cover amongst a shell crater another man seen in hand at some place was fired on by M.G. daily & fell. Enemy Dispositions — None available. Enemy communication — Nothing to report. Aeroplane activity. — (a) Flight on lock positions. Three planes flew over enemy line during afternoon, and two B.E.2c's went shooting Lilli end. — (b) Period of lights seen on front side of our lines about afternoon. Work done — Embrasures at battery. control at alternative position for M.G. R2. — Bryant sheet — nothing urgent at M.G. R5. M.G. R6 emplacement enlarged. Filling bags dug out completed for M.G. R7 & 8. Position at M.G. R3 straightened. Ammunition reserves made at M.G. S6 & 7. Trench cleared in vicinity of position. General wirement and maintenance of posts continued. Material carried to position. Things collected. Gun tested & placed. Bolts filed.	

Army Form C. 2118.

WAR DIARY
INTELLIGENCE SUMMARY

50 Machine Gun Coy.

February 1918

(Erase heading not required.)

Instructions regarding War Diaries and Intelligence Summaries are contained in F. S. Regs., Part II. and the Staff Manual respectively. Title pages will be prepared in manuscript.

Place	Date	Hour	Summary of Events and Information	Remarks and references to Appendices
LEFT BRIGADE SECTOR	12th		Gun indicator - 5. Rounds expended - 750. Gun observation - Ml. Shoop in omeron-ch't. Wind direction - Varying. M.G. R6. sentries a faith at E.27.d. at 11.00am. 200 rounds were fired at their heads. Gun first observed muzzle at J.1. Target - Trenches, tracks, + 3 infantrymen, E.28.L.40.85. M.G. R2. Target - 3 army Aims - Tank, E.27.4.9.72. M.G.85 Target - Entrance to Dugout Trench, Range K3.a.53. M.G. R6 Target - Entrance to dugouts trench K.15.a.75. M.G.27 Target - Lock b. M.G.87 Target - Entrance to dugouts trench M.15.1. - 9.0am + 11.0am - 3.0am Observed - M.G. Trolley - (5) Moveable emplacement - No enemy on a front of Division on either side, small amount of enemy fire observed. Shrapnel bursts slow. (L) Observable observed. 7.00am to 9.00 Enemy 77mm - 7.0am shelled 77Y - Chepot- ridge J. Ridge Lane in K.15.b. Shells sweep in front line + Butler tr. Shells listening posts with machine gun fire carried on by batteries behind Nambreaux. all the afternoon. 1.30 high shrapnel over on K.15.b shelled. 5.0pm-5.30am am K.14.C. shelled. Hot Gun ten rifles enemy defences - None seen + not more observed - the B.M. was sentry at an post. This Afghan sentries shelled from 12.30am - 1.30am. Movement behind enemy line - 11.00am Push of men at E.27.L.90. 2.estual by laying M.G. R6. 10.30 at 2 men running slowly on K.2.a.76. Two rounds half by off. M.G. officer was within enemy departure. Non observed. Enemy communication - Nothing to report.	

A5834 Wt W4973/M687 750,000 8/16 D.D. & L. Ltd. Forms/C.2118/13.

WAR DIARY
INTELLIGENCE SUMMARY

50th Machine Gun Coy

February 1918

Army Form C. 2118.

Place	Date	Hour	Summary of Events and Information	Remarks and references to Appendices
LEFT BRIGADE SECTOR	12th contd.		Aeroplane activity:- (a) Fairly quiet all day. Hostile planes over in afternoon. (b) Flight of 5 planes evidently spotting for hostile artillery shoots over our sector. In attempting to cross our lines they were driven back by M.G's & A.A. Miscellaneous:- Arrangement for alternative M.G. R.1 are now completed. Communication established with O.P. Work on construction of alternative position for M.G. R.2 continued. Work continued on alternative position for M.G. R.3. Telephone & hipflag Gun R.1 tried out with O.P. Sap not completed. M.G. R.6 out level on lateral stdd. mounting completed for M.G. R.7. R.Y. All positions & emplacements Guns, targets & element Belts filled. Ammunition maintained. Guns in action - 5. Rounds expended - 2250. Miscellaneous:- No targets were received for M.G. R6 shifting gun. Guns fired last night as under:-	SAHS
	13th		Targets.	
			Gun M.G.R.1 5.18 & D 40 85 Trenches & Tracks	
			M.G.R.2 E.28 a 10 00 Tracks & X Roads	
			M.G.R.5 K.4 a 30 20 Tracks	
			M.G.R.6 K.4 a 10 50 Strong Points	
			M.G.R.7 K.4 b 10 20 Dew work	
			Irregular fire from 8.0 PM - 2.0 AM Rounds Expended 2250.	SAHS

50 Machine Gun Coy

Army Form C. 2118.

WAR DIARY
INTELLIGENCE SUMMARY

(Erase heading not required.)

February 1918

Place	Date	Hour	Summary of Events and Information	Remarks and references to Appendices
LEFT BRIGADE SECTOR	13		Operations (a) Own: Infantry relief carried out N.E. (b) Enemy: Nil.	
			Artillery (a) Own: Quiet. (b) Enemy: Back areas shelled at intervals. 8.30 PM CANAL CUTTING about LOCK 7 and K15 Central shelled with H.E. 10.30 AM Ditto. 10.0 AM–10.30 AM HUGHES TRENCH shelled with 77-mm. 2.0 PM–4.0 PM BULLEN TRENCH heavily shelled with 77 mm. 4.50 PM Trenches in N½ shelled with 5.9s. 11.40 AM–2.50 PM RAILWAY and Area K14.13 shelled to supply MGR6 from OP.	
			Movement behind Enemy lines: None observed and no targets appeared.	
			Enemy Defences Bail with R and Winter – None observed M.Gs – Heard at night firing through the BK 91B whilst shelled last 2.0 PM of Regimune guide M.s Trenches at Good. S.L.A. & Ground – Good. Enemy Communications – None observed. Enemy Disposition Aeroplane Activity – None observed. Work done: Continuation of yesterday. Work continued on M.G.R.12 alternative position. Sandbag MGR1 improved. General digging of sally of dug-outs positions of the Trenches on ground. Gallery collected and ammunition. Lines tested and cleared. Beth fired. General condition and upkeep of rejoin machines	

A5834 Wt. W4973 M687 750,000 8/16 D.D. & L. Ltd. Forms/C.2118/13.

Army Form C. 2118.

50 Machine Gun Coy

WAR DIARY

INTELLIGENCE SUMMARY.

(Erase heading not required.)

Feb 1918.

Place	Date	Hour	Summary of Events and Information	Remarks and references to Appendices
LEFT BRIGADE SECTOR	13	Genl	Company relieved in the line by S.I. M.G. Coy. Relief complete by 7.30 PM 13/2/18. Teams on relief march back to SANDERS CAMP. Total Casualties for the 12 days in the line. NIL	AHS
SANDERS CAMP.	14TH	8.0 AM 12 noon 2.45 PM	Reveille. Rest for morning. Attention Cleaning Clothing and equipment. Coy Parade. Coy Parade. Coy Sections for DIVL Baths HAPLINCOURT. During afternoon Lewis Gun gear Belts and Belt Boxes cleaned. Huts and Camp generally cleaned and improved.	AHS
	15TH	6.45 AM 8.45 AM 9.15 AM 2.0 PM 3.15 PM 7.0 PM	Reveille. Foot friction drill in Huts. Close order drill mostly by Section. Rest of morning spent in cleaning arms in Cleaning and Overhauling Coy. Special attention being paid to Section Parade. Instruction in cleaning and repacking Belts and Belt Boxes. Gas Chamber for Rapid repacking and also altitude A.B. Bomb Range. Testing also R.H. Helmets on Kit and Iron Ration inspection. An enemy aeroplane (GOTHA) was compelled to land in our lines through engine trouble. The crew 1 officer and 3 Ranks were captured. Believed to belong to No. 1 Bombing Squadron.	AHS
	16TH	6.45 AM 8.45 AM 9.30 AM 10. AM 10. AM 11. AM 7. PM	Reveille. followed by Lecture Economy and Muster Roll call Parade 7.45am Foot friction drill in Huts "A. D." and half B/O Section Parade for Close order drill "B." and half B/O Section Parade for Divl. Baths HAPLINCOURT "D." Lecture and reminder to F O. Sec parade. "A.B." and half of C. Section at disposal of Section Officers. Afternoon. Coy on fatigue work resetting Huts etc. Hostile aircraft very active over our Back area and bombs were dropped in vicinity of YTRES.	AHS

50. Machine Gun Coy.

WAR DIARY
or
INTELLIGENCE SUMMARY

Army Form C. 2118.

Feb. 1918

Place	Date	Hour	Summary of Events and Information	Remarks and references to Appendices
SANDERS CAMP	17TH	7.30 A.M.	Reveille. Voluntary Divine Services as under:—	SMS
		10 A.M.	C. of E. Service and Holy Communion in the "HIP" CINEMA	
		11.30 A.M.	C. of E. Service in 52nd Inf. Bde. Depot Lecture Hut. SANDERS CAMP	
		6.0 P.M.	Evening Service in the "HIP" CINEMA followed by Holy Communion	
		11.0 A.M.	Company paid out. Afternoon Games	
			Enemy aircraft active during the day and small red Balloon dropped by aeroplane landed on SANDERS CAMP and later newspaper printed in French dropped in same locality, and picked up and despatched to 50. Bde. H.Q. for information.	
	18TH	6.45 A.M.	Reveille. 7.45 A.M. Interior economy and Muster Clean Parade. Foot Baths allotted this Unit as follows:— (HERRICK CAMP)	SMS
		8.30 A.M.	'A' 'B' Sections and 'DRIVERS'	
		9.30 A.M.	'C', 'D', and 'H.Q' Sections.	
		10.45 A.M.	Gun drill. Attached men Stoppages Gun gear under Section arrangements.	
		11.45 A.M.	Sections parade for Cleaning Guns and Gun gear under Section arrangements. — Afternoon — Games. —	
	19TH	6.45 A.M.	Reveille. 7.45 A.M. Interior economy and Muster Clean Parade.	SMS
		8.45 A.M.	Physical and Running drill. Vicinity of Camp.	
		10 A.M.	Company parade for cleaning Guns and Gun gear and preparing for the Line.	
		3. P.M.	Limbers packed and Leave for Coy. H.Q. in the Line.	
		5.30 P.M.	Coy parade for the Line. "Battle Order" and march to PHIPPS CAMP and entrain at Station 82.	
		LATER	Coy relieve 52. M.G. Coy in the GRAINCOURT SECTOR	
GRAINCOURT SECTOR	20TH		Relief complete by 11.55 P.M. 19/2/18. Casualties NIL	SMS
			Guns in Action. NIL. Rounds expended NIL. Casualties NIL	
			Change in position. Company moved by night from SANDERS CAMP to Line. (GRAINCOURT SECTOR.)	
			Miscellaneous NIL	

WAR DIARY
INTELLIGENCE SUMMARY

50. Machine Gun Coy.

Feb. 1918.

Army Form C. 2118.

Place	Date	Hour	Summary of Events and Information	Remarks and references to Appendices
GRAINCOURT SECTOR	20	In Contd.	Operations. Relief of HUMOUR completed by 11.55 PM. (a) Ours. (b) Enemy. NIL. Artillery (a) Ours Active on left at 8.0 PM (b) Enemy. Usual night firing - Gas shells at intervals on the Eastern outskirts of HAVRINCOURT Enemy Defences. New work and wire. None seen. M.Gs. Quiet. T.Ms. None located. Dumps None observed State of Ground. Good and firm. Enemy Dispositions. None available. Enemy Communications NIL. Aeroplane Activity NIL. Miscellaneous. NIL. Work done Relief carried out as previously stated and owing to relief not being completed till 11.55 PM prevented any work from being done. Guns in Action 4 Rounds expended. 6,800. Change in Position NIL. Casualties. NIL. Miscellaneous 400 Rounds were fired at Hostile aircraft during the day. Targets engaged last night as under:-	AHS
			Gun. Target. 3 K5.a.80.60. Road, Tracks, + emplacements 11. K5.a.10.00. Track Junction + Roads 13. K12.a.60.90. Tracks and new work. 14. GRAINCOURT. 6,400. Rounds were fired on above Targets from 7.30 PM - 2.30 AM at intervals	AHS
"	21 st			AHS

WAR DIARY

50. Machine Gun Coy.

INTELLIGENCE SUMMARY Feb. 1918.

Army Form C. 2118.

Place	Date	Hour	Summary of Events and Information	Remarks and references to Appendices
GRAINCOURT SECTOR	21st		**Operations.** Both sides NIL.	
		11.15 AM	**Artillery.** Ours Quiet during day shelled enemy front line.	
		1.30 PM	18 Pdrs. Salvo of 18 Pdrs into GRAINCOURT.	
		9.35 PM	Heavies shelled back areas for half an hour.	
			Enemy. Quiet throughout the day.	
		3.0 PM	Odd shells fell in HAVRINCOURT	
		6.30 PM	FLESQUIERES shelled for half an hour.	
		9.35 PM	Salvos into HAVRINCOURT and at intervals till 2.0 AM	
			Desultory shelling of K.15.D during the hours of darkness.	
			Enemy Defences.	
			Dew Work and Wire. None seen.	
			M.Gs. Active against our planes during day but not so usually active throughout the night.	
			T.Ms. OWEN SUPPORT shelled at intervals all the morning.	
			State of Ground. Muddy and heavy	
			Movement behind Enemy Line. Low visibility interferes with observation	
			Enemy Dispositions and Communications. ∴ No information.	
			Aeroplane Activity.	
			Ours. Slight activity during day.	
			Enemy. Ditto – 2 Enemy planes flew over our lines at 1.35 PM, and another one flew over at 6.45 AM, otherwise quiet.	
			Work done. General tidying up. Cleaning and improving dugouts and positions. Latrines constructed for positions StaKen's over. No. 8 emplacement demolished. Nos. 4 and 14 Gun Teams. No. 14 Gun commenced Alternative position for No. 10. Guns tested & cleaned. Maintenance of consolidation upkeep. Belts filled. Salvage collected and sent down the Line.	

50. Machine Gun Coy.   Feb. 1918

WAR DIARY
INTELLIGENCE SUMMARY

Army Form C. 2118.

Place	Date	Hour	Summary of Events and Information	Remarks and references to Appendices
GRAINCOURT SECTOR	22nd		Guns in Action. 6. Rounds Expended. 8,200. Casualties NIL. Change in Position. NIL. Miscellaneous — 70.9 and 70.12. Sniping M. Guns engaged movement during day. Rounds Expended. 200. Guns fired last night as under:—	
			Gun — Target 3 — Trenches in K4.B. 11 — " " " 13 — Strong Point and Tracks in K4a 98. 14 — Tracks and approaches to GRAINCOURT. 7.15 PM — 3.0 AM. Irregular bursts from 7.15 PM — 3.0 AM.	
			Work done. Trenches cleaned, sump pits dug and entrance improved at Coy H.Q. Trench deepened to Div. O.P. from 70.12. Sniping M. Gun. Work on Alternative position for 70.14 Gun continued. General improvement at all positions. Trenches in vicinity of emplacements cleaned. Belts filled. Guns tested and cleaned. Ammunition cleaned and turned. General maintenance of repair and condition. Salvage collected and sent down the line. Both aides NIL.	
			Operations. Artillery. Ours fairly active. The following areas shelled as under:—	
	8.0. AM		GRAINCOURT.	
	2.15 PM		High ground in K.13.	
	3.30 PM		Regulation on LOCK. 6.	
	6.30 PM		Back areas, Tracks and Roads. BOURLON WOOD engaged throughout the day.	

50. Machine Gun Coy. WAR DIARY Feb. 1918. Army Form C. 2118.

INTELLIGENCE SUMMARY.

Place	Date	Hour	Summary of Events and Information	Remarks and references to Appendices
GRAINCOURT SECTOR.	22nd Cont'd		**Artillery** Enemy	
		7.30.AM - 8.0.AM	HAVRINCOURT shelled with 5.9's.	
		9.45.AM	SHINGLER SUPPORT shelled	
		12 noon	Trenches in Area K.17.A shelled with 4.2's.	
		5.15.PM - 5.25.PM	RYDER STREET received special attention.	
		3.0.PM - 3.30.PM	Shell drop on ROAD running NORTH and SOUTH in area K.22.	
		6.20.PM - 6.30.PM	Area K.21.B rather heavily shelled.	
			Usual track areas received attention at intervals. Harassing fire carried out during the night. AA Guns especially active against our planes all day.	
			Enemy Defences	
			Barb work and wire. None seen	
			M.G's. Usual indirect fire carried out during the night on our tracks. Very active during the day against our planes when within range.	
			T.M's. Nothing to report	
			Dumps. None observed	
			State of ground. Soggy and heavy	
			Movement behind Enemy line. Do. 9. Sniping M.G. engaged party of the enemy on the outskirts of GRAINCOURT - Party scattered.	
			Do.12. Sniping M.G. fired on enemy carrying party in E.29.D. They disappeared into shell holes - Two hours later they crawled on to SUNKEN ROAD in E.28.D.B.4. They were again fired on and scattered.	
			Enemy Dispositions and Communications. None available.	
			Aeroplane Activity.	
			Own. Very active all day - especially in rear of Enemy lines. ALL planes being engaged by AA, and S.M.G. fire.	
			Enemy. Quiet. Hostile 'plane 'flew along own front line at 1.0.PM. and passed over DARWIN ALLEY. Five 'planes attempted to cross our lines at 1.0. PM but were driven back by AA, and M.G. fire.	

WAR DIARY

50. Machine Gun Coy

Army Form C. 2118.

Feb. 1918

INTELLIGENCE SUMMARY

Place	Date	Hour	Summary of Events and Information	Remarks and references to Appendices
GRAINCOURT SECTOR.	23rd		Guns in Action 6. Rounds Expended 5,200. Casualties NIL. Change in Position NIL. Miscellaneous No. 9 and 12 Sniping M.G engaged movement during day. Guns fired last night 25-1 as under.	

Target.
Gun.	
3	Trenches in K4.B
11	Tracks and Trenches in K4.a
13	Trenches Dew work, & Tracks in K6.c
14	GRAINCOURT

from 6.0. P.M — 1.0. A.M.

Irregular bursts of fire

Work done. Entrances of dugouts at Coy H.Q revetted cleaned and embrased. Sap head got No. 2 Gun Team strengthened. Trench from No. 12 Sniping Gun to Div¹ O.P. deepened. Alternative position for No 10 Gun commenced. Work continued on alternative position for No. 14 Gun. S.A.A. and material carried from DUMP to Gun positions. Guns tested and cleaned. Belts filled. Salvage collected and sent down the line. General maintenance of repair and condition up Kept.

Operations. NIL. Artillery Own 9.0. Am GRAINCOURT shelled 10.AM-12 noon. Casual shelling of enemy posts in front of GRAINCOURT. 18 Plms and T.M's

Enemy's 8.0. Am-1.0 Am Shells fell in HAVRINCOURT at intervals. 4.0. P.M- 5.0. P.M. Several F.S.9's appeared to fall about Trenches in K.17d area.
8.30. P.M. Shells fell on SUNKEN ROAD in K16d, also to left about near Nos 13, and 14 Gun positions. Same again at 11.0. P.M, and. 1.0. A.M.

50 Machine Gun Coy. Feb. 1918

Army Form C. 2118.

WAR DIARY
INTELLIGENCE SUMMARY

(Erase heading not required.)

Instructions regarding War Diaries and Intelligence Summaries are contained in F. S. Regs., Part II. and the Staff Manual respectively. Title pages will be prepared in manuscript.

Place	Date	Hour	Summary of Events and Information	Remarks and references to Appendices
GRAINCOURT SECTOR	23rd Cont'd		Enemy Defences. New work and wire unobserved M.G's. Usual indirect fire during night particular attention being paid to Area K16c. T.M's Quiet. None located. State of Ground - Improving. Movement behind Enemy Lines. 4.0 P.M. Sniping M.G. D.9 fired on party leaving Trenches in K6. 2.0 P.M. One M.G. well and the next scattered Sniping M.G. 70.12. fired on party of Enemy in E29D. Arty. scattered. Enemy Communications and Dispositions None available. Aeroplane Activity NIL. Miscellaneous NIL.	

Norman Smith
Lieut.
2/o c. 50th M.G. Coy

WO95/2004

50 TM Batty

Dec 1915 - Mar 1916

17 Div - 50 Inf Bde

(No record for Feb found)

~~2 Army Troops~~

17 DIV. 50 Bde

50

TRENCH MORTAR BTY

1915 DEC to 1916 MAR

(1721)

G.B.G.

50th Ionesco Motion Brief.

Dec
vue I

1/
7937

17 Dec

1915

27-28-
AT

Army Form C. 2118

WAR DIARY
or
INTELLIGENCE SUMMARY
(Erase heading not required.)

Place	Date	Hour	Summary of Events and Information	Remarks and references to Appendices
Map 28 Sqrn G18a SE of POPERINGHE	2.12.15		The 50th Trench Mortar Battery was formed and attached to the XVII Division to work with the 27th & 32nd T.M. Batteries. It was composed of 2 NCOs & 10 men R.G.A. just out from Coast defences and 1 NCO & 10 men from the 52 Infantry Brigade. No officers were posted k.t.	
	3.12.15	7 am	Capt. Pratt R.A. T.M.C. & Cpl Needham R.A. and the R.A. personel of the battery were taking up 2" ammunition to the Left T M group of the Division at RAILWAY WOOD. In West Lane Trench they were attacked with shrapnel & Gr Turner R.G.A. was wounded & two men of 32nd Battery. Whilst this wounded man being dressed a whizz bang killed Cpl Needham with a direct hit. He was buried at the cemetry on the MENIN ROAD Igh.	
		11 am		
	4.12.15		The battery was temporarily split up to learn their duties. No 1 Sect under Cpl Millett R.G.A. working with Left group 32 Battery and No 2 Sect under Cpl Watt Notts Fus with Right group 27 Battery	
	7.12.15		Lieut Smart 7th Devons joined the battery and was temporarily attached to Left group	

R.R.T.

Army Form C. 2118

WAR DIARY
or
INTELLIGENCE SUMMARY

(Erase heading not required.)

50th French Mortar Battery

Instructions regarding War Diaries and Intelligence Summaries are contained in F.S. Regs., Part II. and the Staff Manual respectively. Title Pages will be prepared in manuscript.

Place	Date	Hour	Summary of Events and Information	Remarks and references to Appendices
Railway Wood	12.12.16	11.30	Got our left front of Trench Mortars from point Illa & fired 3. y 10 rounds rapid at point Illa 6½ h5 where German Trench Mortar was observed the previous day. Received no reply so presumably it was put out of action by our fire the previous day. Put in a 3.y TM at point I 11 6 6½ 13 to fire in emergency. In afternoon to firing in morning our artillery were withdrawn to shelter owing to our artillery firing on German front line Trenches. Germans opened fire on our Trenches with their artillery. Two men wounded. Pte Darling 7th Yorks & Pte Chivers 9th West Riding. Recommendations:— Corporal Foster 7th Yorks and Pte Kincey 10th Lancs Fusiliers for assisting wounded men to cover under heavy shrapnel fire. One 2" trench mortar either buried or hit – did not have time to find out before relief so reported to 2nd West Lancs who relieved us.	
	13.12.16			
	14.12.16	1.0		

R.H. Mant 2/Lt.
O.C. 50th T.M.B.

Army Form C. 2118.

WAR DIARY
or
INTELLIGENCE SUMMARY.
(Erase heading not required.)

Instructions regarding War Diaries and Intelligence Summaries are contained in F.S. Regs., Part II. and the Staff Manual respectively. Title pages will be prepared in manuscript.

50th Special Trench Battery

Place	Date	Hour	Summary of Events and Information	Remarks and references to Appendices
	19.12.15		Took over from Hunter Weston on the night of the 18th/19th December and carried on with breaking enemy parapet in accordance with minimal orders.	
	19.12.15	10 am	On the 19th fired 12 rounds from 1½ inch gun at Grs C58 and D12 C59 taking away enemy parapet, also fired 6 rounds with 2 inch gun at Grs B67, one of the 2 inch rounds was a blind, all others being effective.	
	20.12.15	1 pm	On the 20th fired 5 rounds from 1½ inch gun at enemy's tin can & implement at Grs D.01 bringing down sides & pounds of same. Observed that a number of stick platts were thrown into the air, and on front last moved, which was blind from the noise of tint-striking metal. Also fired 3 rounds from 2 inch gun at Grs B67, all these rounds were effective.	
	21.12.15	Noon	Fired 12 rounds from 1½ inch gun at Grs D.01 demolishing implacement seen 20th inst. Opened fire with 2 inch gun at Grs B15 B67 but could only fire 2 rounds on account of bad marking.	
	22.12.15		Put in new bed for 2 inch gun. At 4 am opened fire with 2 inch in conjunction with artillery on 6"a trench by mid infantry bombard at Grs B67 fired 12 rounds all were effective. Also firing from 1½ inch gun from Grs C58 and Grs C59 all rounds effective.	

J. Sweeney Lt
OC 50th SM Battery

2353 Wt. W5544/1454 700,000 5/15 D D & L A.D.S.S. Forms/C. 2118.

WAR DIARY
INTELLIGENCE SUMMARY

50th Trench Mortar Battery

Place	Date	Hour	Summary of Events and Information	Remarks and references to Appendices
Ploegsteert Wood	23/12/15 to 27/12/15		Battery at rest 23/12/15 to 27/12/15.	
	28/12/15		Went up to trenches in morning (Enemy shelling Ypres road). With orders from Divst. at 11 a.m. tomorrow morning. Wire received from A + B 2" guns to be of use of Enemy Trench. As enemy retaliates on fired alarm order god effect. Got guns ready. Ran on B. Trench magazine. A gun + fired 13 rounds A gun (12lb gun). Enough enemy trenches about required places. No damage done by enemy return fire.	
	29/12/15		Before return being on emplacements.	
	30/12/15		In evening Capt. Scott came up & pointed out positions for new 1½" + 2" guns. Lieut. Eden came up to select site. Decided to stop in for another day. But unable to get materials for new emplacements. Was given to carrying parties with 2 guns & working on new emplacements. Had to give it about 10 trench in. Shell fire too heavy around us.	
	1/1/16		Got men on C 2" gun. A 2" gun + par/carrying ammunition. Working on 2 new emplacements (1½") ready for humorous shoot. German officer trench fire about 7.30am & as we were asked to retaliate, fired 10 2" rounds with good effect. Lieut. Eden (officer slight wound in hand) decided to stop in for tomorrows shoot. Lieut. Preston relieved Lieut. Eden.	

Army Form C. 2118.

WAR DIARY
of
INTELLIGENCE SUMMARY.
(Erase heading not required.)

Instructions regarding War Diaries and Intelligence Summaries are contained in F. S. Regs., Part II. and the Staff Manual respectively. Title pages will be prepared in manuscript.

Place	Date	Hour	Summary of Events and Information	Remarks and references to Appendices
Railway Woods	2/1/16	6.30 a.m.	Opened fire at enemys front line Trench as per peace arranged, having first put the guns pointing in rifle directions. In magnetic angle. As Trench opened fire before we intended of after us, two rather spoiling effect of our guns at first. Ceased firing at 7 a.m. Left Trenches at 10 a.m. after the firing, after having ascertained that the enemys parapet was down in several places.	

R Stanley Smart
Capt
50th North'd Fus
O.C. 50th North'd Fus

1/1/16

1577 Wt. W10791/1773 500,000 1/15 D. D. & L. A.D.S.S./Forms/C. 2118.

Army Form C. 2118.

WAR DIARY
or
INTELLIGENCE SUMMARY.
(Erase heading not required.)

Instructions regarding War Diaries and Intelligence Summaries are contained in F. S. Regs., Part II. and the Staff Manual respectively. Title pages will be prepared in manuscript.

Place	Date	Hour	Summary of Events and Information	Remarks and references to Appendices
Irraga	27th	10 am	Took over from the Manchesters on the night of the 22nd & 23rd. 5 rounds from 15 inch gun used towards frequented gun at 1/2 D 91. Did not do much damage to parapet effectives.	Reminder
	28th	—	Did not fire on the 28th December, spent the day in preparing ammunition and guns for the expected bombardment which was to take place on the 29th. 9.00	
	29th	11 am	Received notice to open fire at 11 am on Bagnotth (J12 c 93) and trench north of it, in conjunction with artillery. Bombardment opened using ammunition I fired 11 rounds from 15 inch gun and 24 mounds from 3 inch gun. A great deal of damage was done to enemy trench not what showing first hour a number of the enemy running from J12 c 93. The enemy retaliated at 3 pm but (their reply only lasted ?) an hour and did no damage. He had no kind of	
	30th	12 pm	fired 5 rounds from 15 inch gun at J12 D 91, one of which ricocheted E and burst, all remaining rounds did damage to enemy parapet.	

R. J. Adams 2nd Lieut.
13th Hampshire Regt. / 504 S.M. Battery.

WAR DIARY or INTELLIGENCE SUMMARY.

Army Form C. 2118.

Place	Date	Hour	Summary of Events and Information	Remarks and references to Appendices
RIGHT SECTOR ARMENTIERES	March 19th	A.M. 10.30	Took over Rif & Grse & Light Trench Mortars from South Scottish of 21st Div. Battery consists of 2 Stokes guns and 2x 3.7" howitzers. All the guns and also were complete and in good order. There was no munition made on the Brigading of the Light T.Ms. but for use in Trenches there were 107 Stokes Shells complete and 100 rounds 3.7" ammunition available. The mortars were set to work at once to thicken movement engagements in the 2 Stokes Guns behind the sub-section near LOTHIAN AVENUE, in front of the Defence Scheme. The 2 Stokes Direction Scheme then arrived so there was to hand all guns that & Subsits on prearranged positions so that they could fire on critical spots of our own front line in case of an enemy attack, also to being brought to bear on enemy lines opposite shown in the Scheme were [Shet 26] I.10.D.4.5 posn (M) and I.10.D.2.5, 6.3 right but the house was laid on PIGGOTTS FARM and on R.H side in firing LOTHIAN AVENUE, the LH3 on the MUSHROOM.	

Place	Date	Hour	Summary of Events and Information	Remarks and references to Appendices
RIGHT SECT ARMENTIERES	19th	Noon	Relief carried. Relieve 6 T.M.C. CRA 7th L.I. there was formerly to 7th Division in F.R.S. Coffin Hay. / the bad secondment the front Commenced to check stores etc of Heavier Battery in Right Sector.	
	20th		Took carbrind [carbonised?] on stores employments. One employment picked.	
	21st		Took over from 2nd Regt the Heavier T.M. Battery consisting of 1 2" Gun and 2 15" Japan Stokes it was in 6 [?] positions Ammunition	
	22nd		Stores as to follow — 2nd 15" rounds 15" Heavy 413 rounds 15"	
			Rifle 50 rounds Ball shrapnel. There were 3 Ammunition employment	
			Emplacements at the follow points:— 15" (Rifle [Ry]) I 16.d 65.63.	
			2" mortar I 10.D 1/5 53. 15" Petrol [Ry] I 16.B 53 93. There were 4	
			employments immediately behind the firing line viz. J Stores	
			position — A gun [2" mortar plus no bed.] I 16.B II, 5m. B" gun	
			2 mds & mortars gun. I 10.D.a.33. C gun 15 mds. ½ beds. I 11.C.d.3.	
			D gun — Old position — not used. I 11.A 1.63.	
	23rd	2.30 AM	Reported relief carried to T.M.C. CRA and S.C.O [?]	
			Carried out ammunition of 15" to make at least 50 rounds Contents	

WAR DIARY
or
INTELLIGENCE SUMMARY.
(Erase heading not required.)

Army Form C. 2118.

Place	Date	Hour	Summary of Events and Information	Remarks and references to Appendices
RIGHT SECTOR KNIGHTSBRIDGE	March 23 24	10 a.m. 3 p.m. 20th 6.15 by 5 p.m. 5 p.m.	Air Service continues hostile to send over Jasckin. Proceeded to KNIENTIERES in relief and to Dinsrard nearly to fire artillery in a Crash Medic left Coll Evans Found NCO in charge. Returned to the trenches. Enemy shelled Position 14 and western K. MUCH MUCH Longer was a water by SX. Sight on things from and delivered to Trench 76 and free it in Bruys Link and a h Rhue rule Gra (Bht?). 23 rounds use fired Most what book actually in the enemy trench as on the carpets. Ground drive to India Ate a small breakfast. The next am a match. Very	Sgt. C.P. Durgan T.M. Battery 50th T.M.